MW01114100

The CDU and the Politics of Gender in Germany
Bringing Women to the Party

This book develops the concept of the corporatist catch-all party to explain how the German Christian Democratic Union (CDU) has responded to changing demands from women over the past forty years. Otto Kirchheimer's classic study argues that when catch-all parties reach out to new constituencies, they are forced to decrease the involvement of membership to facilitate doctrinal flexibility. In a corporatist catch-all party, however, societal interests are represented within the party organization and policy making is the result of internal party negotiation. Through an investigation of CDU policy making in the issue areas of abortion policy, work-family policy, and participation policy, this book demonstrates that sometimes the CDU mobilizes rather than disempowers membership. An important lesson of this study is that a political party need not sacrifice internal democracy and ignore its members in order to succeed at the polls.

Sarah Elise Wiliarty is Assistant Professor of Government at Wesleyan University. Her research interests include political parties, women and politics, and Christian Democracy. Professor Wiliarty has published articles in *German Politics* and *Politics and Gender* and co-edited *The Transformation of Postwar Germany: Democracy, Prosperity and Nationhood* (1999, with John S. Brady and Beverly Crawford).

The CDU and the Politics of Gender in Germany

Bringing Women to the Party

SARAH ELISE WILIARTY

Wesleyan University

CAMBRIDGE UNIVERSITY PRESS
Cambridge, New York, Melbourne, Madrid, Cape Town, Singapore,
São Paulo, Delhi, Dubai, Tokyo, Mexico City

Cambridge University Press
32 Avenue of the Americas, New York, NY 10013–2473, USA

www.cambridge.org
Information on this title: www.cambridge.org/9780521765824

First published 2010

Printed in the United States of America

A catalog record for this publication is available from the British Library.

Library of Congress Cataloging in Publication Data
Wiliarty, Sarah Elise, 1968–
The CDU and the politics of gender in Germany: bringing women to the party / Sarah
Elise Wiliarty.
    p.   cm.
ISBN 978-0-521-76582-4 (hardback)
    1. Christlich-Demokratische Union Deutschlands – Membership.
    2. Women in politics – Germany.   3. Women – Government policy –
Germany.   4. Women – Government policy – Europe, German-speaking.   I. Title.
JN3971.A98C49   2010
324.243′04082–dc22   2010008594

ISBN 978-0-521-76582-4 Hardback

For Kevin, Patrick, and Geneva

Contents

List of Figure and Tables

Acknowledgments

Writing may be a solitary enterprise, but books do not get written alone. Many people have supported me in this project from its infancy as a dissertation to its maturation into a book. I would like to thank the members of my dissertation committee for their support and intellectual guidance throughout. My chair, Jonah Levy, provided the kind of feedback and support that many graduate students can only dream about. Andrei Markovits shared his excellent insights about German party politics with me at personal meetings in Berkeley, Berlin, Bonn, and Ann Arbor. Henry Brady taught me how parties and their organizations work. Margaret Anderson provided the wisdom of a historian and shared her fascination with politicized Catholicism.

My field research for the dissertation enjoyed the support of a Federal Chancellor's Scholarship from the Alexander von Humboldt Foundation. The Humboldt Foundation also facilitated a return trip to Germany in the summer of 2008. I am grateful to Jörg Niewöhner for arranging an institutional affiliation at the Institute for European Ethnology during that time. At Berkeley I received support from the Center for German and European Studies, the Institute for International Studies, and the Department of Political Science. A Small Research Grant from the American Political Science Association funded my work in Austria. Wesleyan University provided me with multiple project grants and an inspiring semester as a Faculty Fellow at the Center for the Humanities.

I am grateful to the many people who took time out of their busy schedules to answer my questions about the internal life of the CDU. I would particularly like to thank those I interviewed, who shared their time with me and provided me with insights into the Christian Democratic

Union that would have been otherwise unavailable. Special thanks go to Kristel Bendig, former business manager of the Women's Union, who arranged for me to attend countless meetings of both the Women's Union and the CDU. Thank you also to the staff members of the national office of the Women's Union, who were generous with their time and their knowledge, and to the members of the board of directors of the Women's Union, who were very welcoming of an American traveling with them.

Many people have read portions of this manuscript as it evolved. Several Berkeley faculty members beyond my dissertation committee have shared their wisdom and their time in supporting me and this project. Chris Ansell, Pradeep Chhibber, and Nick Ziegler all gave very helpful feedback. Thank you to Alisa Gaunder, Tomek Grabowski, John Leslie, Mark Vail, and Sara Watson for reading multiple versions and chapters. Their often challenging questions greatly improved the quality of this work. Without Alisa, there probably would not be a book at all. I am so grateful to her for her enduring friendship, her generosity with her time, and her confidence in me.

I benefited furthermore from many conversations about parties and German politics with John Brady, Ken Greene, Abe Newman, and Anna Schmidt. Judy Gruber, Alan Karras, and Nelson Polsby helped me negotiate the dissertation writing process in ways that I am sure they did not fully appreciate. I was honored and humbled to follow in Nelson's footsteps when I took up my position in the Government Department at Wesleyan University.

At Wesleyan I have been welcomed into an exceptionally supportive department. Daunting as it may sometimes be to write about parties in a department that was once home to E. E. Schattschneider, I have been greatly encouraged by the enthusiasm of my colleagues. Jim McGuire, Don Moon, Russ Murphy, Peter Rutland, and Nancy Schwartz have all read substantial sections of the manuscript and given me invaluable feedback. Katherine Kuenzli has been a friend, a loyal reader, and a fabulous support in matters both professional and personal. Beyond Wesleyan, Louise Davidson-Schmich, Myra Marx Ferree, Miki Caul Kittilson, Kimberly Morgan, and Joyce Marie Mushaben have cheered me on at numerous conferences and given me reason to hope that there is an audience for the final product. Thank you also to two anonymous reviewers, whose comments improved the book enormously. I was also lucky enough to work with two excellent editors at Cambridge University Press, Lew Bateman and Eric Crahan. It goes without saying that whatever errors remain in this work are entirely my own.

In this age of the Internet, not all support is given face to face. Three online communities have helped see me through this project. The November Dumplings have listened to my complaints, shared my joys, and bolstered me with their confidence. The August Angels saw me through a very difficult time of personal loss in 2006. Finally, the group at Academic Ladder has provided writing support, Saturday morning challenges, and row after row of little green checkmarks as the manuscript emerged.

My friends and family have provided both support and welcome distraction. Alisa Gaunder and Katherine Kuenzli have served dual roles as companions in both academia and motherhood. Sue Imai, Irene Thelen, and Stephanie Speicher helped me keep my perspective and my sense of humor. Jack and Emelie Moriarty helped at every turn with both practical and emotional support. And of course it is impossible to enumerate the many ways in which my parents, Pat and Ted Wilson, have contributed to this project. They are the ones who were brave enough to let their then-fifteen-year-old daughter venture off on her first explorations of Europe. Little did they know then that they would still be supporting that project into their retirement. They have my gratitude for all they have done.

My wonderful husband, Kevin Wiliarty, has given me the greatest inspiration and also borne the greatest burden of my frequent absences and frustrations. His faith in me is unwavering. He has also read the manuscript numerous times. His suggestions have brought elegance to my prose and clarity to my thoughts. He even helped design the cover and watched the kids during a research trip to Berlin. He is my hero and my great love and I am more grateful to him than I have words to say. My son Patrick managed my absences with mostly good humor, and I am thankful to him for telling me how "cool" he thinks it is that I'm writing a book. My darling Geneva Rose is too little to understand all of this, but she makes me laugh and brings light to my heart every day. I dedicate this book to Kevin, Patrick, and Geneva and promise them that they will be seeing more of me in the future.

The CDU and the Politics of Gender in Germany

Bringing Women to the Party

Introduction

A Democratic Paradox?

The summer of 2005 was an exciting one in German politics. On May 22, the Social Democratic Party (SPD) suffered a serious defeat in its electoral heartland, North Rhine-Westfalia, which led Chancellor Gerhard Schröder to call for surprise early elections in the fall. The Christian Democrats chose to run Angela Merkel, chair of the Christian Democratic Union (CDU), as their candidate. After starting the summer with a 25 percent point lead, Merkel lost ground throughout the campaign. From her controversial choice of Paul Kirchhof as future Finance Minister to her poor performance in the televised debate, it seemed Merkel could do nothing right. On September 18, the Christian Democrats received 35.2 percent of the vote and the Social Democrats received 34.2 percent. Neither major party had sufficient votes to form a government with its preferred coalition partner. After two months of wrangling, Merkel finally emerged as the leader of a grand coalition made up of the Christian Democrats and the Social Democrats.

Merkel may have seemed like an odd choice for the Christian Democrats. After all, the CDU is a traditionally Catholic party and she is a Protestant. The CDU has traditional social values, yet it elected a woman. The CDU has struggled to gain votes in the former East Germany and has often seemed ineffective when campaigning there, yet the party elected the first eastern Chancellor. How did this conservative party come to make such an unusual choice for the most important position in the country? The answer cannot be that Merkel is such a good campaigner. While she has consistently won her own constituency seat, her lack of charisma and difficulty in the public arena were well known prior to the election.

CDU policy making on "women's issues" also presents a puzzle. The party has historically had a traditional take on women's roles in society, yet it expanded parental leave, introduced a gender "quorum" and signed on to reform that liberalized access to abortion. What is driving the CDU's agenda on these issues?

Both the CDU's personnel choices and the party's policy making are guided by a logic that can only be understood through studying the party's internal organization. The party's internal structure empowers some groups while disempowering others. I introduce a new theoretical model of party organization, the corporatist catch-all party model, to describe this internal structure. I argue that this form of organization affects party decision making on both policy and personnel issues.

Corporatist catch-all parties represent important internal party groups on the party's decision-making bodies. These parties contain vertically integrated internal groups that have multiple ideological orientations. That is, the groups may be directed at particular societal actors – women, youth, Protestants – but they must also differ from each other in terms of their positions on political issues. Furthermore, in a corporatist catch-all party, these internal groups have some form of assured representation on the party's internal decision-making bodies.

Personnel choices are driven by the party's internal structure. Recognized groups need people to represent them on the party's decision-making bodies. These internal quotas are typically unspoken, but they are reliably followed nonetheless. Merkel's success resulted from her ability to fulfill three important internal party quotas: women, Protestants, and easterners. Because of this, Merkel was frequently a natural choice when an opening became available. Because the CDU strives to maintain a balance in leadership, Merkel sometimes advanced in the party hierarchy ahead of more experienced and better connected men (Wiliarty 2008a).

A related logic applies to policy making. The CDU strives to represent its diverse internal groups on important policy-making bodies. Representation guarantees voice, not outcome. The actual policies advocated and implemented by the CDU are a result of bargaining among these internal party groups.

This form of organization has several important implications for theories of democracy. Conventional wisdom on democratic party theory contains a normative paradox. On the one hand, it is not a good idea for party activists to gain too much power because party activists tend to hold more extreme views than voters (May 1973).[1] If activists' views prevail in policy making, a political party will be less likely to win. If such a party is

---

[1] See Kitschelt 1989 for an expansion and partial rebuttal of May.

elected, it will be less likely to implement policies favored by most voters. Underlying these ideas is the assumption that party leaders are more in touch with ordinary voters and that – if they can only steer around their own activists – they will promise and implement policy that is more acceptable to most citizens than party activists would.

On the other hand, political parties themselves are not internally democratic if party leaders are able to impose their preferences on party activists. As we know from the work of Robert Michels and his Iron Law of Oligarchy, party leaders are likely to prevail over activists because they are better informed and have more resources at their disposal (Michels 1962). Therefore party leaders control a party's policy-making agenda. The problem with this view of party politics, from a democratic standpoint, is that there is a normative preference for parties in a democracy to have internal democracy as well. Yet it seems that if activists are in charge, they will lead parties away from winnable policies – and indeed away from the preferences of voters.

This book does not promise to overcome the normative paradox just described. Instead, it examines empirical patterns of policy making in parties in western Europe and finds that the paradox itself may have been falsely stated. A closer look at policy making – and the links between party leaders, party activists, and voters – reveals a more complex, yet possibly also more democratic dynamic. This dynamic can be observed by studying how parties respond to societal change.

This book develops a theory explaining how a political party decides how to respond to societal changes by investigating how the German CDU has responded to new demands from women since the 1960s. After using the German case to generate this theory, I test it by examining Christian Democratic parties in Austria, Italy, and the Netherlands. Women's roles in most western democracies have been transformed since the 1960s. Women are participating in the labor force in much greater numbers. They are going to school longer and having fewer children. They are much more likely to get divorced or never to marry. They are more interested in being politically active. These changes have caused women to want different things from political parties, but not all women want the same things. How is a party to respond to these changes and still recruit a significant number of votes from women?

The paradox about who controls party policy making has been posed as a conflict between leaders and activists. Who will be triumphant in shaping party policy? Whose view *should* prevail for a satisfactory democratic outcome? Empirical study of the CDU's policy making on women's issues reveals a different sort of dynamic. The struggle within the CDU does not pit activists against leaders. The internal politics of the CDU are more accurately described as groups of activists and leaders struggling with other groups of activists and leaders within the party in an effort to control policy making. This insight about party politics has implications for the quality of democracy. If policy outcomes are determined by internal power struggles, we need to understand how and whether these internal struggles are linked to the preferences of voters. I argue that there is a link though not always a direct one. Furthermore, activists may not be such a bad influence on a party's chances of success after all because they may actually be *more* in tune with voter preferences than party leaders. An examination of how political parties incorporated women's demands can yield new insights on the previously discussed democratic paradox.

Gender and Politics

Incorporating women has been a difficult challenge for political parties, yet this is an area in which enormous progress has been made in recent years. Scholars of gender and politics have developed a rich literature on how to get women's concerns heard by the political system and what role political parties can play. Important insights from this literature include the idea that a strong women's movement can create genuine pressure on political parties and that parties of the left are more likely to be favorably disposed to women's political demands (Duverger 1955: Katzenstein and Mueller 1987; Lovenduski and Norris 1993: Lovenduski and Randall 1993: Caul 1999, Banaszak, Beckwith, and Rucht 2003). An additional strand of the literature, led by the Research Network on Gender Politics and the State (RNGS) group, argues for the importance of women's policy agencies (Stetson and Mazur 1995; Mazur 2001; Stetson 2001a; Outshoorn 2004; Lovenduski 2005b; Hausmann and Sauer 2007). These are offices within the state bureaucracy that are created at the urging of state feminists with the purpose of enacting public policy favorable to women. In some cases, women's policy agencies are able to act as insiders and advance the cause of women's movement activists. In an ideal case, a strong feminist movement can work together with a favorably inclined left-wing party and an active women's policy agency to pass and implement policy in line with the goals of the women's movement.

The findings of the gender and politics literature are crucial in delineating the conditions under which activists in the women's movement can positively influence policy making. This literature does not have much to say, however, about how to understand empirical outcomes under other circumstances. A strong and well-organized women's movement can successfully influence politics, but what happens when the feminist movement is weak or not engaged in party politics? Although it is true that parties of the left are generally more favorably inclined to the demands of the women's movement, left parties are not equally interested in women's issues. What about cases where left parties are disinclined to work with the feminist movement? Or time periods when conservative parties are in power? Furthermore, as the RNGS scholarship shows, women's policy agencies can be co-opted by conservative governments and used to legitimate and implement policy that the women's movement disagrees with. Politics on women's issues does not come to a standstill in the absence of a strong feminist movement or a cooperative left-wing party, yet existing scholarship does not give us many tools to understand conservative party policy making on women's issues.

In many ways, Germany is not a favorable environment for the three-way partnership of women's movement, left-wing party, and women's policy agency. These three actors – movement, left-wing party, and women's policy agency – have not always behaved in a way conducive to cooperation with each other and achievement of the goals of the women's movement. This situation warrants elaboration.[2]

The first weak link in the chain is the West German feminist movement. Owing partly to the complete break of the Nazi era and World War II, the second wave West German feminist movement has been generally considered weaker than its counterparts in many West European countries (Schenk 1981; Gerhard 1982; Altbach 1984; Lovenduski 1986). One product of this comparative weakness is that feminist consciousness was less widespread in Germany than its European neighbors in the 1970s and 1980s (Katzenstein M. 1987: 15). Support for the feminist movement has historically also been lower in West Germany than in other countries (Klein 1987).

The "problem" with the West German feminist movement was not just its weakness, but also that the movement's orientation has not been conducive to increasing its political influence. Feminism everywhere is a movement with multiple internal tendencies. Three of the most prominent of these are radical feminism, socialist feminism, and liberal feminism (Ferree 1987: 173; Tong 1998). While liberal feminism and socialist

---

[2] The next section draws on Myra Marx Ferree's forthcoming book on the German women's movement.

feminism are likely to encourage feminist engagement with politics, radical feminism, the dominant strain in West Germany, often does not.

Liberal feminists, the group most prominent in the United States, believe that women, like men, should be able to realize their full potential as human beings. What sets humans apart from animals is our capacity for rational action. The state should provide a framework within which women (and men) can pursue their own goals, their own idea of "the good life," but state interference should otherwise be kept as small as possible. Liberal feminists pursue women's liberation through sexual equality. They are divided on how to achieve that goal. Some liberal feminists prefer to treat women the same as men and are satisfied with removing discriminatory policy. Other liberal feminists argue that treating women and men the same will not have the same effect because it is women who bear (and often raise) children.[3]

In both cases, however, liberal feminists focus on removing legal barriers to women's liberation, and this approach has generally led liberal feminists to engage in the mainstream political process. The American women's movement is dominated by liberal feminists. Through the National Organization for Women and a strong connection to the Democratic Party, liberal feminists in the United States have worked for policies such as equal pay for equal work, recognizing sexual harassment, and access to safe and legal abortions. Liberal feminists are interested in making society's rules fair for women and men and this desire generally leads them to engage in politics as a way to influence those rules.

Radical feminists, on the other hand, begin with different assumptions about the source of women's oppression and these beliefs lead them to different actions. Radical feminism, the strand of the movement most prevalent in West Germany, assumes fundamental differences between men and women (Ferree 1987). For radical feminists, women's oppression stems from the entire system of distinguishing men and women, the sex/gender system. This is true whether the differences between men and women are rooted in biology or socialization.[4]

Radical feminists do not usually believe that women's emancipation can be achieved through changing a particular set of rules or policies. Instead,

---

[3] Classic texts on liberal feminism include Wollstonecraft 1975, Mill 1970, and Friedan 1974. For overviews of liberal feminism in much more detail see Eisenstein 1986, Kensinger 1997, and Tong 1998.

[4] Radical feminist texts include Firestone 1970; Millet 1970; Daly 1973, 1978, 1984; and French 1985. For more information on radical feminism see Echols 1990, Tong 1998, Crow 2000.

radical feminists argue that women's liberation is achieved through some resolution that addresses the sex/gender system (Tong 1998: 46). Some radical feminists have found the path to women's liberation in androgyny. Others have advocated scientific research designed to find a way to free women from child bearing through the invention of artificial wombs (Firestone 1970 in Tong 1998: 52). What radical feminists have in common is the belief that the sex/gender system is the cause of women's oppression. To overcome this oppression requires some kind of much more fundamental change than can be achieved through policy shifts.

German radical feminists adopted the concept of autonomy to help overcome the sex/gender system. They believed that because contact with men would inevitably involve women's oppression, the only available solution was separation. Through the pursuit of autonomy, West German feminists hoped to find liberation. Autonomy could be found in a variety of areas of life – from demanding control over their bodies and the complete decriminalization of abortion to consciousness-raising groups to separate bookstores, cafes, hotels, and publishing houses. This form of feminism did not lead activists in the German women's movement to make very many demands of the state (Rucht 2003). Instead, feminists feared that working with state institutions might prove to be contaminating.[5]

Partly because of the prevalence of radical feminists in the German women's movement, Germany has no counterpart to the American National Organization for Women. There is no national level organization that might create serious organized pressure from outside the political parties. The *Deutscher Frauenrat* (German Women's Council) is an umbrella organization to which nearly all women's organization in the country belong. However, that means that the *Deutscher Frauenrat* itself is nonpartisan.

Second wave feminism in West Germany has its beginnings in the New Left movement of the late 1960s and the abortion protests of the early 1970s (Ferree 1987: 183). Although the feminist movement helped bring the abortion issue to the political agenda and keep it there, the ultimate legislation was shaped nearly exclusively by the political parties and the Federal Constitutional Court (Kamenitsa 2001: 116–7). (For more on the abortion debates of the 1970s, see Chapter 4.) The lack of influence

[5] West German feminists were willing to accept state funding for their feminist projects. For more information on the West German feminist movement see Doormann 1980, Schwarzer 1981, Doormann 1983, Ferree 1987, Kaplan 1992, Nave-Herz. 1997, Ferree, forthcoming. For a perspective that blames women's exclusion from politics on the gender bias of the German state rather than the factors discussed here, see Young (1999).

of the abortion campaign combined with the conflict with the New Left contributed to the women's movement's commitment to autonomy (Ferree 1987; Ferree forthcoming).

Following the closure of the abortion debate in 1976, the West German feminist movement chose to work for "islands of utopia" – areas of life in which they could live as loyally to feminist ideals as possible – rather than choosing engagement with political parties or the state (Ferree, forthcoming). West German feminists focused their energies on independent projects such as cafes, women's bookstores, and shelters for battered women. Continuing the theme of autonomy, these organizations were run by women, for women. Men were generally not allowed, even as paying customers. The goal of the projects was to provide women the chance at self sufficiency and to make a political statement by showing the possibility of an alternative reality. Projects were generally locally based and run in a nonhierarchical manner, in keeping with feminist values. One result of the focus on the creation of an autonomous feminist sphere, of course, is that political parties did not feel much pressure from the feminist movement to work for particular policy outcomes.

Although the goal of the projects was to create a separate feminist "space" for the various activities, ironically the project work led feminists to begin to make demands on the state after all, in the form of funding. Many projects were funded largely or entirely by the government. Feminists involved with the project work were well aware of the contradictions inherent in attempting to be autonomous while being financially dependent on the state.

Throughout the project phase, then, the feminist movement was not very engaged with the state. Individual projects petitioned for and received funding, often fairly substantial funding, but this situation should not be characterized as a feminist movement moving toward cooperation with a party of the left, even though governments controlled by the SPD were more likely to provide funding for the projects. Instead, the women's movement was situating itself as a client of the state rather than an interest group able to exert pressure to bring about policy change.

Over the course of the 1980s, feminists began to turn more seriously toward the state. For a variety of reasons – the funding issue, the difficulty of sustaining a nonhierarchical organization, the gradual professionalization of some project workers – the project work of the feminist movement began to decline. The new Green Party provided a political opportunity for feminists willing to engage more directly with the state. The Green Party shared many of the values of the feminist movement. Feminists could become active in the party without becoming members and thereby potentially diluting their feminism. Like the feminist projects, the Green Party attempted to maintain a nonhierarchical organization. The Green Party gave feminist activists a way to begin to pressure the state without having to compromise their core values (Ferree, forthcoming).

The Greens did more than provide an opportunity for feminists to engage with the state; the party actively promoted women's and indeed, feminist, participation. The Green Party promoted women to leadership positions and was the first party in West Germany to implement a gender quota (McKay 2004). The party's "zipper" system, implemented in 1986, called for alternating male and female candidates on the party's electoral lists. The party's caucus in the Bundestag jumped from 26 percent women in 1985 to over 50 percent, where it has remained with the exception of the 1990–4 legislative period. Furthermore, the SPD quickly also implemented a gender quota and the CDU adopted policies to promote women as well (see McKay 2004, and Chapter 5). With feminists more ready to pressure the state and the Green Party (and to a lesser extent the SPD) ready to provide them with a channel to do so, the possibility of a partnership between feminist activists and the parties of the left became more viable. Although the history of the focus on autonomy can still be felt in the German feminist movement today, by the late 1980s, West German feminists were becoming much more comfortable working within state institutions and within political parties. (Ferree, forthcoming; Rucht 2003).

German unification interrupted the coming together of feminist movement, political parties, and the state. The life experiences of women in East and West Germany differed dramatically and the values and goals of their respective feminist movements reflected these differences. In the west, lack of affordable child care and irregular school hours made it exceptionally difficult for women to combine family and career. In this context, feminists in the West tended to view paid employment as the path to emancipation. In the east, paid employment was the norm for women and inexpensive child care was widely available. Feminists from the east were more concerned with the burden of the "second shift" because men in the east were not expected to make any significant contribution to housework or child care. As Myra Marx Ferree puts it, women in the west were dependent on their husband and subject to private patriarchy, while women in the east were dependent on the state and subject to public patriarchy (Ferree 1995; 1997). These differences made it difficult for feminists from east and west to find common ground.

The abortion issue following unification made it even clearer that feminists in East and West Germany had different perspectives. At the time of unification, abortion was legal during the first trimester in East Germany, but illegal in West Germany and only permitted under certain well-defined conditions. The new law ultimately adopted in the mid-1990s marked a liberalization of the West German law, but a severe restriction of East German law. Once again, the different life experiences of east and west sometimes made East and West German feminists mutually incomprehensible (Ferree 1997; Rohnstock 1994; Helwerth and Schwarz 1995).

The process of unification made it more difficult for feminists to pressure the state. Despite some brief initial success at influencing the course of events – most notably through the founding of the Independent Women's Organization (UFV) – unification was difficult for women in the east, who have been characterized as "victims of unification" (Ferree 1994; Maleck-Lewy 1997). Eastern women were hit particularly hard by the massive unemployment that emerged in the early 1990s. A major reduction in the availability of child care for all ages has left women scrambling to find alternatives. As women's share of household earnings decreased, their power within their marriages declined as well (Meyer and Schulze 1998). Under these conditions, feminist agitation was not the top priority for many women.

Meanwhile, in both halves of unified Germany, as the women's movement became more institutionalized, it also became more dependent on state funding. As feminist projects have become more institutionalized, they have lost much of the utopian character that drew activists to them in the first place. Fewer women are involved in these projects and of those that remain involved, many are seeking employment opportunities rather than "feminist havens" (Lang 1997).

If we consider the chain proposed previously – feminist movement pressures left-wing political party that works through women's policy agency – we see that in Germany the feminist movement often did not choose to pressure German political parties. Instead, the West German women's movement frequently worked outside of mainstream politics to pursue its ends in very different ways. The East German feminist movement was quickly marginalized after unification.

The next actor in the chain, the party of the left, has also not had an easy relationship to the feminist movement. In the United States, the women's movement has often benefited from close cooperation with the party on the left, the Democrats. In Germany, on the other hand, the relationship between feminists and the main party of the left, the SPD, has historically been more contentious.

Dating back to the nineteenth century, the SPD has tended to prioritize the interests of workers over the interests of women. Although the SPD was initially divided on the "woman question," in 1891 the party officially adopted the position that women should pursue their emancipation by supporting the socialist struggle (Ferree, forthcoming). Despite protests from socialist women who wanted women's political self-determination and economic independence, the Social Democratic Party favored the male breadwinner model with women at home as housewives. This was the model pursued by middle class parties; the SPD preferred to extend this vision to include working class families rather than pursue women's economic independence.

The divide between middle class and socialist feminist movements in Germany dates back to this conflict at the turn of the twentieth century. Some socialist feminists agreed with their party that women should put class struggle ahead of feminist struggle. The main middle class women's organization, the *Bund deutscher Frauenvereine* (BDF), considered the socialist feminists too radical and actually excluded them from joining the BDF, which was supposed to be an umbrella organization of women's groups (Ferree, forthcoming). From the late Imperial Germany through the Weimar Republic (and beyond), women's groups in Germany were divided by class.

Political parties, on the other hand, managed to cross class divides in order to institutionalize policies based on a male breadwinner model. Already in 1900 when conservatives reformed the Civil Code (*Bürgerliches Gesetzbuch*), the SPD agreed with laws allowing husbands to control their wives' property and to forbid their wives from employment. Despite some isolated protests, the SPD as a party did not challenge these laws during the Weimar Republic. In the early years of the Federal Republic, the Social Democrats approved adopting portions of the Civil Code giving fathers authority over mothers and approving the male breadwinner model (Moeller 1993).[6] Across the twentieth century, then, in a wide variety of regime types, the SPD cooperated with conservative parties to reinforce women's economic dependence on men.

Given this history, it is not that surprising that the West German second wave feminist movement was born out of conflict with the new left, or that

---

[6] The SPD did favor equal rights for men and women, but the party consistently differentiated itself from the more radical claims of "women's righters." The SPD supported both equal rights in the Basic Law and "functional differentiation" of men and women in policy and day-to-day life. See Moeller 1993 and Ferree (forthcoming) for more detail.

feminists did not form a strong partnership with parties on the left. When the left was in power in Germany, it did not do much to further the feminist cause. The historical distance and tension between feminists and the SPD closed off the possibility of these two actors working closely together as happened in some other advanced democracies.

In (West) Germany, then, the hoped-for partnership between the feminist movement and the party of the left did not come to fruition because of characteristics of both actors. The feminist movement was dominated by radical feminists who largely viewed the risk of contamination of working through mainstream political channels as not worth the potential payoff, which was likely to be small. The Social Democratic Party had almost a century-long tradition of favoring workers' rights over women's rights and was therefore not a likely partner for feminists.

Another body of literature, generated by the RNGS group, argues for the importance of state feminism in understanding policy outcomes (Stetson and Mazur 1995; Mazur 2001; Stetson 2001a; Outshoorn 2004; Lovenduski 2005b; Hausmann and Sauer 2007). Many western democracies have established women's policy agencies. These bureaucratic entities are designed to further the interests of women in policy making. When feminists inhabit these offices, they can have a significant positive impact on policy making, particularly when supported by a unified and committed women's movement. The RNGS project investigates (and argues in favor of) the state's ability to further the feminist cause.

The state feminist literature makes a strong contribution to our understanding of feminism and policy making. However, this scholarship sometimes struggles with analyzing politics in Germany. Two of the books in the RNGS series directly address policy areas under investigation in this book: abortion and representation (Stetson 2001a; Lovenduski 2005b). In both cases, insights from the RNGS research leads to the conclusion that further investigation of the German case would be warranted. The cross-national analysis in *Abortion Politics, Women's Movements, and the Democratic State* places Germany in its own category, as the only country in which abortion policy did not coincide with the goals of the women's movement. The German feminist movement is characterized as the most divided of all countries analyzed (Stetson 2001a: 280). The chapter on Germany makes it clear that power is in the hands of the political parties on this issue (Kamenitsa 2001). Furthermore, during much of the abortion debate in Germany, the women's policy agency is controlled by the Christian Democrats, giving this agency a quite different role than it has when controlled by parties of the left. To understand abortion policy, then, it would be well worth considering the actions of the German Christian Democratic Union.

On representation, too, the RNGS scholarship concludes that "parties make all of the most important political decisions" in Germany (Kamenitsa and Geissel 2005: 106). One of the insights of Lovenduski's volume, *State Feminism and Political Representation*, is that women's organizations within political parties may act as "quasi-women's policy agencies" (QWPAs) (Lovenduski 2005a: 14). That is, the parties' own organizations for women may be working to improve women's status and influence within the party and within the state. Recognizing the importance of these organizations within political parties is a critical insight, especially in a country like Germany where parties are so important.

Having recognized the potential role for QWPAs, *State Feminism and Political Representation* analyzes a variety of debates about quotas and other mechanisms for improving women's representation in a variety of arenas. However, none of these analyses focus on a conservative political party. While this omission makes perfect sense from the perspective of the state feminism research – after all, parties of the left have been much more likely to implement quotas than parties of the right – it leaves a large gap in our knowledge about what might be going on with women's representation in parties of the right.

While the gender and politics literature provides a wide range of important ideas about how women engage in political action and under what conditions they are likely to meet with success, this literature also reveals some important questions that remain unasked, particularly when we consider politics in Germany. If the typical or desirable pathway for women's concerns to enter politics is for the women's movement to pressure the party of the left and then for these actors to engage in policy making through the women's policy agency, what happens when one or more of these actors does not fit this model? What if the women's movement has little interest in mainstream politics and the party of the left is not particularly friendly to feminism? What if the women's policy agency is often under the control of the conservatives? It is not that no policy on "women's issues" gets made under these conditions, but we have little information on *how* it gets made or indeed on *what kind* of policy gets made.

This book investigates what conservative women want from politics and under what conditions they have been able to get what they want. It focuses on (West) Germany, a country in which the standard actors on women's issues have been especially weak – or to put it another way, a country in which conservative, Christian Democratic actors have been especially strong. The book focuses on Germany's Christian Democratic Union, the CDU, and its policy making on women's issues with a particular emphasis on the party's organization for women, the Women's Union.

The book analyzes policy making in the areas of work-family policy, abortion policy, and participation policy. I selected these policy areas in consultation with policy makers in an effort to cover a wide spectrum of policies relating to women. The policy areas include some that involve serious economic outlay (parental leave and child care), important moral issues (abortion), and internal party power (participation policy/quotas). While I considered other policy areas – particularly policies on pensions and rape in marriage – these three areas cover the widest spectrum and also include a range of debates over a significant time period, from 1968 to 1998.

These policies have also been important in how they have influenced the lives of millions of women in Germany. In the mid-1990s over 95 percent of those eligible took parental leave and 99 percent of leave takers were women (Krug and Rauter 1998: 10). Parental leave and child care policies are likely to influence women's labor market participation, the gender wage gap and even the decision of whether and when to have a child, which affects the overall fertility rate (Morgan and Zippel 2003; Hank, Kreyenfeld, and Spiess 2004; Lewis, Knijn, Martin, and Ostner 2008: 263). The length of parental leave can also affect breastfeeding rates, child health, and infant mortality (Galtry and Callister 2005). Despite some revisions during the Red-Green coalition of 1998–2005, it has largely been the vision of the CDU that has shaped these policies in (West) Germany since the mid-1980s.

As abortion policy has been gradually liberalized since the 1970s, it is the CDU (in conjunction with the Federal Constitutional Court) that has determined how far to go during a particular time period. Twice the CDU asked the Federal Constitutional Court to review legislation that eased access to abortion and both times the FCC overturned the new law. The CDU has not been the source of new abortion reforms, but the party has acted as the brakes during the process of liberalization. It was only in the 1990s, after unification, but also after the CDU had undergone important internal modernization on this issue, that access to abortion was made significantly easier, at least in West Germany.

Finally, participation policies such as gender quotas have mostly been implemented at the party level in Germany. Parties act as gatekeepers to political participation. The percentage of women in the Bundestag increased from 9.8 percent in 1983 (the last year in which no party used a quota) to 32.8 percent in 2009 (Hoecker 1995: 135; *Parliamentary Democracy – Inter-Parliamentary Union*). During that time period the CDU's percentage of women in the Bundestag went from 6.7 percent to 21.6 percent (Hoecker 1995: 137; *Bundeswahlleiter* 2009). By adopting measures designed to increase female participation, the CDU contributed to a normalization of women in politics, a normalization that arguably played a role in the election of the country's first female Chancellor. In short, the three policy areas represent critical political issues that were significantly, even predominantly, shaped by Christian Democratic perspectives. To understand the politics of gender in Germany, we must understand the actions of the CDU.

This book proceeds as follows. In Chapter 1 I chart the CDU's pattern of policy making on three women's issues: abortion, work-family policy, and women's quotas. This empirical information initially serves to make the situation more puzzling. The CDU did not gradually become more progressive on women's issues over time. It did not simply imitate parties of the left. It did not implement only symbolic policies that cost little money. After exploring what policies the CDU pursued on this issue, I examine some possible existing explanations from the literature, including theories about electoral response, party ideology, and party organization. However, I conclude that existing theory is inadequate for understanding the empirical puzzle of how the CDU behaves toward women. Instead, we can best understand the CDU's policy making by understanding which internal groups hold the most power within the party.

Chapter 2 presents my corporatist catch-all party model. A corporatist catch-all party differs from a classic catch-all party, as defined by Kirchheimer (1966), in terms of party organization, leadership, membership, and party policy making. After discussing the internal organization of corporatist catch-all parties, the chapter goes on to discuss how this structure affects policy making.

Chapter 3 explores the historical background that led to the CDU's organization as a corporatist catch-all party. As we will see, the CDU did not design its corporatist catch-all organization in order to facilitate policy making. Rather two important historical events led to the party adopting this organization. First, the CDU has its roots in the Center Party, which followed the Social Catholicism model of auxiliary groups. Therefore, there was a precedent for the party to have important suborganizations. Second, in its founding moment, the CDU became a catch-all party with widespread appeal by integrating a variety of groups that would not necessarily come together easily in a political party: business and labor, Protestants and Catholics, northerners and southerners. An important technique for integrating diverse groups into a single political party was to form internal party organizations with representation on the new party's important decision-making bodies. The CDU also used this technique for its women's organization.

The next section of the book examines CDU policy making on three women's issues over three different time periods. Chapter 4 illustrates how societal changes increased the power and political presence of the CDU's auxiliary group for women. This chapter looks at the CDU during the 1970s. During this decade the reverberations from the women's movement were just beginning to be felt within the party. The CDU's women's organization, the Women's Union, was moving from a primarily coffee-serving society to a significant internal party actor. Much of the energy of the Women's Union during this decade was devoted to claiming its place as a recognized group within the CDU. The CDU itself, partially in response to pressure from the Women's Union, began work on policies to decrease the conflict between work and family. Although there was significant conflict over abortion during the 1970s, the CDU maintained its traditional pro-life stance. Gender quotas were not yet an issue. This chapter illustrates how societal changes can activate a previously latent group within a political party and significantly increase that group's internal leverage.

Chapter 5 demonstrates the ability of a group with a strong position within the party to have a major influence over party policy making. This chapter analyzes CDU policy making during the 1980s, the heyday of the Women's Union. Having claimed their place within the party, women developed a powerful alliance with the Social Committees, the CDU's internal group for labor. Together with the Social Committees and sometimes with the party's group for youth, the Women's Union successfully advocated for significant parental leave policies. The Women's Union also convinced the CDU to pass measures to encourage women to participate in the party. The Women's Union was divided on abortion and the CDU remained pro-life. This chapter shows the ability of an advantageously situated internal interest group – made up of both activists and leaders – to reformulate party policy significantly.

Chapter 6 shows the much more limited policy gains that are possible when an internal group is not dominant within the party. This chapter looks at the 1990s. While 1989 represents a critical year in German politics because of the Berlin wall coming down, internal CDU politics also saw an important shift at this time. The powerful internal coalition, made up of the Women's Union, the Social Committees, and the Youth Union, dissolved in the wake of an attempt to oust Helmut Kohl from the party chair position. The 1990s, then, were a more difficult time for the Women's Union and for the CDU in general. The party's internal constellation was shifting. The presence of easterners presented a new internal party group with different demands, especially on women's issues. Women in East Germany generally worked full time and had complete access to abortion. The 1990s witnessed the Women's Union working on a more ad hoc basis with the Social Committees and the eastern Germans. The Women's Union successfully got the CDU to pass a gender quota (albeit without sanctions), to add child care to the party's platform for the first time, and to sign on to legislation significantly increasing access to abortion in the west (while decreasing access in the east).

Chapter 7 illustrates the importance of internal party dynamics for personnel decisions instead of policy making. The CDU lost the national election in 1998 and entered the opposition for the first time since 1982. This chapter examines the rise of Angela Merkel, beginning in the unification period and continuing until her election as Chancellor in 2005. I show how the corporatist catch-all party model is particularly favorable to talented leaders who represent internal party minorities.

Chapter 8 uses cross-national comparison to illustrate the importance of the corporatist catch-all party model. Here I examine Christian Democratic parties in three additional countries: Austria, Italy, and the Netherlands. As in Germany, the Austrian Christian Democratic Party (the People's Party) has a corporatist catch-all party organization. As in the German case, this type of organization facilitates the input of various internal party groups, including women. The policy preferences of Christian Democratic women are acknowledged by their party. Italy and the Netherlands both have important Christian Democratic parties, but these parties do not represent women through a corporatist catch-all party organization. The Italian Christian Democratic Party is a corporatist catch-all party, but it does not represent women. The Dutch Christian Democratic Party is only weakly corporatist in its organization. These countries certainly have plenty of Christian Democratic women, but their views do not have much political impact.

Chapter 9 concludes by discussing the broader implications of this argument for theories of democracy and party organization. These are, in short, that internal party politics have a critical effect on policy making, but that internal party dynamics have previously been inadequately conceptualized. Importantly, existing theories of party organization tend to inappropriately pit activists against party leaders when in fact internal party groups may be based more around policy orientation than around position in the party hierarchy, at least in political parties with the corporatist catch-all party model.

I

The Puzzle of CDU Policy Making on Women's Issues

At the beginning of the twenty-first century, it is easy to take for granted a "natural" affinity between women and parties of the left. Particularly from an American perspective, the long-standing partnership between the (mainstream) feminist movement and the Democratic Party substantiates this relationship. Yet in most western democracies, including the United States, from the time women were granted suffrage until at least the 1970s, the "natural" affinity was between women and parties of the right (Duverger 1955; Campbell, Converse, Miller, and Stokes 1960; Lipset 1960; Butler and Stokes 1974). Inglehart and Norris call this voting difference the "traditional gender gap" (Inglehart and Norris 2003).

Germany was no exception to this trend. Once women in Germany gained the vote in 1919, they tended to support conservative parties, especially if those parties were religious in orientation (Molitor 1992: 24; Bremme 1956: 71). During the Weimar Republic, women voted for the Center Party and the German National People's Party. In the first decades after World War II, women were more likely than men to support Christian Democratic parties (Molitor 1992: 25).

Women were more likely to vote for conservative parties in general (and the CDU in particular) for a variety of reasons. Women tend to live longer and older people are often more conservative; women also tend to be more religious; women were less likely to be employed outside the home and housewives were particularly likely to be conservative (Bremme 1956; Lipset 1960; Molitor 1992: 33–6; Inglehart and Norris 2003: 77). In West Germany in particular, women may have voted for the CDU because of the party's promises to return the world to "normal" (Moeller 1993: 112). During the war, with men absent from Germany, women had stepped into the void in a variety of ways, working in fields and factories. Rather than rejoicing in their newfound empowerment, the German counterparts of Rosie the Riveter voted for the CDU because of the party's promises to return the country to more traditional gender roles.

The CDU's view of the proper role of women was based on the "3K" image: *Kinder, Kirche, Küche*, or "children, church, kitchen." Women's proper place was in the family, taking care of the children and other family members, or in the church, possibly performing community service and once again, taking care of others. CDU ideology quite explicitly placed a very high value on these activities. These care-taking activities were regarded as being at least as important as the more public world of work and politics, a world populated primarily by men.

Societal changes of the 1960s and 1970s led many women to want something different from the "3K" image the CDU had on offer. Notable changes included the emergence of the women's movement, the increasing number of women in the work place, and the secularization of society. These trends decreased the importance of women's traditional activities and increased the likelihood that women would be involved in what had been viewed in the past as male activities. During the same time period, the rise in the numbers of single parents and the declining birthrate disrupted traditional family structures. These changes made the CDU's stances on women's issues seem increasingly out of touch to substantial segments of society.

With growing numbers of German women less attracted by the 3K image, the CDU began to receive fewer votes from women. Table 1.1 illustrates the so-called "women's bonus" over time. The CDU has a "women's bonus" when it receives more votes from women than from men.

In 1953 the CDU received 47.2 percent of women's votes and only 38.9 percent of men's (Ritter and Niehuss 1991: 224). Until 1972, the CDU regularly received 8 percent to 10 percent more from female voters than from male voters. Indeed, the difference in support from women and men was actually growing throughout this period. In 1972 an abrupt change occurred, and the difference between women's and men's support dropped dramatically. During the CDU's stint in the opposition in the 1970s, the party's women's bonus was significantly smaller and shrinking. While the CDU never recovered the levels of support from women that the party enjoyed in the 1950s and 1960s, the party did nonetheless do better with women throughout the 1980s, only to suffer another turnaround in the 1990s. Note that when the CDU's women's bonus is *declining*, the party

TABLE 1.1 *CDU's Women's Bonus over Time*

Year	% Women voting CDU	% Men voting CDU	Difference
1953	47.2	38.9	8.3
1957	53.5	44.6	8.9
1961	49.6	40.4	9.2
1965	51.7	42.1	9.6
1969	50.6	40.6	10.0
1972	46.0	43.0	3.0[a]
1976	48.8	47.2	1.6[a]
1980	43.7	44.2	−0.5[a]
1983	49.2	47.7	1.5
1987	45.1	42.5	2.6
1990	44.9	42.0	2.9
1994	42.2	40.6	1.6
1998	35.0	34.9	0.1[a]
2002	37.8	39.2	−1.4[a]
2005	34.5	34.7	−0.2

For 1953–87 calculated from results in Ritter and Niehuss (1991: 224). 1990 results calculated from Claus Fischer, Konrad Adenauer Stiftung (1997: 78). 1994 results calculated from Ritter and Niehuss (1995: 51). 1998 results calculated from Molitor and Neu (1999: 255). Election results from 2002 and 2005 calculated from information found at http://www.election.de/cgi-bin/news1.pl
[a]represents CDU defeat.

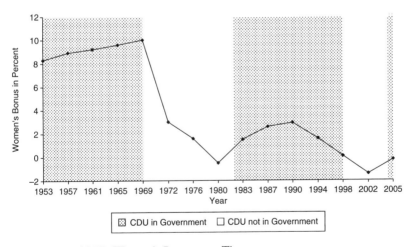

FIGURE 1.1 CDU's Women's Bonus over Time

has lost. When the party begins to receive more votes from women, it has been able to return to government.

The dramatic shift in electoral support in 1972 did not go unnoticed by party strategists, who realized that societal changes were contributing to women's abandonment of the CDU. However, it was unclear how the party should respond. After all, many women were still supporting the CDU. The CDU found itself caught between loyal voters who preferred the party's traditional policy stances on women's issues and an emerging constituency with different policy preferences.

Conservative parties in many western democracies have faced a similar dilemma. As the "traditional gender gap" has given way to the "modern gender gap," women have begun to favor parties of the left rather than parties of the right (Inglehart and Norris 2003: 73–100). Conservative party responses to this dilemma, however, have varied from country to country (Maguire 1998; Melich 1998; Young 2000; Rymph 2006).

The CDU has offered a mixed strategy for confronting these changes. Sometimes the CDU resisted the new ideas about women and tried to promote its traditional image. Other times, the CDU accommodated the new ideas and incorporated the new themes brought up by society. What is behind this variation in response?

I investigate this question by examining three issues: work-family policy, abortion policy, and political participation policy.[1] Each issue has presented a challenge to the CDU's traditional stance. In the case of work-family policy, the traditional CDU view is that women should not be employed outside the home. Therefore, they do not need any benefits or policies to facilitate combining work and family. Indeed, public policy should encourage mothers to remain at home with their children. With more mothers employed outside the home and more single parents, however, voters demanded policies to help women combine work and family. Christian Democratic doctrine clearly opposes all moves toward liberalizing abortion access. The women's movement, however, made liberalizing access to abortion a centerpiece of its demands, and many voters agreed with this stance. Finally, while there is nothing in CDU ideology that directly opposes women's political participation or office holding, the CDU (and its predecessor, the Center Party) has historically had a significantly smaller number of active women than the parties of the left. Women

---

[1] Political participation policy is policy designed to increase the number of female office holders, either in the party itself or in government. Quotas are one well-known type of participation policy. In any case, this type of policy applies to participation in addition to voting.

TABLE 1.2 *CDU Policies Toward Women*

Period	Work-Family Policy	Abortion Policy	Women's Representation	Overall Women's Policy Outcome
1969–82	1	0	–	1
1982–9	2	0	2	4
1989–98	1	1	1	3

0 = No Reform
1 = Minor Reform
2 = Major Reform

were not expected to be active in the public sphere. Therefore, the CDU was not interested in any measures to increase women's political participation. Women had other ideas and began to be politically active in much greater numbers, particularly in the 1980s.

These challenges to traditional CDU policy caused and continue to cause significant internal party conflict. At times, on some issues, the party shifted its policy. On other occasions the CDU strenuously resisted change. How can we explain the variation in response? The first step in understanding how the CDU responded to new demands from women is to examine what that response was.

The transformation of CDU behavior can be broken into three time periods. The first period I investigate is 1969–82, the CDU's first stint in the opposition. The second time period, 1982–9, marks the party's return to government as the dominant partner in the Christian Democratic-Liberal coalition under Chancellor Helmut Kohl. Finally, the third time period, 1989–98, begins with German unification and ends with the CDU's electoral defeat in 1998.

The pattern of CDU behavior is complex. I have coded the CDU's response in each policy area for each time period as no reform, minor reform, or major reform (Table 1.2). I have also added the extent of reform in each policy area together for a given time period to create an index for overall women's policy outcomes. The following section briefly summarizes CDU responses chronologically.

Despite significant societal pressure from the late 1960s through the 1970s, during the first time period, 1969–82, the CDU resisted change and offered primarily traditional responses to new demands from women. With regard to work-family policy, the CDU began advocating child-raising money for parents (in practice, mothers) who stayed home with their children. Although this policy represented a reaffirmation of the traditional gendered division of labor, some actors within the CDU had resisted child-raising money as unnecessary and expensive, because mothers would stay home with their children even without the money. In the face of intense protests to liberalize the abortion law and the party's own strong desire to get credit for designing new legislation, the CDU remained unyielding on abortion. Political participation policies were not yet on the agenda. For this time period, I have coded the CDU's overall women's policy outcome as a 1 because the child-raising money represented a new benefit to women, albeit one in keeping with traditional gender norms.

The 1980s were the heyday for the CDU's efforts to modernize its women's policies. After returning to power in 1982, the CDU created West Germany's first Women's Ministry. The entire party congress of 1985 was devoted to women's issues. The CDU also passed a significant package of work-family policies, including not only child-raising money, but also job guarantees for parents who take time off to care for their children and pension credits for time spent caring for children. In the late 1980s, the CDU adopted a series of measures designed to boost women's participation in the party. On abortion, however, the CDU remained recalcitrant and even considered reversing the policies enacted when the party had been in the opposition. I scored the CDU's overall women's policy outcome as 4 for this time period because of the significant reforms on both work-family policy and participation policy.

In the 1990s, the CDU continued to accommodate working women by passing a law mandating the creation of Kindergarten spots for all children aged three to six. In terms of political participation, however, the CDU voted down a measure that would have given women at least one-third of party offices and every third slot on the electoral lists. Instead, the party adopted a much weaker, nonmandatory measure to increase women's participation in the party. In the 1990s, the CDU also signed an abortion law that transferred the abortion decision from the doctor to the pregnant woman. However, abortion remained a criminal act (though one that would not be punished). For this third time period, I scored the CDU's overall women's policy outcome as 3 because of the modest reforms in all three issue areas.

As is clear from even this short policy summary, the CDU response to changing demands from women is not uniform and does not follow an obvious pattern. The party has not become more accommodating over time, for example. Nor has it responded consistently on individual issues. For any given issue area, the CDU has both resisted change and embraced reform at different moments. The following section explores three rival hypotheses that seek to explain CDU behavior.

ALTERNATIVE HYPOTHESES

Existing theory offers three main arguments for explaining how a large conservative party might respond to change. First, theories based on ideology claim that the CDU is primarily a *Catholic* party. The party's response to societal changes will be guided by its Christian-based ideology. Second, spatial voting literature sees the CDU as part of an oligopolistic system of parties competing for government office and predicts that the CDU's response to societal changes will be driven primarily by concerns for electoral advantage. Finally, catch-all party theories posit that the CDU will try to appeal to new groups in society by making its ideology vaguer and by loosening its ties to party activists. In the end, none of these hypotheses provides a satisfactory answer to our puzzle.

An Essentialist Christian Party

Essentialist theories view parties as deeply embedded entities with strong links to their core subcultures (Lipset and Rokkan 1967; Przeworski and Sprague 1986). These theories predict that the CDU will not respond to new demands from women with any serious adjustment (although the party may respond symbolically). Theories that envision little change highlight the party's ideology as a *Christian* Democratic party. Because of the CDU's roots in Christianity and the party's links to Catholic subculture, the party is expected to cede little ground in terms of modernizing the CDU's stance on women's roles. Particularly on moral issues, such as abortion, the CDU will resist change, even if resistance is electorally costly.

Essentialist theories focus on a party's ideology. The existence of a core constituency virtually guarantees the party a certain level of support and parliamentary representation. When society changes, however, parties face a dilemma if their base is declining. Reaching out beyond core supporters requires parties to moderate their ideologies and their policies. But, moderation implies that essentialist parties sacrifice their identity, which they are unwilling to do. Furthermore, moving away from the party's ideology will alienate the party's traditional voters, also causing electoral decline. For the CDU, societal changes such as secularization and increasing female workforce participation mean that its traditional policies toward women have declined in popularity. Many CDU members and voters continue to support the party's more traditional understanding of women's roles, however, and they may withdraw their support if the CDU decides to compromise on these issues. Przeworski and Sprague (1986) identify a similar dilemma for working-class parties faced with a declining working class. Trade-offs between old and new supporters will be difficult, if not impossible, to pull off successfully. According to essentialist theories, the CDU will ensure the loyalty of these core supporters by remaining true to its Christian ideology.

One possible way out of this dilemma is for the party to offer symbolic policy. Symbolic policy is designed to have little or no real effect (Edelman 1964; Elder and Cobb 1983; Mazur 1995). By offering symbolic policy, the CDU can try to appear to accommodate new demands from women while actually remaining loyal to its traditional position. Of course, this technique involves the tricky undertaking of fooling new supporters into thinking the party has changed, while simultaneously ensuring that old supporters know the party has not changed. This balancing act will probably be difficult to maintain in the long run, but that does not mean parties will not attempt it.

The CDU has certainly passed symbolic policy on women's issues, which might lead observers to believe that the party is only responding symbolically. The CDU's programmatic statements in 1975, "Woman and Society," and 1985, "A New Partnership," clearly served symbolic purposes. "Woman and Society," for example, declared that women were to have an equal role in political, economic, and all other aspects of society. The statement also assigned the task of child rearing to men and women equally (CDU National Party Congress 1975). "A New Partnership" stated that the CDU's Christian understanding of humanity cannot be reconciled with continued discrimination against women. It called for more women to be active in political parties and the media and for men to take over more responsibilities in the household and in child care (CDU National Party Congress 1985). Both of these statements called for dramatic changes in how German society is organized but did little to translate these ideas into practice.

While the CDU certainly passes symbolic women's policy on occasion, the essentialist Christian party theory leaves much CDU behavior unexplained. The party is considerably more flexible than this theory predicts, often responding to societal changes by passing policies that accommodate women's new demands. Many of these policies have had a real, even dramatic, impact on women. For example, in the 1990s, the CDU supported the abortion compromise that significantly eased access to abortion (at least in West Germany). The work-family policy package passed by the CDU in the 1980s provided for parental leave that has been used by nearly 95 percent of mothers since it was implemented (Engelbrech, Gruber, and Jungkunst 1997: 161). From 1985 to 1988, approximately 80 percent of these mothers used the job guarantee to return to work after the parental leave ended (Speil 1991: 72). This policy package cost around 7.2 billion DM in 1995 (Wingen 1997: 214). While the CDU has not given in to every new demand from women, it has clearly responded to some demands, and these responses have been much more than symbolic. Clearly, CDU actions on women's issues are driven by forces beyond an unyielding commitment to Christian doctrine.

Spatial Voting Theory

The spatial voting literature argues that the CDU's behavior, including the party's choice of women's policies, is influenced by voter preferences and the actions of other parties (Downs 1957). This approach views the CDU as a leading player in an oligopolistic system in which the goal of parties is to maximize votes. The most famous result from this approach to studying politics is the median voter theorem. Originally formulated by Downs and made more precise by subsequent authors, the median voter theorem states that political parties will cluster around the median voter; in other words, in the center of the policy space.

Applied to the example of the emergence of women's issues in Germany, we might have the following expectations: New issues were raised by societal changes and by the women's movement of the late 1960s and early 1970s. Voters desired new policies on women's issues and were potentially willing to vote for parties that offered such policies. As a party of the left, the Social Democrats were initially more open to these demands. When the SPD adopted policies attractive to the newly emerging constituency of female voters, women began to shift their votes. As the CDU began to lose votes, it would imitate the SPD and the two main parties would converge around the political center.

This spatial model was developed with the idea that parties could be envisioned to be taking positions along a single line. It was based primarily on the two-party system of the United States. Attempting to apply spatial modeling to the German political system is a complex undertaking. For a variety of reasons, the expectation of convergence of the policy positions of the two main political parties does not necessarily hold. As recognized by theorists working with this approach, under the circumstances of German politics – namely more than two political parties and a multidimensional political space – it is difficult to know what to expect. While a simplistic use of spatial voting theory argues that we should expect convergence, a more sophisticated examination of the theory notes that it is difficult to say whether to expect convergence, divergence, or no stable result at all.

As mentioned earlier, the bulk of the spatial voting literature was developed to describe a two-party system. Moving from two to three parties exponentially complicates the situation. First, for multiparty competition, equilibrium locations do not always exist (Shepsle 1991: 28).[2] If an equilibrium exists, which means if all parties take the positions described in the equilibrium, then no party has an incentive to change its policies because no party can gain an advantage by changing its position. It is a stable outcome. If no equilibrium exists – as is *generally* the case with more than two parties – then it is not predictable what positions parties will take. In other words, under normal circumstances, with multiparty competition, spatial voting theory cannot predict what policies parties will offer.

Until the early 1980s, there were three parties in West Germany's party system. The two large parties, the CDU and the Social Democratic Party (SPD), competed for the dominant position in government. The small liberal Free Democratic Party (FDP) played the role of junior coalition partner to both of the large parties. According to Shepsle (1991: 23) there is no equilibrium in a three-party system. In the 1980s, the Greens, a second party of the left, entered the political scene. With unification in 1990, the Party of Democratic Socialism (PDS), the successor to the old Communist Party of East Germany, became an important regional party in the Eastern states. The PDS subsequently merged with Labour and Social Justice – The Electoral Alternative (a party founded largely by disaffected SPD members) to form the Left Party. Today, Germany is closer to a multiparty system than to a two-party system, albeit with two parties that are significantly larger (25–40 percent of the vote) than the other three (5–10 percent of the vote).

Spatial voting theory predicts that the CDU will respond to changes in the electorate, such as new demands from women, by positioning itself in whichever fashion offers the largest electoral payoff. The difficulty is that

---

[2] Shepsle is assuming a plurality election rule and Germany's electoral system, of course, is generally classified as proportional representation. Cox (1997: 81) argues, however, that the first-past-the-post aspects of Germany's system are sufficient to perform a spatial analysis as if it were a plurality system.

the optimum strategy is not always obvious. In the German context, two issues make it difficult to predict the optimum electoral strategy. First, coalition government is the norm. Second, there are multiple dimensions of competition.

In many multiparty systems, including Germany's, most governments are coalition governments. Governing by coalition, however, is more complicated than governing alone and "makes rational behavior difficult for parties" (Downs 1957: 156). To ease tension with each other, coalition partners may try to find agreement on policy. On the other hand, to appeal to a variety of voters, coalition partners should engage in "product differentiation" and offer a range of policies. Furthermore, each party would prefer to maximize its own power within the coalition, which could mean moving close to or apart from its prospective coalition partner (Downs 1957: 157–9).

The CDU is often pulled in opposite directions on women's issues by its sister party, the Christian Social Union (CSU), and its preferred coalition partner, the FDP. The Christian Social Union is a regional party in conservative Bavaria. It has the most traditional stance of all German parties on women's issues. The FDP, on the other hand, is more likely to advocate a progressive vision on women's policies. There are too many conflicting pressures to predict party behavior with only the information provided by the distribution of voters and other parties. To give just one example, in the late 1970s, there was a serious conflict between the CDU's desire to be more accommodating of societal changes (including, but not limited to, the role of women), and thereby win back the cooperation of the FDP, and the CSU's desire to rally sufficient numbers of conservative voters to get back into government. The CDU and the CSU nearly ended their sisterly relationship over this conflict. Both parties thought their strategy would be more likely to win the election. Clearly, the politicians themselves are often unsure what the best strategy might be.

Another problem for spatial analysis occurs if there is more than one dimension to competition. Again, most of the theorizing of this type assumes a single dimension of competition. Often this simplifying assumption is entirely appropriate. In many industrialized democracies, most voting is structured by issues of socioeconomic class. While multiple issues certainly exist, they can be collapsed onto a single issue without any loss of content. This is not true in Germany, however. While socioeconomic class is certainly an important dimension in German politics, religion has been at least as good – and often better – at predicting how people would vote (Saalfeld 2005: 75).

In political systems such as Germany's, with more than one dimension of competition, most of the theoretical insights from spatial voting theory no longer apply.

The addition of a complicating feature from the real world makes it difficult for spatial voting theory to be useful to us in attempting to understand empirical politics. If we allow for more than one dimension in politics, then we lose the existence of a political "middle" where voters and parties could cluster (Hinich and Munger 1997: 63). In this situation, "majority rule processes can be arbitrary" and chaotic (Hinich and Munger 1997: 63). Worse still, there is no guarantee that the outcome is one that will be preferred by a majority of voters. In fact, it is possible that the outcome will be one that the entire society thinks is worse than some other available policy choice (Hinich and Munger 1997: 64). While regular voters surely sometimes feel this way, it comes as a surprise that it is possibly a correct interpretation of what is happening. In any case, when there is more than one dimension of competition, politics is much more complex.

Spatial modeling certainly helps explain some of the actions of the CDU. On certain issues, such as participation policy, the CDU has clearly imitated policies initiated by left-wing parties. However, this approach also has significant limitations. It is not at all clear, for example, that the best strategy in response to a left party challenge is to imitate the left. In some cases, the CDU may choose to move to the right. For example, in the 1980s, the CDU responded to the SPD's initiatives to liberalize abortion access by radicalizing its position in an attempt to mobilize conservative voters. Spatial voting theory cannot distinguish between moments when the CDU will respond by moving to the left and moments when the CDU will respond by moving to the right.

While it is certainly true that other parties and electoral concerns can provoke a response from the CDU, it is not clear what that response will be. Sometimes the CDU will move toward the left in an effort to blur the differences between the parties. Other times, the CDU will move in the opposite direction to clarify the difference. The primary limitation of spatial voting theory is that it underspecifies how the CDU will respond. Of course the party cares about election results, but this concern does not necessarily tell us whether the CDU will accommodate or resist new demands from women.

Theories of Party Organization

The third alternative hypothesis considered here stems from theories of party organization. Most theories of party organization take an evolutionary approach that describes how party organization has changed over time (Katz and Mair 1995; von Beyme 1996). At different stages of evolution, political parties have had different internal organizations. The various organizational forms affect the relative power balance between leaders and members. A party's internal structure can also determine a party's incentives and ability to respond to societal change. Arguments about party organization also have implications for which groups within a political party have the power to shape party policy.

Theorists working in this tradition often try to categorize party organization based on chronological time period. For example, Duverger has identified elite or cadre parties as typical of the nineteenth century (Duverger 1954). These parties were often loose groupings of notables working together on particular issues without much connection to society outside of the party. They belong to an era when mass suffrage was an exception, not the rule.

At the turn of the twentieth century, as the franchise was extended to working class men (and sometimes women) in many western democracies, a new form of political party arose. Parties of mass integration generally lacked financial resources but by recruiting large memberships they could compete with and even supplant the cadre parties of the earlier era (Neumann 1956). In order to motivate supporters politically, this new kind of party supplied many social needs. Parties of mass integration proved successful in the electoral arena. While working class parties were frequent initiators of the new organizational style, this model was soon copied by parties of the right as well. Denominational parties had often followed this path anyway because in some countries Catholics, like workers, were socially disadvantaged. The conventional wisdom on these parties is that there was not much internal conflict because they were fairly homogenous. Parties of mass integration are usually presumed to have targeted the desires of their memberships in terms of policies both because these desires were fairly straightforward to discern and because these parties were (supposedly) internally democratic.

Parties of mass integration were formed as a strategy for beating the older form of political party, the cadre party, at the polls. Similarly, catch-all parties, the next evolutionary stage in party organization, took shape as a response to parties of mass integration and an effort to beat them at the electoral game (Kirchheimer 1966). While parties of mass integration had their particular constituencies sewn up, each party only catered to one constituency. In other words, a party of the working class was a party only of the working class. Therefore, a party which could appeal to multiple constituencies could generate more votes and win more elections. According to Kirchheimer, this appeal outside the core constituency had both costs and benefits. By exchanging the depth of the mass integration party for the breadth of the catch-all party, the new catch-all parties could get more votes (Kirchheimer 1966: 184). But party leaders would be less closely in tune with what their supporters wanted and their supporters would now potentially be in conflict with each other.

Catch-all parties addressed these problems with two basic techniques. First, they offered generalized appeals that everyone would surely agree with. Calling for prosperity for all would not likely dissuade voters. Second, since internal conflict now presumably would be a problem, catch-all parties disabled their memberships. Whereas in mass integration parties, members could contribute to lively internal party debate (at least in this somewhat stylized analysis), in a catch-all party, members did little to shape party policy. Kirchheimer predicted that this form of party would triumph at the polls, so much so that most parties would adopt this form of organization. He feared that democracy would subsequently suffer (Kirchheimer 1966: 200).

The term "catch-all party" has been popular since Kirchheimer introduced it in 1966. Scholars have subsequently focused on different pieces of Kirchheimer's rather complex argument.[3] Kirchheimer's arguments about how catch-all parties de-emphasize ideology have received significant attention.[4] Scholars have worked to refine Kirchheimer's arguments and highlighted the fact that some of his predictions did not come to pass (Smith 1990). In particular, catch-all parties à la Kirchheimer have turned out to be less omnipresent and more vulnerable that he predicted.[5]

---

[3] Wolinetz (1979) and Dittrich (1983) both break Kirchheimer's argument down into a series of propositions.

[4] Indeed, Smith (1982) argues that catch-all parties may not even exist. He finds scant evidence for a move to catch-all parties outside of West Germany and provides an alternative explanation for centripetal parties in West Germany. However, Smith is not concerned with the organizational aspects of Kirchheimer's theory, which are the focus of this analysis.

[5] The continued presence of non-catch-all parties is not that problematic for Kirchheimer's thesis. As Wolinetz notes, particular electoral and societal conditions allow for the emergence of catch-all parties (Wolinetz 1991). Writing in 1966, Kirchheimer could not have predicted the rise of the post-materialist cleavage (Inglehart 1977) or the new radical right parties (Betz 1994; Kitschelt 1995; Betz and Immerfall 1998; Norris 2005). If not all parties became catch-all parties, certainly some parties in some places developed from something like parties of mass integration to something like catch-all parties. That other parties continue to exist or even arise to challenge catch-all parties simply shows that some political organizations figured out ways to take on the supposed catch-all leviathans.

Kirchheimer's argument is that leaders of catch-all parties disempowered membership to help limit internal conflict. Other scholars have noted that catch-all parties may be more vulnerable than Kirchheimer expected because decoupling from membership may not be possible. Despite the desire to adopt a catch-all party strategy, some parties may not be able to. As Kitschelt notes, even if leaders are able to determine the optimal electoral strategy, in some parties constraints may prevent leaders from making the appropriate policy adjustments. If leadership is insufficiently "autonomous" or if membership is too "entrenched," then members will be able to prevent the party leadership from responding to societal changes (Kitschelt 1994).

Another possibility is that an overly "entrenched" membership will force through an inappropriate response. Both Kitschelt (1994) and Koelble (1991) examine the difficulties of the British Labour Party in the 1980s in this light. A takeover by the radical left rendered the party unelectable, even against the less-than-congenial Margaret Thatcher. If either constraint – insufficient leadership autonomy or overly entrenched membership – prevents the party from responding to voters (rather than members), then the party will lose electoral support as its position becomes increasingly disconnected from the preferences of wide segments of society. These theories share the ideas that membership acts only negatively on a party and that leaders should try to deactivate membership (though they may not succeed).

What Kirchheimer and his followers have in common is that they highlight the importance of party organization for determining the quality of party response to society and the quality of democracy. The internal dynamics of a political party have a significant effect on how and whether that party responds to changing societal demands. Of course parties want to win votes, but the internal life of a political party is a critical filter between the demand coming from society and the output (policies or policy proposals) the party eventually generates.

The CDU is frequently considered to be a catch-all party (Schönbohm 1985; Chandler 1988; Haungs 1992). In terms of CDU response to new demands from women, catch-all theory predicts that the CDU would issue statements on women's policies that are so vague they are hard to disagree with, while simultaneously demobilizing membership in an effort to dampen any tensions with membership over these issues. This hypothesis will investigate whether the CDU fits the catch-all party model as stipulated by Kirchheimer (Kirchheimer 1966).

Catch-all party theories draw our attention to the importance of organizational factors for analyzing party response to societal changes. The relative influence of leaders and members is important and affects what kind of strategy a party will adopt. These theories have too narrow a vision of the role of party members, however. According to these theories of party organization, the best thing a party can hope for from its membership is that it does not seriously constrain the ability of leaders to enact their strategy. This vision is problematic on two counts. First, like spatial voting theory, it assumes that only one best strategy is available and that leadership knows what it is. Second, the only role allowed for membership is as a negative constraint; members may or may not prevent leaders from implementing the "correct" strategy, which is identified by the leadership. This vision ignores the possibility that successful new ideas and strategies might come from membership groups, rather than party leaders. As Mair (1990) points out, decoupling membership from the party organization makes catch-all parties vulnerable to a decline in voter loyalty.[6]

Scholars working from the evolutionary perspective are currently engaged in a heated debate about the possible emergence of the next type of party, the cartel party (Katz and Mair 1995).[7] The cartel party thesis builds on the idea of catch-all party vulnerability. Because catch-all parties had decoupled themselves from their members, voters became freely available and could be courted by any party. Parties could therefore easily lose support. In an effort to maintain positions of power – and also to maintain the wealth of politicians – some parties converted to cartel parties. In a cartel party system, the major political parties live off of state subsidies, which they conveniently approve for themselves. While they may not work

---

[6] Susan E. Scarrow's excellent book, *Parties and Their Members: Organizing for Victory in Britain and Germany*, fits uneasily in this typology (Scarrow 1996). Through an investigation of the Labour and Conservative parties in Great Britain and the CDU and the SPD in Germany, Scarrow finds that party leaders still value party members, particularly as a source of legitimacy. She does not view members as detracting from a party's chances at success and her research reveals multiple ways in which parties have attempted to maintain or even increase membership. Furthermore, in keeping with the argument of this book, Scarrow finds evidence of increasing intraparty democratization in some of the parties in her study. She does not, however, analyze conflict among different groups of members or leaders or how this conflict might be regulated through the party organization.

[7] The cartel party thesis has sparked a great deal of scholarly argument (Koole 1996, Katz and Mair 1996; Young, L. 1998; Kitschelt 2000; Blyth and Katz 2005; Scarrow 2006). Discussions have focused on the question of to what extent parties are moving to a cartel-like system and whether the entire notion of a cartel party is a valid one. According to the cartel party thesis, as parties accept more state subsidies they become closer to the state. As Detterbeck (2005) points out, however, closer state ties do not preclude close societal ties. Indeed, it may be advantageous for a party to have both. The ties to both state and society need to be investigated and considered separately until there is good evidence that one kind of link precludes the other.

openly together, cartel parties nonetheless have the effect of colluding to limit competition. In a cartel party system, democracy is seriously degraded as parties become part of the state and responsible only to themselves and not to voters. Like Kirchheimer and the other theorists in the evolutionary tradition, Katz and Mair argue that incentives from party competition are such that an increasing number of parties will evolve into cartel parties.

The evolutionary perspective on party organization envisions that parties will adapt to their environment in similar ways. Although it is sometimes implicit, this perspective generally assumes that parties will respond to shared challenges with shared solutions and therefore that all parties in a particular country (or even all parties in countries at similar stages of development) will have similar organizational structures. These assumptions are actually not in keeping with Darwin's theory of evolution, however. There may be multiple responses to a particular environmental challenge, for example. Different responses will lead parties to develop in different rather than similar ways.

A Different Approach to Party Organization

This book builds on theories of party organization, but takes the developmental approach rather than the evolutionary approach (Panebianco 1988; Harmel and Janda 1994; Wilson 1994). This developmental approach to party organization examines the role of internal party politics in influencing party behavior. Analysts working in this tradition consider whether and how particular internal institutional structures facilitate or hinder adaptation to societal change.[8] These theories argue that parties to some extent shape their own development. Decisions made by actors within the party affect how the party responds to external challenges.

Unlike the evolutionary approach, which assumes that parties will meet external challenges in similar ways, the developmental approach suggests that party response will vary from party to party. From this perspective, then, Kirchheimer has correctly identified a shared dilemma: how could the pre–World War II parties of mass integration expand beyond their original base of electoral support without alienating their core constituencies? Kirchheimer's mistake is in presenting the catch-all party as the *only* response. This book argues instead that multiple responses are possible. When making comparisons to Kirchheimer's model, this research treats it

---

[8] Wilson (1994) focuses particularly on leaders rather than institutions.

as an ideal type, a generalization of how parties responded to the challenge of trying to broaden their electorates. Actual parties may approximate Kirchheimer's model or they might take a quite different approach to the dilemma of expanding support without losing their original voters.

Two factors influence how a party responds: the party's founding conditions and the party's primary goal. Indeed, these two factors are linked, as the circumstances facing a party at its moment of origin will lead to the adoption of goals that are appropriate for that moment in time. The goals of the founding moment are embedded into the party's institutional architecture and will continue to influence how the party responds to challenges in the future. As Duverger puts it, "Just as men bear all their lives the mark of their childhood, so parties are profoundly influenced by their origins" (Duverger 1954: xxiii).

While Duverger distinguishes primarily between parties of parliamentary origins versus parties of extraparliamentary origins, Panebianco has developed a more sophisticated typology of genetic models (Duverger 1954: xxiii-xxxvii; Panebianco 1988: 49–68). Panebianco's analysis examines three factors of party formation: the party's construction through either territorial penetration or territorial diffusion,[9] the presence or absence of an external "sponsor," and the potential presence of a charismatic leader. Each of these factors influences the party's subsequent organization. For example, a party that is formed through territorial penetration – that is, when the central party organization directs the formation of local organizations – is more centralized and cohesive. A party formed through territorial diffusion – meaning that local organizations exist first and work together to create a national organization – will be less centralized and is more likely to be marked by struggles over control of the party leadership. In the case of a party, with an external sponsor, activists may be primarily loyal to the sponsoring organization (such as a trade union or a church) rather than the party and leaders may be legitimated by the sponsoring organization rather than the party's own organization. Finally, a party of "pure" charisma will be inseparable from the charismatic leader who founded it. Panebianco also allows for "situational" charisma, in cases where a leader offers exceptional leadership in a time of extreme social stress (Tucker in Panebianco 1988: 52). These three factors, the process of party construction, the potential presence of an external sponsor, and the

---

[9] Panebianco views territorial penetration or diffusion as distinct from Duverger's notion of parliamentary or extraparliamentary origins (Panebianco 1988: 50).

potential presence of a charismatic leader, determine a party's "genetic model" (Panebianco: 1988: 50–3).

In addition to its founding conditions, a party's goals influence its behavior. A range of theorists have considered a variety of party goals such as vote seeking, office seeking, policy seeking, and democracy seeking (Budge and Keman 1990; Laver and Schofield 1990; Strøm 1990; Schlesinger 1991; Harmel and Janda 1994; Harmel et. al. 1995; Müller and Strøm 1999). Vote-seeking parties, obviously, prioritize winning votes over all other goals. In a two-party system, office-seeking parties are essentially the same as vote-seeking parties. In multiparty systems, however, office-seeking parties may act to maximize votes for their preferred governing coalition rather than for an individual party. Policy-seeking parties work to maximize their ability to influence public policy. Exactly how parties do this may involve complex strategic calculations, however, particularly in terms of how to elicit policy concessions from potential coalition partners (Müller and Strøm 1999: 5–9). Finally, democracy-seeking parties attempt to maximize internal party democracy (Harmel and Janda 1994: 269). Parties with different goals are likely to behave differently when facing a similar stimulus from the external environment. Parties will evaluate the meaning of the external challenge differently based on their particular goals and parties will have varying capacities to respond to the challenge based on their institutional structures (Koelble 1991; Kitschelt 1994; Levitsky 2001; Leslie 2002; Burgess and Levitsky 2003; Leslie and Wiliarty 2009).

Panebianco classifies the CDU as being constructed through territorial diffusion ("in the purest form" no less), lacking an external sponsor, and having a "situationally" charismatic leader in Konrad Adenauer at its founding. Thus, we can expect the party to be decentralized, to exhibit leadership conflict, and not to have activists who are more loyal to some other organization. Panebianco notes that leaders with situational charisma cannot mold their organization as they see fit, but rather must "*bargain* with many other organizational actors" (Panebianco 1988: 52). Even Adenauer, who so thoroughly dominated much of the CDU's early development, had to negotiate many of his policies with other internal party actors.

In terms of party goals, the CDU is usually classified as an office-seeking party (Panebianco 1988; Harmel and Janda 1994: 284). The goal of the CDU is certainly to win elections and gain executive office. But the founding conditions of the CDU embedded an additional goal in the party's institutions, that of internal balancing of a range of societal interest groups.

As noted previously, the CDU was founded as a decentralized party. Although Adenauer was a powerful party leader, he had to bargain with multiple internal groups when making decisions for the party. One of the CDU's primary strategies for managing rival tendencies within the party was to institutionalize representation for various groups on the party's internal decision-making bodies. To give just one example, in an effort to convince Protestants to support the party, the CDU formed an internal group for Protestants and guaranteed this group access to party policy making (Bösch 2001). While the party's *goal* is to win elections, its *strategy* for achieving that goal is to represent and balance societal groups internally. This strategy led the party to develop what I call a corporatist catch-all party structure.

While the book primarily analyzes the organization and behavior of the CDU, it is interesting to note that the SPD also does not fully conform to Kirchheimer's expectations for a catch-all party. Panebianco classifies the SPD as having been formed through territorial diffusion because it was formed from the merger of the ADAV (General German Workers' Association) and the SDAP (the Social Democratic Workers' Party) in 1875 (Panebianco 1988: 70). This originating condition is similar to the CDU's formation. However, Bismarck's persecution of social democrats led to the party being thoroughly centralized and thus counteracted the decentralized tendencies created through the merger. The unions in Germany were more dependent on the SPD than the other way around so the SPD (like the CDU) was not legitimated by an external organization. Finally, while the CDU was founded in the context of Adenauer's situational charisma, the SPD did not have charismatic leaders. This combination of founding conditions led to a highly institutionalized party, much more so than the CDU. Neither the SPD nor the CDU developed in exactly the way Kirchheimer predicted, but with its greater centralization and greater institutionalization, the SPD is closer to Kirchheimer's model. Although internal structure of the SPD has been described as "loosely coupled anarchy" (Lösche and Walter 1992: 173) the leadership is still more able to control party policy making than is true for the CDU.

Like the CDU, the SPD is an office-seeking party, but the SPD has struggled with the question of what strategy would be most successful in gaining office, particularly in response to the rise of the Green Party. In contrast to the expectation of catch-all party theory that party leaders would know what strategy would lead to electoral victory, the SPD has vacillated between leaning left and leaning right. The party pursued *both* options in an effort to gain office, but switching frequently between these strategies had the unintentional effect of hurting the party's electoral chances (Kitschelt 1994).

The SPD also places a high priority on the goal of internal party democracy, stemming at least partially from the Social Democrats' post-war conflict with the Communist Party (Kaden 1964; Leslie 2002). In an effort to differentiate the party from the Communists, the leadership of the SPD implemented an internally democratic organization. Interestingly, Koelble found that this structure made it more difficult for the New Left to take over the party because the New Left had to conquer the SPD district by district, which proved too difficult (Koelble 1991).

The SPD's commitment to an internal representative hierarchy means activists from outside the party perceive the SPD as potentially open to new ideas. While activists from the libertarian left were ultimately unable to penetrate the party, feminists willing to join the SPD's women's organization had better luck (Koelble 1991; Leslie and Wiliarty 2009). A group's chances of getting its views established within the SPD depend on the group's success at persuading party members.

The different internal organizations of the SPD and the CDU contribute to differences in how these two parties address challenges. While the details of the policy outcome in question depend on the particular issue and the arrangement of interests within the party, in general, conflict within the SPD is likely to be more intense. Once the conflict is settled, though, the central leadership is more likely to direct policy making. The CDU, on the other hand, is more likely to moderate conflict through a process of granting internal representation and the chance to shape policy. Conflict is less intense, but the policy direction of the party may be less clear.

The following chapter describes the corporatist catch-all party structure that characterizes the CDU and considers its implications for policy making. Chapter 3 then looks at the CDU's founding moment and how and why the party chose this form of internal organization.

2

The Corporatist Catch-All Party Model

This chapter accomplishes three goals. It begins by developing the corporatist catch-all party model through a comparison with Kirchheimer's vision of a catch-all party. I call Kirchheimer's version of a catch-all party a "classic" catch-all party. The chapter goes on to explicate the policy-making dynamics in a corporatist catch-all party. Finally, it offers a preliminary explanation of the CDU's behavior on women's policy, based on this new model of party organization.

My concept of the corporatist catch-all party differs from the concept of the classic catch-all party in four ways: 1) party organization, 2) leadership, 3) membership, and 4) party policy making. These differences are summarized in Table 2.1.

A classic catch-all party has the following features. First, the primary internal party division is horizontal. In other words, the party has a leadership and a membership. Second, in a classic catch-all party, leadership is unified. Third, the membership of a classic catch-all party can only affect the party negatively by forcing leadership to follow a losing strategy. Fourth, a correct, i.e. winning strategy exists and the leadership knows what it is. The important question is whether or not the membership can prevent the leadership from pursuing this correct strategy.

A corporatist catch-all party differs from a classic catch-all party on all four dimensions. First, the party is organized both horizontally and vertically. Corporatist catch-all parties are divided into leaders and members, but also into internal party groups. Drawing on the corporatism literature, I note that corporatist catch-all parties have much in common with corporatist political systems. The insights from the corporatist literature point to particular types of interest representation (Schmitter

TABLE 2.1 *Differences Between Classic Catch-All Parties and Corporatist Catch-All Parties*

	Classic Catch-All Party	Corporatist Catch-All Party
Party Organization	Horizontal divisions only	Horizontal and vertical divisions
Leadership	Unified	Divided
Membership	Negative contributions only	Positive and negative contributions
Party Policy Making	Leadership knows winning strategy. Membership may prevent implementation of winning strategy.	Leaders disagree about winning strategy. Actual party behavior depends on internal party dynamics and alliance building. Members are a significant source of new ideas and strategies.

1979: 13) and policy making (Lehmbruch 1979: 150).[1] In a corporatist political system, the state recognizes certain interests, but not others. State recognition brings with it a variety of potential benefits, including policy influence, but state recognition also entails costs, such as diminished autonomy from the state.

In a corporatist catch-all party, membership is organized into interest groups that are recognized and sanctioned by the party. Some (but not all) interest groups are acknowledged in this fashion and gain representation within the party. The party offers recognized groups both inducements, such as subsidies and logistical support (administrative personnel, printing

---

[1] Schmitter and Lehmbruch emphasize these different aspects of corporatism through their definitions. Schmitter defines corporatism as "a system of interest representation in which the constituent units are organized into a limited number of singular, compulsory, non-competitive, hierarchically ordered and functionally differentiated categories, recognized or licensed (if not created) by the state and granted a deliberate representational monopoly within their respective categories in exchange for observing certain controls on their selection of leaders and articulation of demands and supports" (Schmitter in Schmitter and Lehmbruch 1979: 13). Lehmbruch's definition focuses more on the policy making aspects of corporatism: "Corporatism ... is an institutionalized pattern of policy-formation in which large interest organizations cooperate with each other and with public authorities not only in the articulation ... of interests, but ... in the 'authoritative allocation of values' and in the implementation of such policies" (Lehmbruch in Schmitter and Lehmbruch 1979: 150). The authors agree that they are focused on different aspects of the same phenomenon. I will be discussing both features of corporatism as I transfer these ideas to the realm of party organization.

and mailing costs, office space), and constraints, such as control over the interest group's selection of group leaders (Collier and Collier 1979). Recognized groups have institutionalized representation on the party's decision-making bodies. Unrecognized groups have neither the benefits nor the constraints that come with recognition. They are not represented in the party's governing structure. Thus, the existence of party recognition sorts all societal interests into those that are recognized and those that are not.

Groups represented on a party's decision-making bodies participate in policy making. Policy making happens through a bargaining process in which represented groups negotiate with each other and with party leadership. Representation on the party's decision-making bodies, therefore, is not merely symbolic. A corporatist catch-all party's interest associations do more than just lobby the party; they are integrated into the party's decision-making process. Represented groups are not guaranteed that the final outcome will go their way, but they are guaranteed the right to participate in the bargaining process. The party adopts the results of the bargaining process as party policy.

The second distinctive feature of a corporatist catch-all party, as compared to a classic catch-all party, is that its leadership is divided. The leaders of the internal party groups sit on the party's decision-making bodies. These leaders do not agree with each other about the optimal strategies and policies for the party to pursue. They must negotiate with each other to determine party behavior.

Corporatist catch-all parties have an additional feature that classic catch-all parties lack. Corporatist catch-all parties may have a leader or leaders (often the party chair), who manage the conflict among the internal party groups. Much as the state in a corporatist economic system may ensure the fairness of the conflict between labor and capital, the party chair in a corporatist catch-all party may balance internal party groups and prevent the exclusion of an important group.

In a corporatist catch-all party, there is a balance of power and a division of labor between the internal party groups and the party chair. The party chair is a different type of position than leadership of an internal party group. An effective party chair acts as a manager and is therefore somewhat apart from internal alliance building (Clemens 1994; Ansell and Fish 1999). He or she may favor one alliance or another, but is unlikely to be a leading member of an alliance.

The relationship between the party chair and internal groups is one of interdependence. The party chair has a certain amount of power to balance among the various groups. He or she tries to prevent any particular group from becoming too powerful. The party chair can increase the power of an internal group by giving the group's leader an office over which the party chair has control. The party chair can decrease the power of an internal group by demoting the group's leader to a less desirable position. However, the party chair cannot eliminate the group's representation in the party's internal decision-making process. Furthermore, the party chair should not vacillate so frequently among groups that he or she appears to have no backbone. On the other hand, if most groups turn against the chair, he or she will be removed from office.[2] Internal groups can lessen the power of the party chair by publicly criticizing him or her or by organizing events and issuing policy or strategy papers that oppose the chair's position.

The third feature of a corporatist catch-all party is that members can help the party win elections rather than just hurt the party's chances at the polls. Because of its distinctive internal organization, a corporatist catch-all party responds to new issues and electors in a different manner than the classic catch-all party. When a classic catch-all party reaches out to new groups, it demobilizes membership. For classic catch-all parties, this demobilization is necessary because of potential conflict between loyalists and floating voters. Loyalists would prefer that the party remain true to its founding ideals. New supporters are interested in the party only if it changes its original doctrine. Theories based on the classic catch-all party model assume that when a party appears internally conflicted, it will suffer at election time. The conflict is resolved by making the new tenets of the party so abstract that everyone can subscribe to them and by decreasing the power of both loyalists and potential new supporters, so that neither can significantly influence the party's actions. Because old members will resist the move to broaden the appeal, classic catch-all parties must limit the power of membership if they wish to adapt successfully (Kirchheimer 1966).

Corporatist catch-all parties operate according to a different logic. They respond to change by incorporating the groups advocating change into the party's governing structure. Instead of weakening the links to both loyalists and floating voters as a classic catch-all party would, a corporatist catch-all party maintains organizational links to the loyalists, but also offers links to floating voters as these voters coalesce into interest groups.

---

[2] CDU Chancellors have much more frequently lost their office because they lost internal party support than because they lost an election (Padgett 1994: 8).

Through its recognition process, the party controls which groups gain representation. Pre-existing groups may or may not attempt to resist the party's recognition of new groups, depending on whether they view the new groups as potential competitors or allies. The recognition process will therefore likely be contentious. Once both loyalists and new groups have access to the party's decision-making structures, however, they must reach some kind of compromise with each other on what the party's position will be. Represented groups are central players in defining party policy.

This method of incorporation allows a corporatist catch-all party to reach out to new societal interests without demobilizing membership. If the party considers new interest groups important enough, it will give them representation on party decision-making bodies and the influence over party policies that comes with this position. This method of representation means that it is not necessary for the party to take power away from members when it reaches out to new societal interests.

The fourth feature of a corporatist catch-all party is that party leaders disagree on the correct strategy for the party.[3] The question is not whether or not party leaders have managed to discern the correct strategy for winning, but rather how can we explain what strategy a party actually pursues. The party will pursue the strategy chosen by the dominant coalition, the group of party leaders who occupy sufficient party offices to control party behavior. The party's behavior cannot be deduced from changing voter demands, but depends on the party's internal organizational dynamics.

Policy Making Within a Corporatist Catch-All Party

Policies (and more general strategies) in a corporatist catch-all party are largely the result of negotiations among internal party groups. It is not that party ideology or electoral pressures are irrelevant to party behavior. But these factors are significantly refracted and mediated by internal party dynamics.

A variety of internal party groups are represented on the decision-making bodies of a corporatist catch-all party. To discover what policies a party will choose, we need to know both the policy preferences of the internal party groups and which groups will prevail. Internal party groups

---

[3] In a political system in which the voter preference distribution is not unimodal and the party system contains multiple parties that must form a coalition in order to govern, the assumption that there is no a priori "correct" winning strategy is more accurate.

may have preferences over either general party strategies or particular policies. In fact, they are likely to have preferences over both, and these preferences are most frequently linked. Learning the policy preferences of particular groups entails reading their policy statements or talking with group leaders.

Two factors influence the power of a particular party group and its ability to convince the party to adopt its policy priorities: whether the group is mobilized on an issue and its alliance situation.[4] For a group to be mobilized on an issue, it must both care about and have a clear position on the issue. If a group cares about an issue, it might still not have a cohesive position. A party group with a higher level of consensus among its membership is more likely to be effective than a group that is internally divided. In the CDU, for example, women in the 1970s were often divided, and therefore their influence during this time period was limited.

The second factor shaping a group's influence is its alliance opportunities. In thinking about a particular group's alliance situation, it is helpful to consider two possibilities. A group may be part of the dominant coalition or it may be excluded from it (Panebianco 1988: 37–8). The dominant coalition is a subset of party leadership that controls critical offices and works together over time to control party behavior in major decision-making arenas (Panebianco 1988: 38). If a group is in the dominant coalition, then it will be fairly easy for that group to convince the party to implement its policy agenda. This situation describes women in the CDU in the 1980s. The women's auxiliary organization was both mobilized on women's issues and was a part of the dominant coalition. These factors explain why women in the CDU made significant gains during this time period.

If a group is excluded from the dominant coalition, mostly it will be frustrated in its attempts to persuade the party to implement its agenda. Outsider groups will be permitted to voice their preferences, but insider groups will prevail in policy decisions. The only opportunity for outsider groups to make policy is for them to form what I call a "cobbled coalition."

A "cobbled coalition" is a short-term or punctual alliance formed by groups outside of the dominant coalition. Cobbled coalitions are usually capable of only modest reforms. They may have to resort to nonstandard policy-making procedures, such as working with opposition parties, in order to realize even a small part of their policy agenda. And they are

---

[4] For more on what influences the power of the CDU's auxiliary organizations, see Schönbohm (1985: 228–229).

unlikely to be able to sustain reforming initiatives over time. Women in the CDU during the 1990s were not in the dominant coalition and had to resort to cobbled coalitions in order to make progress on their policy agenda. Their successes during this time period were therefore more modest, even though their ideas had become more mainstream in German society.

A dominant coalition will remain in place until something occurs to affect the internal balance of power within the party. For example, if the party loses an election, the existing dominant coalition will be weakened (Panebianco 1988: 243–4). Minority elites – those outside of the dominant coalition – will then have the opportunity to take over the party and form a new dominant coalition. This internal shifting can happen after a national-level election, but it might also occur following a scandal. In a federal system, the internal balance of power may also be affected by state-level elections. In particular, a series of losses at the state level may be sufficient to bring about a change in the dominant coalition. Furthermore, the dominant coalition might be able to hang on, even after an electoral loss, depending on how that loss is perceived within the party. As will be shown in the coming chapters, the CDU's dominant coalition did not change after its initial electoral loss in 1969, but only gradually shifted after a second loss in 1972. The dominant coalition changed again in 1989, but in the context of Kohl's reaction to an attempted internal takeover of the party, not in response to unification. Electoral results are only one force among several that might cause changes in a party's dominant coalition.

Explaining Christian Democratic Policies Toward Women

This book investigates the German Christian Democratic Union's response to the challenge of new demands from women on work-family policy, abortion policy, and participation policy. As noted earlier, the party's behavior is not consistent regarding either issue area or time period. This pattern of policy making is the outcome I am seeking to explain. I argue that because the CDU is a corporatist catch-all party, its response to new demands from women is shaped by the mobilization and alliances of the party's internal groups.

As a corporatist catch-all party, the CDU contains internal party groups that are represented on the party's decision-making bodies. The CDU contains two kinds of internal groups: regional organizations and auxiliary organizations. In the CDU the leaders of regional (*Land*) organizations are quite powerful, particularly if the interests of the *Land* are clear. The regional leaders also play an important role in selecting the central party leadership. The auxiliary organizations are sometimes effective on national level issues because auxiliary organizations are formed around some kind of common interest or shared group identity (the labor group, the youth group, the business group, etc.), which may allow these groups to build support across regional lines. On the other hand, auxiliary organizations may be very weak or even not present in certain regional organizations. The leaders of auxiliary organizations also exert influence over the central leadership selection process.

In a corporatist catch-all party like the CDU, policies on women's issues are largely the product of internal interest group politics. It is not that Christian Democratic ideology or the changing place of women in German society or SPD initiatives are irrelevant, but these forces are strongly channeled by internal bargaining among the major interest groups that shape policy within the CDU. In particular, the CDU's women's policies depend on the success of the party's women's auxiliary organization, the Women's Union, in forging alliances with other groups within the party. In order to understand the CDU's policy making on women's issues, it is important to understand both the policy agenda of the Women's Union and whether or not the Women's Union is in a position to realize its policy agenda.

The policy agenda of the Women's Union is not identical to that of the feminist movement. While activists in the Women's Union were often quite appreciative of the agenda-setting ability of the feminist movement, the Christian Democratic women did not always hold feminist positions. As one member of the Women's Union board of directors put it:

We're not women's libbers. We're not radical like the women's movement. But they also helped us. One has to acknowledge that. (Renate Diemers, personal interview)

Activists in the Women's Union thought the feminist movement was raising important questions, but they did not always agree with the answers the feminists were giving. Sometimes, the Women's Union had different answers to these questions; other times its position was fairly close to the position of the feminist movement. Determining the policy preferences of the Women's Union is the first step in determining how the organization influenced CDU policy making.

The second step to understanding how the Women's Union affected CDU policy making is to discover whether the organization was in a sufficiently powerful position within the CDU to drive the party's policy.

TABLE 2.2 *Is the Women's Union Mobilized?*

	Work-Family Policy	Abortion Policy	Participation Policy
1970s	Yes	No	–
1980s	Yes	Yes	Yes
1990	Yes	No	Yes

Two factors influence the power within the party of the Women's Union. The first is the mobilization of the Women's Union and the second is the alliance position of the Women's Union.

The mobilization of the Women's Union is fairly straightforward. If the organization is united behind a particular policy goal, it will be easier for the Women's Union to achieve that goal. If the Women's Union is internally divided, it will be more difficult to convince other actors within the CDU to follow the Women's Union's policy preferences.

As Table 2.2 indicates, the mobilization of the Women's Union varied by issue area. The Women's Union consistently put forward a policy agenda with full membership support on both work-family policy and participation policy. While the Women's Union occasionally experienced internal conflict over both of these issue areas, some kind of compromise that united the organization could always be found. On abortion, on the other hand, the Women's Union was generally divided. Only in the 1980s were the women of the CDU united on this issue.

The alliance situation of the Women's Union is the second factor influencing the ability of the organization to affect CDU policy making. Women in the CDU are not a majority within the party. To accomplish anything, they must form alliances with other groups. Because women's preferences may not be shared by other groups, compromises and log-rolling are often necessary. The selection of an alliance partner will likely influence which part of an interest group's agenda will be enacted.

In thinking about the opportunities for the women's interest group to shape CDU policy, it is helpful to distinguish between two situations: 1) when the Women's Union is in the dominant coalition and 2) when the Women's Union is not in the dominant coalition. The dominant coalition is a subset of the party leadership working together over a period of time to control party behavior in major decision-making arenas (Panebianco 1988). This kind of alliance is stable over time and works together on multiple issues. The dominant coalition has sufficient control over the internal workings of the party that it can generally make party policy.

TABLE 2.3 *Alliance Situation of the Women's Union*

	Women's Union in the Dominant Coalition?
1969–82	Yes
1982–9	Yes
1989–98	No

TABLE 2.4 *CDU Policy Making and the Influence of the Women's Union*

	Issue Area	Women's Union Mobilized	Women's Union in the Dominant Coalition	Extent of Reform
1970s	Work-Family	Yes	Yes	1
	Abortion	No		0
	Participation	–		–
1980s	Work-Family	Yes	Yes	2
	Abortion	Yes		0
	Participation	Yes		2
1990s	Work-Family	Yes	No	1
	Abortion	No		1
	Participation	Yes		1

0 = No Reform
1 = Minor Reform
2 = Major Reform

The dominant coalition does not consist of the entire party leadership. Because all important interest groups continue to be represented in decision-making bodies, these groups are now divided into insiders, who are members of the dominant coalition, and outsiders, who are not. Insiders will find it relatively easy to get the party to adopt their policies; outsiders will find it extremely difficult.

The only real option for outsiders to get the party to adopt their policies is to form a "cobbled coalition." Unlike the dominant coalition, a cobbled coalition exists only on a single issue, on which all involved groups must agree. A cobbled coalition will find it much harder to get its policy passed and this type of coalition is capable of only modest reforms. If a cobbled coalition is successful in passing its policy, the coalition will generally dissolve afterwards.

As Table 2.3 summarizes, the alliance situation of the Women's Union varied by time period. In the 1970s and the 1980s, the Women's Union was part of the dominant coalition. In the 1970s, the Women's Union cooperated with the Social Committees and the Youth Union to make CDU policy. The policy agenda of the Women's Union during this time period was fairly narrow and traditional. The Women's Union cooperated on the policy agenda of its alliance partners, however, and its partners backed the Women's Union's increasing prominence within the party. In the 1980s, the Women's Union was again in the dominant coalition with the same alliance partners, the Social Committees and the Youth Union. By this time, however, the Women's Union had a more wide-reaching policy agenda of its own, which was also significantly less in keeping with traditional CDU women's policies. In the 1990s, the Women's Union was no longer in the dominant coalition. It was able to form cobbled coalitions on child care policy and abortion policy.

Chapters 4 through 6 provide in-depth analysis of the CDU's policy-making behavior on women's issues during these time periods. The outcomes are summarized in Table 2.4. These three chapters also pit the corporatist catch-all party hypothesis against rival explanations of CDU behavior. Prior to these empirical chapters, Chapter 3 provides an overview of the origins of the CDU, explains how the CDU became a corporatist catch-all party, and discusses the relationship between the CDU and women in the years prior to the advent of the women's movement.

3

The Postwar CDU

Origins of a Corporatist Catch-All Party

Angelo Panebianco argues that "a party's organizational characteristics depend more upon its history, i.e. on how the organization originated and how it consolidated, than upon any other factor" (Panebianco 1988: 50). To the extent that a party's beginnings continue to shape its organizational form over time, examination of a party's origins can inform our understanding of internal party dynamics. An awareness of the origins of the CDU in particular can also shed light on one pattern of genesis for corporatist catch-all parties in general.

What are the origins of a corporatist catch-all party? How does a party come to take on this kind of structure? This chapter begins with the general conditions under which a corporatist catch-all party is likely to emerge. Then it discusses the origins of the CDU and how the party set up internal representation for important societal groups at its founding. Finally, it considers the early relationship between women and the CDU.

The most important factor contributing to the emergence of a corporatist catch-all party is what Panebianco terms "territorial diffusion" (Panebianco 1988: 50–1). He distinguishes between organizations developed through territorial diffusion versus those developed through territorial penetration. Territorial penetration occurs when the center controls the organization's development and extends this control to the periphery. Territorial diffusion, on the other hand, refers to cases in which the organization develops from the spontaneous formation of associations that then merge into a larger organization. Panebianco also uses the term territorial diffusion more broadly to describe parties that form through the merger of separate national organizations. I will use territorial diffusion to refer to cases in which a party forms through the merger of existing organizations, not all of which must be national (or, indeed, based on territorial divisions). A corporatist catch-all party is much more likely to emerge under conditions of territorial diffusion than territorial penetration.

To become a corporatist catch-all party, the groups that merge to form the national party must retain their identities within the party and be represented on the party's internal decision-making bodies. It is not necessary for every small group to be internally represented and the party may create and represent new groups but the general trend should be clear. Furthermore, these internal groups should represent general differences of policy. It is not enough for groups to be personalized factions around a particular leader. The form of internal representation required by a corporatist catch-all party comes about as a way of managing the differences among these multiple internal groups.

While territorial diffusion is the most important factor contributing to the emergence of a corporatist catch-all party, pressure to exhibit democratic norms also increases the likelihood of the formation of a corporatist catch-all party. Even if internal representation of important party subgroups does not conform to the expectations of liberal democratic individualism, it does ensure that important groups within the party get a voice. Regardless of whether party elites are genuinely committed to party democracy or not, the corporatist catch-all party structure appears democratic and is therefore an appropriate response to pressure to democratize. Furthermore, this form of party organization decentralizes power and can be used as a safeguard against concentrating too much power with the party's central leadership.

To return to Panebianco's model, corporatist catch-all parties are more likely to be internally rather than externally legitimated (Panebianco 1988: 51–2). He defines a party as being externally legitimated when it has an external "sponsor" institution. In this case, the loyalty of supporters and the legitimacy of leadership will be more directly tied to the external institution than to the party itself. A corporatist catch-all party is highly unlikely to emerge under these conditions because its internal party structure is defined by the representation of diverse interests. If there were an external sponsoring institution, presumably this institution would shift the internal balance of the party towards its own interests rather than allowing the internal diversity to continue.[1] The conclusion to this book includes

---

[1] A corporatist catch-all party corresponds somewhat to Panebianco's (otherwise unnamed) "case four" which is formed through territorial diffusion, is internally legitimated, and

further reflections on how corporatist catch-all parties emerged under similar conditions in countries besides Germany.

The remainder of this chapter takes a close look at the origins of the CDU. As expected, the CDU was formed under conditions of territorial diffusion "in its purest form" (Panebianco 1988: 116). Konrad Adenauer's leadership of the party was cemented following the Bundestag election in August 1949. He was the clear choice for the CDU/CSU Chancellor candidate and because the Christian Democrats were the largest parliamentary group, his selection as Chancellor was assured. The question of which parties to include in the governing coalition was somewhat trickier because some CDU progressives preferred a coalition with the Social Democrats. The left wing of the party was weakened by the decline of one of its most important leaders, Jakob Kaiser, however. Furthermore, the SPD made its participation in the governing coalition contingent on several demands, which the CDU regarded as outrageous, including that the SPD control the Economics Ministry (Pridham 1977: 61). The weakness of CDU progressives and the aggressiveness of the SPD tipped the balance in favor of a conservative coalition consisting of the CDU/CSU, the FDP, and the small German Party.[2] The Christian Democrats and the Free Democrats became the dominant alliance in German politics and governed together from 1949 to 1966, with the exception of the 1957–61 legislative period when the Christian Democrats nearly had an absolute majority and governed with only the German Party.[3]

Adenauer was elected Chancellor prior to the official formation of the CDU's national party organization. The first party congress was held in Goslar from October 20–2, 1950. Adenauer was elected party chair with 302 out of 335 votes (Pridham 1977: 67). The Goslar congress also ratified the CDU statutes the leadership had drafted. While CDU leaders made

---

weakly institutionalized (Panebianco 1988: 64). Corporatist catch-all parties are not necessarily weakly institutionalized, however. Indeed, with time it is likely that the corporatist catch-all party structure becomes institutionalized in the party. Panebianco further discusses the potential role of charisma in a party's genetic model (Panebianco 1988: 52–3, 65–7). I agree with his assessment that Adenauer had situational charisma. François Mitterrand, leader of the French Socialist Party (PS) at the time it adopted a corporatist catch-all party structure, can also be said to have possessed situational charisma. (See conclusion chapter). Helmut Kohl and Angela Merkel – subsequent successful leaders of the CDU – are clearly not charismatic, however. Charismatic leadership can be helpful for a leader attempting to balance the internal forces in a corporatist catch-all party but it is not necessary.

[2] The German Party was a nationalist party that was later absorbed into the CDU.

[3] The German Party had only 17 representatives in the Bundestag, while the CDU/CSU had 270 (Ritter and Niehuss 1991: 101).

plans at this congress for developing a party organization, including the creation of a national headquarters, actual implementation of these plans proceeded slowly.

The CDU's extraparliamentary organization remained fairly weak over the course of the 1950s, but that was not the case for the parliamentary caucus. With each election, the Christian Democratic parliamentary group grew in size and diversity. As the parliamentarians became more experienced, they were also less likely to yield to Adenauer on all issues. The Bundestag delegates continued to back Adenauer on foreign policy, but were sometimes resistant on social or economic policy (Pridham 1977: 79).

With Adenauer as Chancellor, the CDU/CSU laid the building blocks for West German politics and society. In foreign policy, West Germany reentered the western alliance and also rearmed itself. With major contributions from Ludwig Erhard, the CDU/CSU set up the social market economy and experienced the economic miracle (*Wirtschaftswunder*). The gross national product of West Germany grew at an average rate of 8 percent per year during the 1950s (Edinger and Nacos 1998: 147). Largely because of the policies of the CDU, West Germany emerged from the 1950s as an economic and democratic success story and as a much-rehabilitated member of the community of western nations.

One of the reasons that the CDU was able to dominate German politics so thoroughly during the 1950s was that the party successfully reached out to and integrated societal groups that might have offered opposition. The party recognized important groups by founding auxiliary organizations that were affiliated with the party.[4] The CDU originally had seven auxiliary organizations: the Youth Union (*Junge Union*), the Women's Union (*Frauen Union*),[5] the Social Committees of the Christian Democratic Workers (*Sozialausschüsse der Christlich-Demokratischen Arbeitnehmerschaft*), the Municipal Politics Association (*Kommunalpolitische Vereinigung*), the Middle Class Association (*Mittelstandsvereinigung*), the Economic Council

---

[4] I follow Zuckerman (1979) in distinguishing between factions and other kinds of groups within a political party. When compared to factions, nonfaction groups such as the CDU's auxiliary organizations have 1) greater emphasis on member equality and the normative claims of members of the group; 2) for nonfaction groups, personal gain is associated with policy success; and 3) loyalty is less person-specific and more closely related to issue or policy agreement.

[5] The Women's Union went through a series of name changes as will be discussed later in the chapter.

(*Wirtschaftsrat*),[6] and the Refugees Union (*Union der Vertriebenen und Flüchtlinge*). In 1972 the party added an additional auxiliary organization, the School Pupils Union (*Schüler Union*),[7] and in 1988 the newest auxiliary organization was created, the Seniors Union (*Senioren Union*). Additionally, two older CDU organizations do not have the official status of auxiliary organizations, but often act similarly: the Protestant Working Circle (*Evangelischer Arbeitskreis*) and the Ring of Christian Democratic Students (*Ring Christlich-Demokratischer Studenten*) (Pridham 1977: 291 and CDU Web site).

While many parties have auxiliary organizations, the CDU's are more autonomous from the main party than is generally the case. The auxiliary organizations have their own statutes, their own leadership, and often their own publications. Many are open to people who are not members of the CDU, and CDU members are not required to join an auxiliary organization. Auxiliary organizations may issue their own policy statements, which, however, may not contradict CDU principles (CDU Statutes, section F, paragraph 39). They also administer their own finances although some of the money comes from the main CDU; many auxiliary organizations also receive dues from membership. The auxiliary organizations vary quite a bit in their assertion of autonomy from the CDU (Pridham 1977: 292). Some auxiliary organizations have been more active than others have and a particular auxiliary organization may be more active at certain times than others.

The auxiliary organizations themselves are not decision makers within the party. Rather, they are a way for the CDU to recognize the importance of a societal interest. The auxiliary organizations allow the CDU to stay in touch with social changes and to influence how certain interests are organized within the party. The auxiliary organizations also serve as a forum for CDU activists who want to promote a particular societal interest to meet and strategize with like-minded activists. The auxiliary organizations can influence the behavior of the CDU because the auxiliary organizations are represented on the party's decision-making bodies.[8]

The CDU's corporatist catch-all party organization is a product of the party's founding moment in postwar Germany. In the chaotic postwar

---

[6] The Middle Class Association and the Economic Council later merged to create the Middle Class and Economic Association.

[7] The School Pupils Union was later subsumed into a subsection of the Youth Union.

[8] For more on the role of auxiliary organizations, see Chandler (1989: 304).

years, the future Christian Democrats worked to create a new kind of party, one that would overcome various failings of the prewar party system. Getting the forces on the conservative side of the spectrum to coalesce into a single political party was an exceptionally difficult project. The nascent Christian Democratic party was divided by issues of region, religion and class. The organizational structures and policy-making practices developed in order to bridge these divides laid the foundation of the CDU's approach to politics for the decades to come. This approach did not follow a "one man-one vote" theory of democracy, but it did ensure that important voices across the internal political spectrum were heard and represented within the party.

Groups of female Christian Democrats also met and organized in the early postwar period. Women were generally quite supportive of the CDU at the polls, but these Christian Democratic women's groups demanded representation within the party. Because Christian Democratic women were largely supportive of the party's traditional stance regarding appropriate roles for women in society and drawing on the Center Party's tradition of its women's association, the CDU created an internal group for women. This group was represented on the CDU's policy-making boards as early as the 1950s. Christian Democratic women did not become a politically salient group until the 1970s, however.

This chapter traces the emergence of the corporatist catch-all party structure as the party worked to overcome internal divisions based on region, religion, class, and gender. This process involves answering three questions. First, why did the CDU recognize this group with internal party representation? Answering this question requires explaining the internal party tension generated by this societal divide. Second, how did the CDU set up internal party representation for this group? In other words, what form did internal party representation take? And finally, what were the effects of establishing the corporatist catch-all party structure for this group? Here, we expect to see four possible effects. First, we expect to see less internal party tension as the group in question receives established representation within the party. Second, we may see policy effects as the CDU adopts some or all of the agenda of the newly-recognized group. Third, there may be voting effects. If voters within a particular societal group believe the CDU is paying attention to their group's interests, they may increase their support for the party. Finally, we may see mobilization effects. If leaders of the party's internal subgroup see it as beneficial to their own position within the CDU, they may try to mobilize their group's membership.

MANAGING REGIONAL DIVIDES

Regional divides presented a serious challenge to the early CDU. The party was founded nearly simultaneously in different areas of occupied Germany. Early attempts at organizing the new party occurred in Cologne (June 1945), Berlin (June 1945), Frankfurt (September 1945), and Munich (September 1945) (Becker 1987: 32). The difficulties in merging these separate Christian Democratic organizations in the circumstances of late 1940s postwar Germany were significant. In the period immediately following World War II, the Allies divided Germany into four zones. The various Christian Democratic movements across the country developed locally and idiosyncratically before they merged nationally (Pridham 1977: 48–9). Communication and travel were difficult because the normal infrastructure had been destroyed by the war and because the allies limited movement across the zones. The postwar conditions also meant that the CDU lacked basic resources, which hindered communication among the various groups. Paper shortages meant that posters and pamphlets could not always be produced (Pridham 1977: 45–6). Because of this delay, when the CDU did finally form a national organization – in October 1950, a year after the party began governing West Germany – regional differences were strongly established (Bösch 2001: 51). The resulting regional organizations remained strong and contributed to the CDU's eventual federal character. This internal heterogeneity was later an electoral advantage, but it also made forming the new party more difficult.

Scholars disagree about the importance of the Allies licensing policy in the CDU's ability to overcome regional differences. Each occupying country had the right to license political parties in its zone, which led to conflicting pressures. On the one hand, Allied zoning policy meant each zone had its own Christian Democratic party and no national party emerged (Gurland 1980: 14; Jesse 1985: 91). On the other hand, the Allies tended to license only one Christian Democratic party in each zone even if several groups were active (Bösch 2001: 52). This latter policy was especially helpful in overcoming divisions between the old Center Party and the new Christian Democratic Party.

While the founders of the CDU agreed that they wanted to create a Christian party, they disagreed on most everything else. The various groupings in different parts of the country did not make up a coherent ideology (Pridham 1977: 33). One observer found the CDU to be "socialist and radical in Berlin, clerical and conservative in Cologne, capitalist and reactionary in Hamburg and counter-revolutionary and particularistic in Munich" (cited in Pridham 1977: 23).[9] When the diverse elements eventually merged into a single party, they were helpful in appealing to a heterogeneous electorate, but this heterogeneity also sometimes made it difficult to discern the party's position.

Early CDU leaders were not always eager to centralize their new party. Konrad Adenauer, in particular, acted to slow the emergence of a national party organization (Bösch 2001: 68). In Adenauer's efforts to preserve his own leadership of the CDU in the British zone, he sometimes worked against tendencies toward a national party. Adenauer tried to limit communication and travel between regional CDU organizations and Berlin and tried to portray Jakob Kaiser, a left-leaning leader of the Berlin Christian Democrats, as too close to the Soviets (Bösch 2001: 66). When Frankfurt began to emerge as a possible counterweight to Berlin and a potential future capital city, Adenauer insisted on the independence of the CDU in the British zone (Bösch 2001: 67). Adenauer was not the only leader to prefer a less centralized party. By maintaining separate local and regional organizations, more groups and people within the party could remain in leadership positions. Many of the elites from the former Center Party were skeptical of centralization philosophically in any case (Bösch 2001: 68).

Even when party leaders favored the creation of some kind of central party organization, they differed on what form it should take. Debates over whether to centralize or federalize the party took place simultaneously and overlapped with debates over what structure the new country should take (Ley 1978: 19–31). In general, leaders in the north, especially in Berlin, were more in favor of a central party organization (Becker 1987: 216). CDU leaders in southwestern Germany and in Bavaria preferred a more federal solution with greater independence for the *Land*-level actors (Becker 1987: 219–21). This conflict increased the regional friction within the party. These were not just disagreements over the party's internal structure, but also over the future organization of the state. Divisions on questions of centralization versus federalism prevented the CDU from forming a unified position on issues such as what form a second parliamentary chamber should take and which territorial units should have the power to tax (Ley 1978: 142).

---

[9] Bösch argues that the main difference among the various local CDU chapters was whether they were predominantly Catholic or Protestant (Bösch 2001: 70).

The difficulties with the internal structure of the party were not simply about the relative power of the *Land* versus the national level. Often the CDU did not even have a strong organization at the *Land* level. Except for Bavaria and the city-states, most of the postwar *Länder* were new creations without historical traditions (Becker 1987: 216). The CDU maintained separate organizations in the Rhineland and Westphalia until 1985. Baden-Württemberg had four separate CDU organizations until 1971 (Kleinmann 1993: 292). Of course the continued existence of a separate party, the Christian Social Union, in Bavaria, is the best evidence of the exceptionally strong federalist tendencies within German Christian Democracy.

The Christian Democrats overcame these regional divides only slowly and with a certain amount of difficulty. Future Christian Democrats across Germany came together in June and July of 1945 to begin local chapters of a new kind of party that would combine both Protestants and Catholics. Early meetings occurred in Cologne, Dusseldorf, Berlin (Wieck 1953: 54, 77, 207) and many other places. The first push for a national organization came from Berlin. The Berlin organization was made up of a wide range of political elites who happened to be in Berlin at the end of the war. Because Berlin had been the capital and because the founding Christian Democrats in Berlin represented many regions in Germany, the founders of the Berlin Christian Democrats claimed to be starting a national party (Wieck 1953: 207–8). This leadership claim was not accepted by Christian Democrats elsewhere. Nonetheless, the Berliners organized the first national level meeting of the various local and regional Christian Democratic parties that had formed throughout 1945. This meeting took place in Bad Godesberg in December 1945.

The Bad Godesberg meeting marks one of the earliest moments of the emergence of the corporatist catch-all party structure. Indeed, the Bad Godesberg meeting served as an impetus for some *Land* organizations to constitute themselves in order to send representatives to the national meeting (Becker 1987: 224). The federal structure of the party was quickly emerging. This process was not simply a matter of calling a federal organization into existence. The subnational units of the party were clearly representing their constituencies, in this case geographic territories. This initial meeting led to the creation of the Zone Coordination Committee (*Zonenverbindungsausschuss*) to facilitate cooperation among all CDU organizations (Becker 1987: 224). The Zone Coordination Committee subsequently led to the creation of the Working Association of the CDU/CSU (*Arbeitsgemeinschaft der CDU/CSU*) in February 1947

(Becker 1987: 226). The Working Association represented the break-through of the principle of federalism as a guideline for the party (Becker 1987: 227).

Federalism was the main tool for managing the regional divides within the CDU. Unlike the Weimar Republic, the new (West) Germany was going to have a federal system of government. The CDU was also becoming a federal party with representation based on region. A possible alternative organizational structure for the CDU would have been representation of the four zones. Both the British zone and the Soviet zone were fairly cohesive by 1947. In 1946, however, activists attempting to form an American zone organization for the CDU failed to do so. Advocates of an American zone organization ran into difficulties with both the relationship this potentially new CDU organization would have with Christian Democrats in Berlin and with the problem that the Bavarian Christian Social Union was not interested in merging with other organizations to create an American zone CDU (Becker 1987: 221). Efforts to make zone-level units the CDU's primary subnational units failed but by 1946/47, the debate within the party was about *what kind* of subnational unit would be represented in a future national party. The *fact* of subnational representation was not in question.

With the creation of the Working Association of the CDU/CSU in 1947, the CDU committed itself to internal representation of the *Länder* (rather than the zones). The Working Association of the CDU/CSU gave the same representation to each *Land* with extra for Berlin (Becker 1987: 226). The Working Association did not make committee assignments at the February 1947 meeting because not all of the *Länder* had sent representatives (Ley 1978: 35). Federalism within the young CDU was not so much about representing existing territories with existing identities. The new German states – the *Länder* – were mostly not based on previous geopolitical territories, as evidenced by the frequent use of hyphens in their names. Instead, this form of internal federalism was a method for distributing power in a way that was perceived to be fair (Becker 1987: 216).

The Working Association met several times over the course of 1947 and 1948. The primary issues it confronted included the pending division of the country, further clarification of the internal organization of the party, and preparing for the election of August 1949 (Becker 1987: 224–30, 246–54). The status of the East CDU and of the Bavarian CSU continued to be problematic. The electoral victory of the combined forces of the CDU and the CSU in August 1949 gave impetus to continue the project of developing an internal party organization (Becker 1987: 254).

By this time the division of Germany was clear. East Germans were no longer permitted to travel to West Germany for party conferences (Becker 1987: 258). In keeping with its emerging corporatist catch-all party structure, the CDU came to terms with the division of Germany partly by giving representation within the party to representatives from the East. Neither the SPD nor the FDP did this. The slots within the CDU for East Germany were held by refugees residing in the west. The CDU used its corporatist catch-all party structure to give at least some form of recognition to Christian Democrats in the East.

The continued existence of the separate Bavarian CSU is evidence of the difficulty regional divisions presented to the Christian Democrats. No other party in Germany maintained separate organizations in any of the *Länder*. The separatism of the Bavarian organization was solved by having two parties, which ran separate election campaigns, but then formed a single caucus in the Bundestag (Becker 1987: 253).

The structure of the corporatist catch-all party was developed at the very founding moment of the party. The rather difficult birthing process of a party that emerged during the immediate aftermath of the war is apparent here. The separate regional organizations did not truly merge into a national party until after the CDU held elective office. The new statutes were approved in October 1950 (Becker 1987: 260). In the meantime, giving representation to the *Länder* (and indeed, sometimes to sub-*Land* organizations) was a technique that allowed the CDU gradually to coalesce into a single party. The strong regional tendencies of the party are very much still in evidence today.

OVERCOMING CONFESSIONAL DIVIDES

One of the most difficult divisions for the CDU to overcome was the confessional divide. It was a new idea to organize Protestants and Catholics – together *as Christians* – in the same party. As will be seen, tensions between the two confessions often ran high in the early postwar years. In particular, there was a near-constant fear that the CDU was actually a Catholic party masquerading as a biconfessional one. The CDU's solution to this problem was to create an internal organization for Protestants, the *Evangelischer Arbeitskreis* or EAK. The EAK worked to recruit Protestants into the CDU and to highlight the importance of Protestant views and politicians within the party. The EAK also served as a liaison to the Protestant church, especially when there were political differences between the church and the party. The creation of the EAK was an important instance of the CDU's development toward the organizational structure of a corporatist catch-all party.

Protestants and Catholics had traditionally been organized separately in Germany. The CDU has its origins in the Catholic Center Party (*Zentrum*), which had been an important party in both Imperial Germany and the Weimar Republic. The Catholic Center Party existed prior to Bismarck's *Kulturkampf*, a cultural battle against Catholics started in the early 1870s, but the party's cohesion was greatly strengthened by the *Kulturkampf* (Schmidt 1987: 68).[10] In an effort to win the loyalty of the Liberal Protestants, Bismarck initiated a campaign of discrimination against Catholics, aimed at constraining the influence of the Catholic Church. Catholics responded by strengthening their own political movement, the Center Party, to defend their interests (Anderson 1981: 134). Center Party elites considered some kind of merger with Protestants after World War I, but this idea did not go very far because many within the party feared that such a development would sacrifice important characteristics of the party (Schmidt 1987: 96). The Center Party maintained its prewar structure and went on to become a principal actor in the parliament of the Weimar Republic.

Given this history, it is not surprising that Catholics and Protestants rarely cooperated politically during imperial Germany and the Weimar Republic. During the Weimar Republic, it became clear that although organized Catholicism was a significant political force, Catholics did not make up enough of the population to form a majority on their own. While many factors contributed to the rise of Hitler and the National Socialists, the weakness and internal divisions on the political right certainly played a critical role in leading Germany into this disaster.

Ironically, because of Hitler's persecution of the parties of the left, these parties emerged after the war relatively untainted by cooperation with the Nazis and with organizations that had either gone underground or into exile. The parties of the political right, however, including eventually the Catholic Center Party, were discredited by their compromises with National Socialism (Pridham 1977: 21). When the leader of the Catholic Center Party, Heinrich Brüning, became Chancellor, he resorted to emergency powers and called for new elections while support for the National Socialists was growing (Feutchwanger 1993: 220–4). The Center Party also later voted for the Enabling Act that conferred dictatorial powers on

---

[10] Even prior to the *Kulturkampf*, many Catholic organizations were formed in the years following Prussia's defeat of Austria in 1866 (Kalyvas 1996: 204–5).

Hitler. After World War II, many conservative activists were eager for some kind of new movement that would overcome previous failings.

Historical tensions around the issue of a biconfessional party carried into the postwar period. Because the early initiators of the idea of a Christian Democratic party were activists from the old Center Party, some Protestants viewed the CDU more as a successor to the Center Party than as a genuinely biconfessional party. Catholics had been better organized than Protestants both before and during the Weimar Republic. Furthermore, the loss of East Germany meant that the confessions were nearly equally balanced in the new Federal Republic, whereas previously Protestants had been a clear majority of the population. Some Protestants feared that the CDU was a thinly disguised Catholic party in which Protestants would never have significant influence (Schmidt 1987: 202).

Catholics also had some trepidation about the idea of a biconfessional party. Some leaders and members of the old Center Party made serious efforts to revive that party.[11] The Center party – political home for Germany's Catholics for decades – had enormous emotional resonance, especially among the grassroots (Schmidt 1987: 202). It was not easy to leave behind a party that had been such an important part of many people's lives. Proponents of reviving the Center Party also feared that Catholic ideas – especially about schools and abortion – would be watered down in a party with Protestants in it (Schmidt 1987: 152). Furthermore, some proponents of the Center Party, especially those with ties to the Catholic trade unions, wanted a party that was further to the left on economic issues than the emerging Christian Democratic Party seemed to be.

With these difficulties on the table, it is in some ways surprising that the CDU managed to overcome these confessional divisions to form a party supported by both Catholics and Protestants. On the other hand, the moral and political pressures for finding a solution to religious tensions were significant. The founders of the CDU were very concerned about the vacuum on the political right in the postwar period. In their eyes, it was critical that the new party be based on Christian doctrine. A politics based on Christianity was the only possible moral response to the sins of the Third Reich (Heidenheimer 1960: 33). They hoped that Christianity would provide an ethical basis for politics and spiritual renewal in Germany.

---

[11] For more information on the history of the relationship between the Center Party and the early CDU see the excellent *Zentrum oder CDU: Politischer Katholizismus zwischen Tradition und Anpassung* by Ute Schmidt.

A Christian party could hopefully avoid the sins of both godless Nazism and godless Bolshevism. Furthermore, by basing the new party on Christianity, instead of either Protestantism or Catholicism, the CDU's founders hoped to overcome some of the problems and divisions that had plagued religiously oriented parties during the Weimar Republic.

Tactical considerations also played a major role in the desire to bridge the confessional divide. A party supported only by Catholics was perpetually too small to govern. The Protestants were too internally divided to be effective. By bringing together all Christians in one party, the early Christian Democrats hoped to create a force strong enough to win elections and govern the new postwar West Germany. In particular, the founders of the CDU hoped the new party would be popular enough to defeat "Marxist" opponents on the left (Bösch 2001: 28).

The nascent Christian Democratic Party confronted confessional conflict immediately. The newly founded Christian Democratic Party (not yet Christian Democratic Union, and not yet organized on a national level) had separate organizations in the Rhineland (Catholic) and Westphalia (Protestant). The initiators of the new party decided to maintain separate organizations, but to work out a shared program for both regions (Uertz 1981: 46). The Program Commission for the newly founded Rhenish and Westphalian Christian Democratic Party met September 28, October 5, and October 12, 1945 (Uertz 1981: 47). One of the main challenges for the Program Commission was different views on the relationship between religion and politics. Protestants and Catholics had different ideas about the ability of humankind to live ethically (Uertz 1981: 44). For religious Protestants, original sin implied that humankind was tainted. The best one could hope for was to live an individually ethical life in a corrupt world. Protestants saw religion and politics as fundamentally separate realms that were often in opposition to each other (Uertz 1981: 50). Catholics were more optimistic. They believed that God had created man in God's image and despite original sin, it was still possible to create an ethical social order; indeed, they felt a moral obligation to attempt to do so (Uertz 1981: 50). In the early Christian Democratic Party, the Catholic label for this moral social order was Christian Socialism.

While this disagreement appears more theological than political, it came to a head during the process of writing a shared program for the Rhenish and Westphalian Christian Democratic Party. The compromise that allowed the Program Commission to continue its work was twofold. First, the term (though not the concept) Christian Socialism was dropped from the program. For Protestants the problem with Christian Socialism was largely theological rather than economic.[12] Political systems could not be Christian because they were the creation of tainted humankind (Uertz 1981: 48–9). Second, the preamble to the program was divided into two parts, the first written by the Protestants and the second by the Catholics. According to the minutes of the Program Commission there was "widespread agreement that the theological reservations of both churches had to be overcome and that in particular the numerically weaker representation of the Protestant side ... should not be manifested in the preamble" (minutes quoted in Uertz 1981: 50). Even at this exceptionally early stage in party formation, Christian Democrats were concerned about whether Protestants would have adequate influence within the party.

Protestants in support of Christian Democracy had been meeting separately from Catholics since August 1945 (Egen 1971: 19). In October 1945, the *Landesvorstand* of the Rhineland Christian Democratic Party asked Dr. Otto Schmidt to organize a meeting with Protestants to discuss any possible difficulties that might arise in forming a political party together with Catholics (Egen 1971: 21). A series of early meetings, beginning in December 1945 and led by Schmidt, focused on issues such as what Protestants would do in such a party, whether to form a purely Protestant party, and how to get more Protestants to engage with politics (Egen 1971: 22–5). These questions were particularly pressing while Catholics were deciding whether to reactivate the old Center Party or whether to form a new biconfessional party. This group, called the *Evangelische Tagung*, continued to meet regularly from 1946 to 1948 (Egen 1971: 45).

The issue of German rearmament increased pressure on the CDU to institutionalize the voice of Protestants within the party. During the occupation period rearmament was not a critical issue, but it became an important question quickly after the emergence of two separate German states and the beginning of the Cold War. Many thought rearmament would help cement West German sovereignty and bind the new Federal Republic to the Western Alliance. Certainly a rearmed West Germany would also feel more secure when facing off against the Soviet Union in East Germany. On the other hand, rearming West Germany implied cementing the division between the two Germanys and giving up the hopes of unification in the near future. The division of opinion within the CDU ran along confessional lines with Catholics (and especially

---

[12] As we will see, the concept of Christian Socialism also lost significant influence within the party, but that was due to conflict with business interests, not Protestants (Uertz 1981: 207).

Adenauer) favoring rearmament and Protestants being far more skeptical (Bösch 2001: 119–20). After all, the new East Germany was predominantly Protestant. The Protestant sections of West Germany were also much closer geographically to the border. Protestants found the division of Germany more difficult to accept than Catholics did (Bösch 2001: 120). The CDU's support of rearmament was seen as further proof that the CDU was dominated by Catholics.

In 1950, significant conflict over rearmament broke out when two leading Protestants began to criticize Adenauer's position on rearmament. Martin Niemöller, who chaired the leadership council of the German Protestant Church (*Bruderrat der Evangelische Kirche Deutschlands*) and Gustav Heinemann, who was the CDU's Minister of Interior Affairs, both criticized the CDU for Adenauer's rearmament policy (Egen 1971: 66–71). Heinemann resigned his position in Adenauer's cabinet over the issue. These serious protests from two of the CDU's leading Protestants raised doubts about the legitimacy of the CDU's claim to be a biconfessional party.

The conflict with Heinemann and Niemöller led some leading CDU Protestants to begin to consider how to give Protestant Christian Democrats a more prominent and visible role within the party. At the meeting in Goslar in October 1950, when the CDU officially organized as a party, Protestant delegates met separately and registered their official approval for the policies of Adenauer and the CDU (Egen 1971: 72). However, Niemöller, Heinemann and their followers continued to agitate against rearmament throughout 1951.

In December 1951, Ernst Bach, the mayor of Siegen and treasurer of the CDU, wrote to Adenauer suggesting the formation of a national-level committee for Protestants within the CDU. Bach feared that the continued agitation from Niemöller and Heinemann would convince Protestants to leave the CDU because the party was too strongly influenced by Catholics. Bach also argued that such an organization would help Protestants form a more unified opinion, which would increase their power and visibility within the CDU. Adenauer agreed and leading Protestant elites planned a meeting for March 1952 in Siegen.

Over 200 delegates attended the Siegen conference from March 14–16, 1952. The delegates officially backed Adenauer's *Westpolitik*, opposed a neutral West Germany, favored rearmament, and advocated for the right to conscientious objection (Egen 1971: 103). This conference is widely regarded as the founding moment of what became the *Evangelischer Arbeitskreis* (EAK).

Immediately following the conference in Siegen, Protestant leaders met with Adenauer to plan the formation of a national-level group for Christian Democratic Protestants. Press reactions to the conference had been very positive. In particular, all rumors of Protestant succession from the CDU were put to rest. The EAK was officially founded on May 27, 1952 with Hermann Ehlers as chair and Bach as General Secretary (Egen 1971: 116). The addition of the EAK to the party's internal organization marks the extension of the corporatist catch-all party structure to include Protestants.

One of the important early goals of the EAK was building up the new organization. The EAK worked to recruit both activists and potential office holders. The group wanted to have more Protestants available to fill the positions it planned to ask for. The EAK also worked to ease tensions between the CDU and the Protestant church (Egen 1971: 156).

The EAK worked especially at preparing for the 1953 national elections. The CDU had fared significantly better with Catholics than with Protestants in 1949. Thirty-nine percent of Catholics had supported the CDU in 1949 while only 25 percent of the Protestants did. For the SPD, the situation was nearly a mirror image. Thirty-four percent of Protestants voted for the Social Democrats but only 26 percent of the Catholics (Egen 1971: 140–1). The EAK wanted to increase the CDU's share of the Protestant vote. This issue was especially pressing because Gustav Heinemann had started a new party, and was claiming in his campaign literature that the CDU was a party for Catholics only.

The CDU's efforts to win more votes from Protestants were successful. The party increased its share of the Protestant vote from 25 percent in 1949 to 34 percent in 1953 (Egen 1971: 173). The SPD did not increase its share of the Protestant vote. The sharp increase in CDU support from Protestants was frequently credited as a main reason for the CDU's significant victory in 1953 (Egen 1971: 175–6).

The EAK put together statistics about the confessional balance of candidates and ministers from the CDU. The organization sent letters to internal party organizations that were deficient in Protestants and asked them to add more. This technique was frequently successful (Bösch 2001: 331). The CDU significantly increased its numbers of both Protestant representatives in the Bundestag and Protestant ministers after the first election in 1949. In the first Bundestag, 70 percent of Christian Democratic Members of the Bundestag were Catholic and only 30 percent were Protestants. Subsequent Bundestag caucuses generally had 62 percent Catholic Christian Democrats and 38 percent Protestant (Bösch 2001:

322). Adenauer significantly increased the number of cabinet seats for Protestants in his second cabinet. In the first cabinet, five out of fourteen positions were held by Protestants. In the second cabinet, it was ten out of eighteen (Egen 1971: 1975).

The emerging corporatist catch-all party structure helped the CDU bridge the difficult confessional divide within the party. CDU Protestants founded the *Evangelische Arbeitskreis* in an effort to counteract frequent allegations that the party was led and controlled by Catholics. The effort was largely successful, especially in terms of personnel politics and on the issue of German rearmament. The corporatist catch-all party structure provided internal influence for the Protestants and external evidence that the CDU was open to both confessions.

OVERCOMING CLASS DIVIDES

In addition to regional tensions and religious tensions, the fledging CDU faced class divisions. The middle class was the CDU's "natural" support base, but early CDU leadership wanted the party to have cross-class appeal for a variety of reasons. The CDU's internal organization for workers – the *Christlich Demokratische Arbeitnehmerschaft (CDA)* – formed prior to the CDU's official coalescence into a party. Once the CDU emerged as an organized party, the CDA was represented on the party's decision-making bodies. When the CDU has been in government, the chair of the CDA has also usually been the Minister of Labor. Scholars have debated the effect of the CDA on the main party. Sometimes the CDA is considered a "fig leaf," used to hide the fact that the CDU ignores workers' interests. Other times the CDA seems to be making genuine contributions to CDU policy making.

Christian Democratic leaders considered the working class an important group to attract. Different leaders were interested in this project for different reasons. Several CDU founding fathers had roots in the Christian labor movement (Pridham 1977: 30–1). When Christian trade unionists gave up the idea of separate Christian labor unions in favor of one large union, they considered having a significant role for Christian workers in the CDU the best way to preserve some of the identity and special features of Christian labor (Kleinmann 1993: 100).

Even CDU leaders without roots in Catholic unions often wanted the CDU to be attractive to the working class. The CDU wanted to portray itself as a *Volkspartei*, or people's party, a party that would represent everyone. For the *Volkspartei* strategy to work, the party had to show that it represented and appealed to classes beyond its natural middle-class base. Furthermore, especially during the late 1940s and early 1950s, CDU leaders felt that there was a real risk of workers voting for the Communist Party or the SPD. By creating a party that appealed to at least a significant segment of the working class, the CDU was building a bulwark against socialism, its chief political rival (Pridham 1977: 28).

Attempting to draw support from across the class spectrum was no easy task, however. Tension between supporters of the working class and supporters of the middle class was so severe in the founding days of the CDU that it was not clear if the party would find a way to overcome this divide. This disagreement was over the fundamental political direction of the party. The differences across the political spectrum manifested themselves most clearly on social and economic issues, and particularly on the question of nationalization of industry.

The internal suborganization for workers in the CDU was founded to ensure a voice for workers within the CDU. The *Sozialausschüsse der Arbeitnehmer der CDU/CSU* (Social Committees for Workers in the CDU/CSU, usually abbreviated CDA for *Christlich-Demokratische Arbeitnehmerschaft*) was founded in late 1945 (Uertz 1981: 65). Johannes Albers was the main force behind the new association. He began by sending circulars to former union members to solicit support for the new organization (Uertz 1981: 66). By February 1946, the CDA was running training weeks at the Cloister Walberberg for former members of Christian trade unions. The *Sozialausschüsse* coalesced from a series of local organizations, much like the CDU. The first meeting of the British zone *Sozialausschüsse* was February 21–2, 1947. The first national meeting was November 28–30, 1947 (Uertz 1981: 67).

The Social Committees' leadership had important positions within the party and the government from the beginning. Jakob Kaiser, one of the founders of the Social Committees, was vice chairman of the party from 1950 to 1958; in Adenauer's first cabinet, the Social Committees held the Labor Ministry (Anton Storch) and the Ministry for all-German Questions (Jakob Kaiser).

The left-leaning Christian socialists battled with more liberal forces in the party over program. The CDU's first program was the "Guiding Principles" of the Cologne CDU (*Kölner Leitsätze*) from June 1945, which was significantly influenced by the principles of Christian Socialism and advocated worker participation in industry (Uertz 1981). When Adenauer took over the leadership of the CDU in the British zone, he put forth a program with greater emphasis on liberal economic ideas (the Neheim-Hüsten program), but this program met resistance within the party. In response to pressure from the Social Committees, Adenauer began including the ideas (though not the name) of Christian Socialism in some of his speeches (Uertz 1981). The highpoint of the power of the CDA was in the writing of the Ahlen program of 1947. This program included demands to nationalize certain industries. The statements of Ahlen were quickly made obsolete when the western Allies agreed to form a West Germany with a liberal economic system. Ludwig Erhard took the lead in designing the new political economy. While some of the dreams of the Christian Socialists – such as nationalization of major industries – were never realized, the CDA continued and continues to have a significant impact on CDU policy making (Uertz 1981).

The CDU also appealed to workers through its economic policies, particularly through the creation of the so-called "social market economy." As envisioned by CDU Finance Minister Ludwig Erhard, the social market economy rejected both laissez-faire, free-market capitalism and socialist economic planning and intervention. Instead, the government set up a regulatory framework that ensured both sufficient competition and adequate social protection. For the working class, the social market economy meant an extensive social insurance system providing generous protection for the elderly, the sick, the injured and the unemployed. The social market economy also included worker participation in company decision making. The CDU passed laws in 1951 and 1952 ensuring that workers had substantial representation on the board of directors of their companies. In the late 1950s the CDU passed a series of laws called "Property Policies" that were directed at the working class. These laws were designed to help workers acquire property through savings incentives, incentives to build private houses, and tax breaks for employers who gave their employees shares in the company (Domes 1964: 150).

One way of measuring the success of the CDU in attracting the working class is to examine electoral returns. While the CDU was not as successful as the SPD, which was after all a workers' party, the CDU did gain significant support from workers. In 1953 35 percent of workers voted for the CDU (48 percent for the SPD). Among Catholic workers, 47 percent voted for the CDU in 1953 (36 percent for the SPD) (Pappi 1973: 580). While the CDU received a higher percentage of the vote from other classes, the CDU cannot be considered a purely middle class party. It achieved its objective of catching at least some of the working class.

THE CDU AND WOMEN

While the CDU struggled to incorporate the different regions, Protestants and workers, women proved to be a far less difficult group for the party to attract, at least at the polls. The party won significant support from female voters in the early years of the Federal Republic. Indeed, it is not going too far to say that the CDU owed its early success to its continued ability to win votes from women.[13] The only major complaint women raised about the new party was lack of adequate female representation in the process of founding the new German state. Partially with the goal of ensuring adequate representation of women (and their vision for politics) in the new party, female Christian Democrats began meeting together before the official formation of the CDU and before the first national elections. They quickly organized a women's association for the CDU and by the mid-1950s, the leaders of the women's organization were automatically members of the CDU's *Bundesvorstand*.

The effects of the corporatist catch-all party structure are more difficult to see with regard to women in the early postwar period. The women's organization for the most part agreed with CDU policy so there was little conflict. When there was disagreement, the women's organization tended to be internally divided and so it was not effective at persuading the main party of its policy preferences. During this period, women consistently voted for the CDU in high numbers. Two of the most important female leaders of this time period – Helene Weber and Elisabeth Schwarzhaupt – gained access to internal power within the party through Adenauer and they were therefore less in need of a mobilized membership base. As we will see in later chapters, in the 1970s the women's organization transformed into a much more cohesive and influential internal party actor. In the 1950s and 1960s, women were part of the CDU's corporatist catch-all party structure, but they were not yet making use of the power that this structure gives them.

Christian Democratic women were largely supportive of the CDU's positions in terms of gender relations. In the early postwar period, the CDU's stance on issues related to women was generally traditional. The policies of the CDU towards women, like those of its predecessor the Center Party, were based on the "3K model." The three K's stand for *Kinder, Kirche, Küche* (children, church, kitchen), referring to the spheres

---

[13] Female support for the CDU is compatible with trends in other countries that show women with strong support for religious parties.

of life in which women were traditionally supposed to be active. The CDU's women's policies in the 1950s focused on promoting this model. Particularly after the difficulties of wartime and the immediate postwar period, many in Germany were eager to return to traditional gender relationships, which to them represented a comforting normalcy.

The CDU advocated a society based on the family as its fundamental unit (Heidenheimer 1960: 41). This vision was contrasted with both National Socialism and Communism as forms of government that violated the sanctity of the family (Moeller 1993: 64). Families were the guardians of traditional, Christian values and were deserving of support and protection.

The CDU vision of these families was quite specific. A "normal" family had a husband, a wife, and at least two children, preferably more. The husband worked outside the home for a wage that was large enough to support himself and his dependents. The wife cared for the children and the household. Although she did not receive a wage, her work within the home was of equal value to his; sometimes this point was made with explicitly economic rhetoric. Wives should not work outside the home because they already had important jobs working inside the home. Part of this work involved watching over the children's development to ensure that German children emerged with the appropriate Christian values necessary for resisting both Communism and National Socialism.[14]

The CDU's position on women's issues in the 1950s was based on a concept of gender relations that was widespread within the Christian Democrats, but also within German society in general. Women and men were seen as inherently different, with women being more natural and men being more rational.[15] This difference was regarded as biological and

---

[14] The Christian Democratic vision of "normal" families ignored the postwar reality of many "non-normal" families. Approximately three million German men were killed in World War II, and at the end of the War, two million more were in prisoner-of-war camps (Moeller 1993: 27). The result was a dramatic "surplus of women" (*Frauenüberschuss*). Even in 1950, for every 100 men between the ages of twenty-five and forty, there were over 130 women (Moeller 1993: 28). These "surplus women" could not be wives in the CDU's "normal" families because there were no men available as husbands. Furthermore, even when husbands returned from the war alive, many married couples found the difficulties of returning to life together after such a long separation too great. The divorce rate sky-rocketed in the postwar period (Moeller 1993: 29). The 1950 West German census counted 15.4 million households, 1.7 million of them women living alone and 2.1 million headed by women with dependents (Moeller 1993: 32). These women did not fit well into the CDU's 3K model.

[15] This view was certainly not limited to Germany.

immutable. While women were not necessarily seen as less valuable, they were regarded as being beneath men in a natural hierarchy.

Both Christian Democratic women and men largely adhered to the vision just stated. The only significant point of conflict raised was that Christian Democratic women active in the party were sometimes dissatisfied with the extent to which women were represented on decision-making bodies, both in the party and in the government. The logic on this point was based on the idea of gender difference. Because men and women were different, it was critical to have women's views represented in the political process. Women were supposedly more peaceful. One Christian Democratic leader argued that women had managed without men throughout much of the war. Indeed, the war itself was evidence that men had failed in politics. Certainly the women who carried on in their absence should be represented in the new democracy (Holz 2004: 231). Unlike the other groups discussed here, Christian Democratic women made no demands beyond increased representation.

Like the internal suborganization for workers, the founding of the CDU's internal suborganization for women predates the founding of the party itself. The women in the CDU initially came together in regional and local associations. The first cross-zonal women's meeting was September 26, 1947 in conjunction with a meeting of the working group of the CDU/CSU (Holz 2004: 75). Over the course of fall 1947 and spring 1948, the women met several times to prepare for the founding of an official women's association of the CDU. The first meeting of the Women's Association of the CDU/CSU (*Frauenarbeitsgemeinschaft der CDU/CSU*) took place on May 1, 1948 in Frankfurt (Süssmuth 1990). The Christian Democratic women wanted their own organization because they wanted to contribute to how political issues of importance to women were handled by the new state and the new party (Süssmuth 1990: 61).

Helene Weber was elected as the first chair of the *Frauenarbeitsgemeinschaft* (Süssmuth 1990: 63). Other members of the Executive Council were chosen to reflect regional and confessional balance. The main CDU party agreed to fund most of the costs of the women's association (Holz 2004: 79–80). The *Frauenarbeitsgemeinschaft* spent the next months formulating position papers on important constitutional issues of particular concern to women, such as political training for women, equality, parents' rights, and media (Süssmuth 1990: 66). The *Frauenarbeitsgemeinschaft* devoted an entire conference to the work of the Parliamentary Council (Süssmuth 1990: 67). The organization also devoted considerable time to preparing for the first national election in August 1949.

When the organization for women had to be refounded after the CDU officially constituted itself as a party in 1950, problems with the relationship between the women's organization and the main party became apparent. In its new party statutes, the CDU called for "appropriate representation" for women on all party committees, but the women did not get a position as deputy chair of the party as some had desired (Holz 2004: 86). Calls for increased financial support for the women's organization showed that the party was not giving the *Frauenarbeitsgemeinschaft* adequate funding (Holz 2004: 87). Christian Democratic women also felt that their work for the party was granted insufficient recognition and that they were frequently chosen as committee members simply because they were women and not because they possessed expertise on a given subject area (Holz 2004: 90–1).

The new CDU women's organization, the National Women's Committee of the CDU (*Bundesfrauenausschuss der CDU* [or BFA]) was constituted at a meeting in September 1951 (Holz 2004: 89). The *Bundesfrauenausschuss* consisted of delegates from each of the *Länder*. It generally met twice a year until 1956 to discuss a variety of political issues. The main CDU's tendency to undervalue the women's contributions was a frequent agenda topic, but the women's organization also discussed education policy, economic policy, social reform, foreign policy, and other issues (Holz 2004: 92–3).

By the mid-1950s it became clear that the internal rules for organizing the *Bundesfrauenausschuss* were inadequate. Questions as basic as how many delegates each *Land* was entitled to and the rules for running meetings did not have obvious answers (Holz 2004: 94). The BFA codified its statutes in 1956–7 in conjunction with rewriting the statutes of the main party (Holz 2004: 95). As part of this reform process, the BFA was reconstituted as an official "association" (*Vereinigung*) of the CDU. Like other associations (for youth, municipal politics, social committees), the chairs (the women had one Protestant and one Catholic leader) of the women's association were automatic members of the National Executive Council of the main party (Holz 2004: 96–7). The statutes for the newly named Association of Women of the German CDU (*Vereinigung der Frauen der CDU Deutschlands*) were passed in November 1957 (Holz 2004: 98). The association maintained this form until 1988 when the name changed again to Women's Union (*Frauen Union*). The 1988 change also allowed people who were not members of the CDU to join the Women's Union (Keller-Kühne and Klein 1998: 135).

For the women of the CDU, the reconstitution of their organization as an official party association marked their incorporation into the corporatist catch-all party structure. While their actual representation in the party hierarchy did not change, the shift to association status meant that the main party could not remove the women's organization from the party's decision-making bodies in a way that might have been possible if the women were only promised "appropriate representation."

Even as an officially recognized party association, however, the *Frauenvereinigung* was not a stronghold of internal party power. Two factors prevented women from gaining more influence. The first is clearly electoral pressure. The main CDU felt no need to respond to internal demands from its organized female membership because it was doing so well with female voters. The second is unity. Women were organized within the party, but they did not yet have a goal that they agreed on.

In terms of policy, the CDU's women's organization was not very effective at influencing the CDU's positions on women's issues in the 1950s. This lack of influence is illustrated through one of the most important debates on women's issues in 1950s West Germany, the question of how to bring the old Civil Code in line with the Federal Republic's new constitution, the Basic Law. The majority of the laws regulating marriage and family relations were to be found in the Civil Code (*Bürgerliches Gesetzbuch*), which had been written in the 1870s and 1880s and had been in effect since 1900 (Moeller 1993: 47). During the Weimar Republic, parliamentarians had begun, but not completed, the task of revising some of these provisions to make them less patriarchal. The Civil Code explicitly gave husbands extensive rights over their wives and gave fathers (even against the objections of mothers) rights over their children (Moeller 1993: 47).

In the process of writing the Basic Law, the Parliamentary Council undertook a serious debate on the status of women in German society. This was one of the few topics discussed by the Parliamentary Council that the public followed closely (Holz 2004: 117). The Parliamentary Council wrote two contradictory articles directly addressing women's issues. Article Three, backed by the SPD, stated that "men and women shall have equal rights." Article Six, backed by the CDU/CSU, stated that "marriage and the family shall enjoy the special protection of the state," and in a later paragraph of Article Six: "Every mother shall be entitled to the protection and care of the community." Protecting motherhood meant freeing mothers from other responsibilities so they could care for their children – and reinforced the existing law that married women could only work outside the house with their husbands' permission (Moeller 1993: 66). These two sections of the Basic Law represent contradictory prescriptive visions of gender relations in West Germany.

The first elected West German government, a conservative coalition made up of the CDU/CSU, the FDP, and the German Party,[16] was charged with passing legislation to realize the vision of the Basic Law. The CDU/CSU took this as an opportunity to try again to get its vision of proper gender relations written into law. From 1949 to 1953 the Bundestag engaged in a series of debates over how to revise the Civil Code. Because the Parliamentary Council had endorsed both equal rights for men and women *and* special protection for marriage, mothers, and the family, the Bundestag had to decide whether the related clauses in the old Civil Code would have to be revised or could stand as they were. Two sections of the Civil Code were potentially in conflict with the new Basic Law. The Civil Code declared that in case of a conflict, husbands had the final authority over wives. Often it was imagined that the potential conflict would be over where to live. Likewise, fathers were given final authority over mothers when parents disagreed about choices regarding their children.

Most male Christian Democrats, backed by the Catholic Church, argued in favor of the "natural hierarchy" within marriage, proclaimed by both the bible and the Pope, which marked husbands as superior to wives and fathers as superior to mothers (Moeller 1993: 92–3). The CDU/CSU claimed that because husbands were naturally above wives, a law declaring them to be equal would have no effect, even if it were desirable, which it was not.

The CDU's women's association (at this time, the BFA) met twice to discuss these issues, once in February 1950 and once in July 1952 (Holz 2004: 155). The discussion at these meetings was very controversial; the press was not allowed to be present during the debate. The chair of the BFA, Helene Weber, favored retaining the authority of both husbands and fathers, but many women within the organization objected. Activists within the BFA were in open disagreement with the Catholic Church on these points and they were working with cross-party organizations, against the wishes of Helene Weber. The BFA did not vote on these issues because there was too much internal disagreement (Holz: 2004: 165). Despite Weber's attempts to downplay the views of the more progressive

---

[16] The German Party was later absorbed into the CDU.

women, she was not able to claim publicly that her organization was in favor of men's authority, because it clearly was not.

The Parliamentary Council had imposed a deadline of April 1, 1953 for its revision of the Civil Code. The Bundestag failed to meet this deadline, after which the Basic Law took precedence, while parliamentarians continued their attempts to find a compromise. Among CDU women, the conflict over the final authority of husbands and fathers worsened after 1953. Elisabeth Schwarzhaupt, newly elected to the Bundestag, was openly critical of the party's position. In this second round of parliamentary debate, Helene Weber was the only woman who spoke in favor of men having the last word (Holz 2004: 193). Perhaps because even prominent CDU women disagreed on these issues, the BFA did not discuss them again throughout this time period.

When these measures came to a vote in the Bundestag the result was a split decision. Husbands and wives were given equal rights by a majority of twelve votes; fathers' rights trumped mothers' rights by a majority of twenty (Moeller 1993: 203). The majority of the CDU/CSU caucus voted to give both husbands and fathers rights over wives and mothers. The SPD voted for equal rights. Most of the FDP delegation sided with the SPD, against their Christian Democratic partners in the governing coalition. The two issues were decided differently because some Christian Democrats defected from their party to support equality between husbands and wives and a few Free Democrats supported fathers over mothers (Moeller 1993: 203). The new family law was brought before the Federal Constitutional Court. In a 1959 ruling, the court struck down the provisions granting fathers preferred authority over mothers and declared parents to be equal.

As a corporatist catch-all party, the CDU should have given Christian Democratic women a significant role in policy making, especially on women's issues. Yet Christian Democratic women did not play a major part in the CDU's position on who had final authority within a family. There are a variety of reasons for this. First, for most of the debate, the BFA was not yet as firmly rooted within the party hierarchy as it became after 1956. Second, Christian Democratic women were internally divided on the issues of husbands' and fathers' final authority. In particular, members of the BFA diverged more and more from the position of their leader, Helene Weber. That internal disagreement made the organization less effective. Finally, the CDU was not experiencing any electoral pressure from women. The party continued to do well with women at the polls throughout the 1950s. Despite some continued activity on issues of women's representation within the CDU, the BFA and later the *Frauenvereinigung* acted primarily as a social group during the 1950s and 1960s. This would change in the 1970s when the CDU experienced a dramatic drop in electoral support from women. The *Frauenvereinigung* became more politicized and more unified. As a result, the organization moved from its role as a social organization to become a political actor within the CDU.

The genesis of the CDU clearly goes a long way to explaining the party's corporatist catch-all organization. The conditions under which the CDU was founded and the particular challenges the party faced in its initial period led to an internal organization that still shapes party policy making today. Chapter 9 illustrates how similar dynamics at the founding moment contributed to the French Socialist party and the Hungarian Socialist party also adopting the corporatist catch-all party structure. The following three chapters illustrate the effect of this organization on the CDU's policy making on women's issues.

4

The Emergence of the Women's Union, 1969–1982

The late 1960s and early 1970s were a time of change in German politics. New social movements, including the women's movement, entered the political arena. The influence of these changes on the SPD has been noted frequently, particularly as the SPD struggled to come to terms with the Green Party.[1] However, the CDU was also affected by the advent of New Left politics, including the women's movement.[2]

One of the most important effects of the politics of the late 1960s on the CDU was the rise of the Women's Union.[3] This internal organization had been present since the party's founding, but had served primarily as a social organization. The advent of the women's movement helped politicize the Women's Union. Christian Democratic women did not adopt the positions of the women's movement. Rather the women's movement provided the opportunity for the Women's Union to begin to advocate for its own positions on women's issues within the CDU.

The rise of the women's movement coincided with some important changes within the CDU. Helga Wex, a new energetic leader, became

---

[1] See for example, Andrei S. Markovits and Philip S. Gorski, *The German Left: Red, Green and Beyond* (1993), Thomas A. Koelble, *The Left Unraveled: Social Democracy and the New Left Challenge* (1991) and Herbert Kitschelt, *The Transformation of European Social Democracy* (1994).

[2] The German women's movement arose in opposition to some of the New Left organizations. The tension between feminists and New Left movements should not be underestimated and continues through today.

[3] The Women's Union went through a series of name changes. In 1988 it adopted the name *Frauen Union* to bring it in line with the CDU's other auxiliary organizations. During the 1970s the organization was actually called the *Frauenvereinigung* but I will use the term Women's Union from this point forward for simplicity's sake.

chair of the Women's Union in 1971. Turmoil within the CDU and a dramatic increase in female membership both presented an opportunity for the Women's Union to become much more prominent within the party.

The Women's Union's influence on the CDU is apparent in a new work-family policy, child-raising money, which advocated paying mothers who remained home to raise their children. While this policy reinforced traditional gender roles, it also broke with long-standing CDU policy that mothers should care for their children without financial remuneration. Child-raising money was an expensive policy that recognized the value of women's heretofore unpaid labor in the home. The Women's Union successfully convinced the party to advocate spending this money.

As a point of contrast, the Women's Union, like most other internal party actors, did not have a unified position on abortion reform. The Women's Union was not influential in the CDU's internal decision-making process on abortion. Because discussions on abortion reform began during a period of internal instability within the CDU and because few existing internal party actors were unified on abortion, the CDU tended to be reactive. Rather than leading the way, the party acted only when forced to do so. The CDU was internally divided and unable to reach agreement beyond attempting to prevent change to the law.

The first section of this chapter examines the politicization of the Women's Union and shows how this organization became more influential during this time period. The second section investigates the integration of the Women's Union with existing internal CDU groups. The next two sections explore CDU policy making on women's issues during the 1970s. The final section considers alternative hypotheses.

THE POLITICIZATION OF THE WOMEN'S UNION

As noted earlier, in the first two decades after World War II, the CDU had a traditional view of the proper role of women. The "3K" image – *Kinder, Kirche, Küche,* or children, church, kitchen – outlined the appropriate spheres for women's activities according to the party (Moeller 1993). During this time, the Women's Union rarely challenged this idea.[4] The Women's Union was primarily involved in organizing charity events and social gatherings. Its members were far more likely to serve coffee at party events than to advocate for particular policies. As Renate Diemers,

---

[4] One exception was the pressure a group of women activists in the Women's Union put on Adenauer to add a female minister to his cabinet. They were finally successful in 1961.

Member of the Bundestag and the Women's Union board of directors, explained:

> In the 1960s, the CDU had women's afternoons to court women's votes, but they weren't about politics. The politicians invited the women to come to the event and then paid them compliments. (Renate Diemers, personal interview)

Whether because female voters approved of the CDU's traditional take on gender roles or because female voters were more religious and therefore more drawn to the CDU as a Christian party (Bremme 1956), the CDU received significantly more electoral support from women than from men during the 1950s and 1960s. It was not uncommon for the CDU's "women's bonus" to be as large as 10 percent.[5] Clearly, as far as female voters were concerned, the CDU was doing something right. However, the party's women's bonus dropped significantly from the 1969 election (10.0 percent) to the 1972 election (3.0 percent).[6] This drop in support from women posed a serious problem for the CDU and prompted at least some CDU politicians to explore changing the party's stance on women's issues.

Simultaneous with these electoral changes, from the late 1960s through the mid-1970s, the Women's Union became increasingly politicized. No longer willing merely to serve coffee, the Women's Union began to issue position papers independent of the CDU and to work within the party to get its policies adopted (Süssmuth 1990: 122). The CDU's auxiliary organizations are supposed to be transmissions belts, transporting the views of the CDU to their target populations and ensuring that the CDU is aware of and responsive to the views of the target population (CDU statutes). Prior to this time period, the Women's Union's transmission belt operated primarily in one direction, from the CDU to women in Germany. In the 1970s the transmission belt began working in the other direction.

Three factors contributed to the increasing politicization and influence of the Women's Union. The first was the women's movement in West German society. The second was the Women's Union's new leader, Helga Wex. The third was the huge increase in female CDU membership and increased Women's Union representation on the party's decision-making bodies.

---

[5] The women's bonus is the difference between the percentage of women voting for the CDU/CSU and the percentage of men voting for the CDU/CSU.

[6] Some of this shift was due to a change in the voting age between the two elections, from 21 years old to 18 years old. Additionally, Willy Brandt was a particularly attractive candidate to women voters.

The Influence of the Women's Movement

Myra Marx Ferree identifies two sources of the beginning of the feminist movement in West Germany: women in the New Left and the conflict surrounding paragraph 218, the section of the legal code criminalizing abortion (Ferree 1987: 183). Within the New Left, women activists grew angry with their male counterparts. Although this movement was supposed to be emancipatory, the male activists did not take the concerns of the women seriously. Women active in the Socialist Democratic Students (SDS) were frequently given the tasks of child care or typing, while the men wrote pamphlets and made speeches. At an SDS conference on September 13, 1968, one frustrated female activist pelted a male SDS leader with tomatoes after he ignored a female speaker. This tomato-throwing incident was a moment of insight for other women in the SDS who formed women's groups all over West Germany after they returned home from the conference. It is often cited as the beginning of the West German feminist movement (Schwarzer 1981: 13).

The second source of this movement was the struggle to reform paragraph 218, which criminalized abortion. In 1971 Alice Schwarzer, one of Germany's most prominent feminists, organized an article for the weekly news magazine, *Stern*. In a June issue, an article *"Ich habe abgetrieben"* ("I had an abortion") was published, in which 374 women admitted to having had an abortion (and thereby breaking the law) (Hochgeschurz 1995: 162). The point of this article, inspired by a similar one in France, was to show that the law against abortion (paragraph 218) was ineffective and to weaken societal taboos surrounding abortion. Within one month of the article's appearance, activists had gathered 90,000 signatures demanding the elimination of paragraph 218.

In the early 1970s, "women's committees" were founded in Berlin, Frankfurt, and many other towns. These groups were active on several issues, including child care and women's health. While the abortion issue resonated most clearly with the largest number of supporters, the women's movement also had a large number and variety of "projects" which were not linked in any national organization. Projects included consciousness-raising groups, women's bookstores and publishing houses, shelters for battered women, and women's centers at universities. Along with continued protests against paragraph 218, the movement also had two feminist magazines with national circulation, *Courage* and *Emma* (Ferree 1987: 174).

As the women's movement gathered steam, it became increasingly difficult for the mainstream political parties to ignore its activities and demands. According to Annelies Klug, business manager of the Women's Union from 1973 to 1985, the Women's Union decided to take on the issues raised by the women's movement (Annelies Klug, personal interview). While some Women's Union members would have preferred to do nothing, the organization's leadership (especially under Helga Wex) chose to address women's issues, albeit not by embracing feminist positions. Indeed, Wex and the Women's Union activists sought to present a counter image to the women of the women's movement.

Even when the Women's Union women agreed with the problems identified by the women's movement, they frequently preferred different solutions. Some Women's Union activists openly identified themselves with the middle classes (Renate Hellwig, personal interview) while some sections of the women's movement felt closer to the working class. The Women's Union activists were not scornful of men, felt much less comfortable with lesbianism than the women's movement did, and mostly opposed liberalizing abortion access. Women's Union activists were also interested in expanding educational opportunities for women, a position that the middle-class women's movement of nineteenth century Germany also advocated. Only by becoming active themselves could the Women's Union women work to ensure that their views were also heard (Annelies Klug, personal interview).

New Women's Union Leadership

Along with the emergence of the women's movement, the second factor contributing to the politicization of the Women's Union was a shift in the Women's Union's leadership. In the late 1960s, the Women's Union changed its leadership structure and personnel. Both changes pushed the Women's Union into a more politically active role (Keller-Kühne and Klein 1998: 133; Bösch 2002: 246).

Unlike the CDU's other auxiliary organizations, the Women's Union originally had two co-leaders. From its inception in 1948 to the organizational reform in 1969, the Women's Union had one Protestant chair and one Catholic chair. While the Protestant and Catholic Women's Union chairs do not seem to have had serious conflicts with each other, the Women's Union lacked a clear spokesperson who would stand for the CDU's women. In 1969, the Women's Union's leadership was consolidated into a single chair, like all other CDU auxiliary organizations.

The initial change in form did not result in a change in personnel. Aenne Brauksiepe had been the Catholic chair of the Women's Union since 1958, and she continued as single chair after the reform. Already under Brauksiepe's tenure, the Women's Union was becoming more politically active than it had been in the 1950s. Brauksiepe organized two congresses on working women in 1964 and 1969 (Süssmuth 1990: 119–21). The new Women's Union statutes passed in 1969 emphasized that the organization should take positions on political issues (Süssmuth 1990: 112). Despite these efforts, however, the Women's Union was still primarily engaged in social functions and charity activities. The shift of emphasis occurred in 1971 when Brauksiepe retired and Helga Wex took over as chair of the Women's Union.

The Women's Union's new leader was a young, dynamic politician from Cologne. Her entrance onto the national political stage was dramatic: she took over Konrad Adenauer's seat in the Bundestag when he died in 1967. According to Udo Kollenberg, one of Wex's closest coworkers throughout the 1970s, this coincidence brought Wex a great deal of publicity, which she was able to use to increase her profile within the CDU (Udo Kollenberg, personal interview). Wex was in many ways Adenauer's opposite. She was young, female, and Protestant. She embodied many of the voting groups the CDU had struggled to attract. Some CDU leaders thought Wex would make an ideal "Vorzeigefrau" – token woman – and these sentiments helped her move up in the party hierarchy quickly.

Wex was not just a token woman, however. As the chair of the Women's Union in North Rhine-Westphalia, Irmgard Karwatzki, explained, Wex was an ambitious and skilled politician, "the kind of person you couldn't ignore" (Irmgard Karwatzki, personal interview). Udo Kollenberg described Wex as follows:

She had captivating eyes, like in the movie, Halloween. She had the courage to be unloved. She was brave politically. And she was ambitious. (Udo Kollenberg, personal interview)

Wex used women's issues as her ladder to climb the party hierarchy. She managed to represent the potential for CDU adjustment to a changing German society, something the party critically needed. In turn, the party promoted her internally. In 1969, she took over Brauksiepe's position in the Presidium. In 1971, she became chair of the Women's Union. In 1972, she became a deputy chair of the CDU Bundestag caucus. In 1973, she was appointed leader of the CDU's commission on women (Keller-Kühne and Klein 1998: 133).

Wex was too ambitious to chair an organization that sponsored primarily social and charity events. She soon began to try to convince the women of the Women's Union that their organization should take political stands on women's issues (Irmgard Karwatzki, personal interview). Although the Women's Union's members were initially reluctant to change their organization's role, Wex used opinion polls to argue for the growing importance of women's issues and to show that the CDU's positions on these issues were not popular. Furthermore, because no other group in the CDU seemed to be taking on women's issues, the Women's Union was the logical actor to do so (Annelies Klug, personal interview).

Throughout the 1970s, Wex pursued a series of policies and actions on women's issues. In 1973 and 1974, she organized two conferences on work-family policy. Both took child-raising money as a focal point. The idea was to pay mothers who stayed home with their children for longer than the required maternity leave.

Wex raised the profile of women's issues within the CDU. In 1974, Wex requested an Investigative Commission (*Enquete-Kommission*) on "Woman and Society" in the Bundestag. The Commission was charged with investigating how to implement policies to achieve women's equality. In 1975, the CDU national party congress approved a position paper, also entitled "Woman and Society" that was based on the Women's Union's Basic Policy Program. Many of the statements in these programs were incorporated into the CDU's Basic Policy Program in 1978. In 1979, the Women's Union published a paper outlining plans for a new research institute on women's issues. In 1982, the federal state of Lower Saxony followed this suggestion and founded the Institute of Woman and Society (Süssmuth 1990: 122–30). Under Helga Wex, the Women's Union was becoming a serious political player within the CDU, and women's issues were becoming more important to the party.

Female Membership Increase

The third contributor to the politicization of the Women's Union was the extraordinary increase in CDU membership generally and in female members more particularly. From 1969 to 1980 overall membership increased by 129 percent, while female membership increased by 266 percent. Women's share of CDU membership rose from 13.1 percent to 21.0 percent (Schönbohm 1985: 167 and 192).

The influence of the CDU's auxiliary organizations within the party depends partially on how many members the organization has (Schönbohm 1985: 228). In the case of the Women's Union, it is difficult to tell how many Women's Union members actually identify with the Women's Union because membership is automatic for female CDU members. Falke estimates that 36 percent of CDU women identified with the Women's Union in the 1970s (Falke 1982: 170). Schönbohm estimates the identification rate at 50 percent (Schönbohm 1985: 222). However, the increase in Women's Union membership was so enormous that the Women's Union gained in influence, even if only a minority of its members identified with its political objectives.

As the Women's Union grew in size, its leadership could more effectively argue that its positions had to be taken seriously by the party. Furthermore, unlike many auxiliary organizations, the Women's Union's members were more evenly distributed throughout the various *Länder* and its influence was therefore also more evenly distributed (Schönbohm 1985: 232).

Over the course of the 1970s, the Women's Union was transformed from an organization with primarily social functions to a much more active internal political group. Societal pressures to do something on women's issues combined with new leadership, and more numerous and active membership propelled the Women's Union to a more active role on women's issues within the CDU. As the following section discusses, this new group hardly entered a void when it entered party political life. Instead, the Women's Union quickly became a potential new player in the complex internal world of the CDU.

THE EMERGENCE OF A NEW DOMINANT COALITION

From 1966 to 1969 West Germany was governed by a "Grand Coalition," that is, the two main parties, the Christian Democrats and Social Democrats, governed together. Following the 1969 national level elections, the "Grand Coalition" was replaced by an SPD-FDP coalition and the Christian Democrats were forced into the opposition at the national level for the first time since the founding of the Federal Republic.

Loss of the Chancellor's office and governing power brought several problems to the fore for the CDU. Without the Chancellor's office, it was unclear where leadership of the party rested. Was the party chair or the chair of the parliamentary group responsible for leading the CDU? In 1969 the outgoing Chancellor, Kurt Kiesinger, remained party chair because no clear alternative was available (Pridham 1977: 188–94). From 1969 to 1971, it was unclear whether CDU leadership lay with Kiesinger, the party chair, or Rainer Barzel, chair of the parliamentary caucus. During these two years, power gradually shifted to Barzel, primarily because of his independent pursuit of a legislative agenda in the Bundestag (Pridham 1977: 195).

In 1971, when Kiesinger's term as party chair expired, he declined to run again. Barzel's leadership of the CDU was recognized when he was elected as party chair at the 1971 national party congress, despite a challenge from Helmut Kohl, Minister President of Rhineland-Palatinate and an up-and-coming leader within the CDU (Bösch 2002: 104). However, this instability in the party leadership made it difficult for the CDU to act coherently.

A second problem was that the party now needed a strategy for how to behave in opposition. Because the CDU had always been in government, it had no experience with responding to government proposals. Furthermore, the CDU was divided on the best strategy for returning to government. Some sections of the party viewed the 1969 defeat as a historical accident, requiring little change; others called for courting the FDP as a future coalition partner. Unfortunately for the party, these two strategies pointed in different directions (Kleinmann 1993: 316–18).

To make matters worse, internal tensions that had been masked during the period of the Grand Coalition now became painfully clear. The CDU was deeply divided on important questions of the day, such as normalizing relations with East Germany and increasing the power of unions.[7] Different actors within the CDU sometimes advocated contradictory policies. As Rudiger Göb, the CDU Business Manager from 1970 to 1971 observed:

The Opposition is like an automobile that is being driven by several motorists at one time: one is doing the steering, another has his foot on the accelerator, a third is pumping the brakes and yet another is operating the indicator. If this car is first past the chequered flag in 1973, it will be mainly as a result of luck. (Rudiger Göb as quoted in Pridham 1977: 197–8)

Lacking both a dominant coalition and effective leadership, the CDU failed to solve these problems during the 1969–1972 legislative period.

One reason for the failure is that party leaders improperly assessed the results of the 1969 election. Although the move to the opposition eventually proved to be of critical importance for the renewal of the CDU, party leaders initially questioned the legitimacy of the election results (Pridham 1977: 188). The most dramatic shifts in electoral support between the 1965 election and the 1969 elections were the gains of the Social Democrats and the losses of the Free Democrats. The Christian Democrats were able to maintain relatively stable support and remained the largest parliamentary caucus in the Bundestag.[8] Because many in the

---

[7] Keep reading for more on the second issue, worker participation.

[8] When comparing the seat distribution in the Bundestag from 1965 to 1969, the CDU lost three seats (193 down from 196), the CSU remained constant at 49, the SPD gained 22 seats

CDU regarded the loss of power as an accident (*Betriebsunfall*), the party undertook few changes prior to the elections in 1972 (Pridham 1977: 191).

The Election of 1972 and Its Aftermath

The 1972 election was much more devastating to the party than the 1969 election had been. This time, the CDU lost 16 seats as its parliamentary group decreased from 193 members to only 177. The CSU's seat share declined only one seat from 49 to 48. The SPD managed to increase its seats in the Bundestag from 224 to 230, while the FDP improved its position by 11 seats, from 30 to 41 (Ritter and Niehuss 1991: 101). The electoral results caused widespread demoralization within the Christian Democratic parties, especially the CDU. Willy Brandt, the SPD Chancellor, seemed unbeatable, and voters viewed the CDU/CSU as out of touch with a changing world (Pridham 1977: 207). This more serious electoral loss created the impetus for change in the CDU's leadership and its dominant coalition (Panebianco 1988; Harmel and Janda 1994; Harmel et. al 1995).

Rainer Barzel had been chair of the CDU since 1971. In the spring of 1972, prior to the national elections, the CDU/CSU parliamentary caucus had attempted to install Barzel as Chancellor through a constructive vote of no confidence (Pridham 1977: 194). This tactic failed. Barzel had then been the CDU/CSU Chancellor candidate in the elections of 1972. Finally, in the spring 1973, Barzel lost the support of the CDU/CSU parliamentary caucus – his main source of support within the party – over the issue of *Ostpolitik*, or normalizing relations with the German Democratic Republic (Pridham 1977: 202). Barzel was willing to compromise with the governing coalition and desert the CDU's hard-line stance opposing any reconciliation with East Germany. When the parliamentarians refused to follow Barzel's lead by supporting Chancellor Willy Brandt's eastern treaties, Barzel resigned as parliamentary chair and party leader. Helmut Kohl ran for the position of party chair unopposed at the national party congress in June 1973. He was elected with 520 of 600 votes (86.7 percent) (*Süddeutsche Zeitung*, June 13, 1973).

Since losing the election for party chair two years earlier, Kohl had worked to develop the support of regional leaders (Pridham 1977: 213). Once he announced his candidacy for the position of party chair in January 1973, Kohl's standing among regional leaders grew. His choice of Kurt

(an increase from 202 to 224) and the FDP lost 19 seats (a decrease from 49 to 30) (Ritter and Niehuss 1991: 101).

Biedenkopf from North-Rhine Westphalia for General Secretary helped secure the support of the largest regional organization of the CDU (Pridham 1977: 213). With Kohl's election to the party chairmanship, the CDU gained a new, younger leadership team. In addition to Biedenkopf, the new parliamentary caucus leader, Karl Carstens, was also a member of the younger generation. Because Biedenkopf owed his position entirely to Kohl and Carstens was serving his very first term in the Bundestag, neither of them was likely to emerge as a rival to Kohl.

The choice of Biedenkopf and Carstens to head his leadership team illustrated Kohl's commitment to integrating and balancing the divergent forces within the CDU (Pridham 1977: 227). Biedenkopf, a relative newcomer to party politics, was already known as a reformer and an innovative thinker through his position as a professor. Biedenkopf favored courting the Free Democrats as a future coalition partner and helped develop the concept of the "New Social Questions," one of the CDU's major reform ideas of the 1970s. While the "New Social Questions" were also linked to the Social Committees, Biedenkopf remained an independent actor, not tied to any particular auxiliary organization. For example, Biedenkopf was the main architect of the compromise on extending codetermination, a policy by which workers are represented on company boards of directors. Only someone independent of both business and labor could have constructed a compromise accepted by both sides (Pridham 1977: 224–8). Carstens, on the other hand, was known for his conservative positions, especially on defense, and was favored by the conservative wing of the party. By balancing his selection of a leadership team, Kohl broadened his support base and kept communication channels open to all sections of the party.

In addition to new party leadership, the electoral defeat in 1972 led to the emergence of a new dominant coalition in the CDU as well as a new party leader. The former dominant coalition consisted of the CDU's business groups and nationally oriented actors within the party. Because the CDU's electoral defeat in 1972 was much more pronounced than in 1969, it convinced significant sections of the party that reform was now critical to regaining power. Three groups with whom the CDU fared especially poorly in the 1972 election – women, youth, and workers – became more active in the party and led the fight to modernize the CDU's policy stances. The auxiliary organizations for these groups – the Youth Union, the Social Committees, and the Women's Union – formed the new dominant coalition that strongly influenced party policy over the course of the 1970s and into the 1980s.

The new dominant coalition did not secure its power over the party immediately following the 1972 electoral loss. Instead, the alliance of the Social Committees, the Youth Union and the Women's Union emerged during the period 1973–5. In the late 1960s and early 1970s the Social Committees were deeply involved in an internal party battle over the question of whether to extend worker participation. Worker participation refers to an aspect of the German system of industrial relations, which allows workers to participate in company decision making.[9] The Social Committees favored increased worker participation while the CDU's Economic Council opposed it. The ultimate position of the party represented a compromise between these two positions (Kramer and Kramer 1976). While the Social Committees initially appeared to have suffered a defeat in terms of the CDU's final position, they emerged from the discussion process in an improved position within the party.

The CDU's internal debate on worker participation improved the position of the Social Committees in two ways (Kramer and Kramer 1976). First, the organization itself became more dynamic and assertive in its relationship to the main party. Second, through these discussions, the Social Committees and the Youth Union formed an alliance that then served as the basis for the new dominant coalition.

The CDU had initially adopted a position in 1971 on worker participation that was quite one-sided in favor of the Economic Council (one of the CDU's auxiliary organizations for business interests). This early defeat served as a wake-up call for the Social Committees. The Social Committees fought back through a campaign of public criticism of the CDU that included threats to submit its own legislation and try to convince the SPD to approve it. The Social Committees even threatened to split off from the CDU entirely (Kramer and Kramer 1976: 39). These moves challenged the CDU's reputation as a catch-all party, able to represent all segments of society. Furthermore, when Helmut Kohl and Kurt Biedenkopf, the CDU's newly elected chair and General Secretary, respectively, tried to go around the Social Committees and consult directly with union leadership, the unions refused to cooperate and insisted on continued negotiations with the Social Committees (Kramer and Kramer 1976: 26–7). These tactics proved successful, forcing the CDU to change its position on worker participation to a more labor-friendly stance and simultaneously increasing the status of the Social Committees within the CDU.

---

[9] For more on this topic, see Markovits 1986, chapter 3, and Katzenstein, P. 1987, chapter 3.

In June 1973, the CDU's auxiliary organization for young people, the Youth Union, elected a new chair, Matthias Wissmann. This election was the culmination of a lengthy reorientation of the Youth Union towards a more progressive position (Kramer and Kramer 1976: 41). The new leadership and position of the Youth Union made possible an alliance between the Youth Union and the Social Committees, as the two organizations within the CDU most interested in reforming the party. As Wissmann described it:

I believe this is more than a short-term practical alliance. This is a programmatically based cooperation that thrives above all on shared principles. Principles, when it's a question of the realization of the ideas of the social partnership in social policy .... When it's a question of solidarity with marginalized groups in the welfare society. And that's what I especially want to stress. When it's a matter of the realization of the only element in the name of the CDU/CSU that has a basis in theory, in other words, the "C" in practical politics. (Wissmann quoted in Kramer and Kramer 1976: 31)

The alliance Wissmann described here formed the basis of the dominant coalition that controlled much of CDU policy making in the 1970s. The Youth Union and the Social Committees worked together to modernize the CDU's personnel and policies. They were soon joined by the Women's Union, further increasing the power of the coalition.

By 1975, the new dominant coalition was secure in its power. As reported June 26, 1975 in the *Frankfurter Allgemeine Zeitung*:

One of the treats of the party congress was that even before the congress started, the Youth Union demonstrated solidarity together with the Women's Union and the CDA. Here things really came together in the framework of overarching consensus and in solidarity written in big letters and the main party will have to get used to the fact that without this block or against this block, they aren't going to be able to do much.

The new dominant coalition used the increasing power of the party's national-level extra-parliamentary organization to shape CDU policy. Heiner Geissler, CDU General Secretary from 1977 to 1989, described the situation this way:

We had a phalanx in the CDU from the mid-1970s to the early 1980s. The Youth Union, the Women's Union, and the Social Committees. It was pretty powerful at party congresses. It could determine CDU politics. (Heiner Geissler, personal interview)

The new dominant coalition asserted its agenda at party congresses and through thematic conferences over the course of the 1970s. Leaders of this new dominant coalition included leaders of the auxiliary organizations, such as Helga Wex, the chair of the Women's Union, Norbert Blüm and Hans Katzer, leaders of the Social Committees, and Matthias Wissmann, chair of the Youth Union. Other leaders of the dominant coalition were Heiner Geissler, the Social Minister in Helmut Kohl's home state of Rhineland-Palatinate, who became General Secretary of the CDU in 1977; Richard von Weizsäcker, who had been the CDU's candidate for Federal President in 1974; and Ernst Albrecht, Minister President of Lower Saxony. Geissler, Blüm, Weizsäcker, Albrecht, and Wex made up a clear majority of the Basic Policy Commission, an important internal party group that wrote the CDU's first general programmatic paper, passed in 1978 (Bösch 2002: 38).

This dominant coalition focused primarily on domestic policy, which helped it maintain its leading position in the party. The CDU had been losing on foreign policy issues, and many in the party were eager to switch the agenda to domestic issues. The new dominant coalition pushed for policies that would modernize the CDU.

Although the Women's Union was an important member of the reform-oriented dominant coalition, neither the dominant coalition nor the Women's Union itself held values that could be defined as feminist. While this coalition did advocate some policies that would have a significantly greater impact on women's lives than on men's lives, the vision of women's roles was still fairly traditional.

On work-family policy, the dominant coalition developed a policy to pay mothers to stay home with their children. There are many ways that a government can influence the choices parents make about who should work and who should stay home. By giving the stay-at-home parent fairly low monthly payments, called child-raising money, this policy encouraged mothers, almost always the less well paid parent, to stay home. However, by devoting substantial financial resources to mothers, this policy also acknowledged the importance of parenting. Although the child-raising money reinforced the traditional gendered division of labor, it also increased the value shown to the conventionally female part of this work.

The CDU's actions on abortion, meanwhile, were generally less coherent than its actions on work-family policy. One reason for the difference is that the abortion debate began in 1971, during which time no clear dominant coalition existed within the CDU. The Women's Union was also divided on the issue of abortion. Even after the dominant coalition began to exert more influence within the party in 1973, the coalition was itself divided on the abortion issue and therefore unable to pursue a clear policy goal. The remainder of this chapter discusses CDU policy making during the 1970s on the issues of work-family policy and abortion policy.

POLICY MAKING ON WOMEN'S ISSUES: WORK-FAMILY POLICY IN THE 1970S

Contrasting two thematically-related policy areas from the 1970s highlights the important role of the dominant coalition in shaping CDU policy. With respect to work-family policy, the new dominant coalition seized the initiative to propose a novel policy that was eventually adopted as part of the party program. Even after coming into its own, the new dominant coalition remained divided on the question of abortion. Consequently, the CDU's responses to abortion were purely reactive.

The CDU traditionally held that mothers should be at home, not in the workforce. Even at the congress on working women in 1964, the party made it clear that the new openness toward working women should not extend to include mothers (Bundesgeschäftsstelle der Christlich Demokratischen Union Deutschlands 1965). By the early 1970s, however, changes in both societal and political circumstances were pushing the CDU to reconsider its stance (Henry-Hutmacher, personal interview). From the mid-1970s onward, the CDU advocated an interesting compromise: Mothers should receive child-raising money to care for their own children at home. While the CDU had always recognized raising children as work, by offering to pay parents to stay home with their children the party tacitly acknowledged that women had other viable alternatives.

In part, the CDU was reacting to a significant drop in the German birthrate. Between 1965 and 1975, *per anum* German births decreased by 50 percent (Statistisches Bundesamt 1987: 24). At the same time, the debate surrounding abortion reform (see following) had identified financial hardship as a motivation for abortion. The CDU had always supported traditional families, but by the 1970s the idea of the family was expanding, even within certain quarters of the CDU, to include single parents with children. Paying mothers to raise children might simultaneously be an antidote for the falling birthrate and financially motivated abortions.

To some extent, the CDU was also responding to a challenge from its most important political rival: In 1972, the SPD had proposed a "Baby year" that provided for a one-year pension credit for stay-at-home mothers. The SPD's coalition partner, the FDP, found this initial proposal too expensive, but the two parties later implemented an alternative work-family policy: an extended maternity leave that allowed for six months off and provided a payment of 750DM per month from the national government. Crucially, the benefit was available only to women who had been working at the time of their pregnancy. The CDU needed some kind of alternative proposal that would not disadvantage women who had stayed at home all along.

The alternative approaches developed by the CDU and the SPD represent components of different welfare state regimes, as developed by Esping-Andersen (1990). Esping-Andersen's well-known welfare state regimes include liberal welfare states, corporatist welfare states, and social democratic welfare states. The three welfare state regimes have different approaches to the question of what benefits to provide to working mothers. Liberal welfare states leave the choice of whether mothers should work to the market. If child care is available and affordable and their salaries high enough, particular mothers may choose to work. If child care is too expensive or they cannot earn enough in paid employment, mothers can choose to stay home. Corporatist welfare states, on the other hand, are based on the subsidiarity principle. Families are expected to care for their members and the male bread-winner's wage should be high enough to facilitate that arrangement. Sometimes these regimes provide long parental leaves to encourage women to stay home and care for their own children. Finally, social democratic welfare state regimes emphasize the principles of universalism and egalitarianism. To meet those goals, these regimes frequently provide high quality state-funded daycare as well as other policies to encourage women's employment (Esping-Andersen 1999: 74–86).

The SPD's choice not to focus on providing child care confirms Germany's classification as a corporatist welfare state regime. The Scandinavian social democratic welfare regimes started providing extensive state-funded child care in the late 1960s and early 1970s (Esping-Andersen 1999: 55). Even though the SPD is a social democratic party, as noted in the introduction, the party has often taken a relatively conservative approach to women's issues. The SPD-FDP coalition implemented a parental leave for working mothers, but did not increase the provision of child care and did not provide additional benefits for nonemployed mothers.

For the CDU, the main question was whether to pay mothers to stay home or not. Certainly most actors in the party expected mothers to stay home to care for their own children, but if mothers were willing to do so without payments from the state, that was obviously preferable. Within the group of corporatist welfare state regimes, there is extensive variation in parental leave in terms of both the length of time off and the amount of money the stay-at-home parent receives.[10]

Despite the external pressure for the CDU to address the work-family issue through payments to mothers, there was powerful resistance within the party. Many Christian Democrats opposed policies to help working mothers on both ideological and financial grounds. While paying mothers to stay home seems like a policy for stay-at-home mothers, many within the CDU (and the CSU) regarded child-raising money as an admission that these mothers might otherwise be in the workforce. Franz Josef Strauss, chair of the CSU, and Ludwig Erhard, former Chancellor, objected to the CDU's proposal on the basis of cost (Udo Kollenberg, personal interview). Representatives of business, including the leadership of the Middle Class Association and the Economic Council, also opposed the policy change. Some even accused the CDU of becoming more socialist than the SPD (Kleinmann 1993).

On the other hand, the dominant coalition – consisting of the Youth Union, the Social Committees and the Women's Union – favored the policy initially called "family money." Family money, or child-raising money as it came to be called, would pay either a mother or a father 500DM per month for six months. The proposal contained no job guarantee and in fact, made it clear that the policy was partially designed to fight unemployment (Doormann 1980: 30). While the CDU policy paid less money than the SPD policy, the CDU policy was available to all parents, including mothers who had not previously been employed. The child-raising money conveniently coincided with a long-standing demand from the women's movement that women be paid for housework. While the strand of the women's movement affiliated with labor unions had never adopted this demand, many feminists, including the first German feminist magazine, *Courage*, advocated some kind of pay-for-housework arrangement (Hochgeschurz 1995: 174). By responding to this specific demand, the CDU hoped to appeal to this section of the electorate.[11]

Within the dominant coalition, Wex and Geissler had both been developing the idea of child-raising money. Geissler initially envisioned it as a

---

[10] Bussemaker and van Kersbergen (1999) note this variation, but do not provide an explanation for it. They suggest further research into domestic political factors, which is the approach taken here.

[11] While pay-for-housework was never a serious demand of the women's movement in the US, it was in Germany, where feminists were more likely to emphasize the differences between men and women (Ferree 1987: 179).

means to help single mothers, but in the process of working on the policy, he realized that married mothers could also benefit (Heiner Geissler, personal interview). For Wex, child-raising money was part of a more comprehensive attempt to get the CDU to be active on women's issues. It was something she could convince her followers to embrace, as opposed to the more controversial initiatives that favored working mothers. Child-raising money was at once progressive and traditional. Geissler and Wex both argued that child-raising money would win votes for the CDU.

In order to develop support for the child-raising money, Wex mobilized (rather than disempowered) CDU members. After the party's electoral defeat in 1972, the CDU attempted to reach out to voter groups that it was having trouble with. The party set up a series of temporary working groups focused on particular sections of society (Udo Kollenberg, personal interview). As a rising star in the CDU and the chair of the Women's Union, Wex was a natural choice to chair the working group on women. In this capacity, she organized two large meetings, both of which had child-raising money as a primary agenda topic. The first, in Bonn on September 24, 1973, was a hearing held jointly with the CDU's working group on families at which experts discussed the various problems facing families and possible policy solutions (CDU-Bundesgeschäftsstelle 1973). The second, a family politics congress in Münster on October 4–5, 1974, was a large meeting with party members and featured keynote speeches from Wex, Heiner Geissler, and Helmut Kohl (CDU-Bundesgeschäftsstelle 1974). Both events served a joint purpose of gathering feedback on the child-raising money policy and promoting the policy.

Wex also worked to inform and involve members of the Women's Union on the policy of child-raising money. As chair, Wex developed the Women's Union's first Basic Program, which included a demand for child-raising money. The Women's Union adopted the Basic Program at the meeting of its national congress on February 21–3, 1975 in Dortmund.

The Women's Union's demand for child-raising money had a strong influence on the main party. The CDU used the Women's Union's Basic Program as the basis for the party's statement on "Woman and Society." The CDU approved "Woman and Society" in May 1975 at the national party congress in Mannheim. "Woman and Society" then served as the foundation for the section on women in the CDU's Basic Program, adopted by the party congress on October 23–5, 1978 in Ludwigshafen. Both "Woman and Society" and the CDU's Basic Program included child-raising money as a policy favored by the CDU.

In the end, the Women's Union, backed by the dominant coalition, used its increased prominence within the CDU to convince the party to adopt the child-raising money proposal. Annelies Klug described the strategy pursued by the Women's Union as follows:

It's important to set up working groups to develop proposals for regional and national congresses. That gets the discussion going. Then it's important that you guide the discussion. Without guidance, you'll just hit resistance. You need to present a well-argued position over and over again … These temporary working groups develop policies on a particular topic and then you try to get the important parts of them into the party program … That's why it's so important that the leader of the Women's Union is integrated into the party's committees at the national level. The essential elements [of the Women's Union's new positions] were there [at the national party congress in 1975] in Mannheim. (Annelies Klug, personal interview)

Because the dominant coalition was able to control access to important policy-making offices, it could out-maneuver opponents of this policy. It was particularly important that the dominant coalition control such a large majority of the Commission charged with writing the Basic Program. And it is important to remember that – thanks to the CDU's corporatist structure – one of the main techniques for getting the party to adopt this policy was to raise membership involvement through a series of conferences and meetings rather than to demobilize it.

POLICY MAKING ON WOMEN'S ISSUES: ABORTION POLICY IN THE 1970S

In contrast to policy making on work-family issues, the CDU's policy making on abortion in the 1970s is an example of the party's inability to act in a coherent fashion when the dominant coalition is divided. The Bundestag made three attempts to pass abortion reform. On the first and third of these attempts, the CDU was too divided even to submit a proposal. On the second attempt, the CDU submitted two proposals because the parliamentary caucus was unable to unify itself behind a single bill. The CDU was not a policy leader on abortion.

The CDU had no major objections to the postwar abortion law. In the initial postwar period, abortion in West Germany had been illegal. This law was based on a court decision from 1927.[12] In this decision, the judge

---

[12] Laws passed under National Socialism in 1935 and 1943 more seriously restricted abortion, but these laws were repealed at the end of the war.

declared that if the pregnant woman's life or health were seriously in danger, then abortion was not punishable (although it remained illegal). The decision about whether the danger to the woman's health was sufficient to allow an abortion had to be made by a medical doctor (Gante 1991: 16–17). After the war, many women were raped by occupying troops. In these cases, abortion was generally allowed, although strictly speaking the procedure was still both illegal and punishable (Gante 1991: 341–2). As a party with strong Catholic roots, CDU opposition to abortion was a natural stance.

While the CDU was content with existing law, societal and political pressure brought the question of reform to the fore. In 1970, a group of liberal law professors published the "Alternative Proposal," (*Alternativ-Entwurf*) a document proposing that abortion be legalized during the first three months of pregnancy. They argued that fear of punishment was preventing women from seeking counseling that might ultimately lead them to decide *not* to abort. Furthermore, because many doctors were granting abortions for nonmedical reasons, the difference between the practice of the law and the letter of the law had grown increasingly large.[13]

Activists in the German feminist movement were also pressuring the political parties to liberalize the abortion law. The women's movement considered the right to an abortion to be a fundamental right that West German women lacked. Their preference was to eliminate paragraph 218, the paragraph criminalizing abortion, from the legal code entirely. The publication of the article "I Had An Abortion" in the June 1971 issue of *Stern*, brought the women's movement a great deal of attention and many new supporters. This event and the protests that followed it convinced many politicians that abortion reform would have to be addressed (Gante 1991: 123–9; Ferree, forthcoming, Chapter 3).

The main line of debate in the early 1970s was whether the reform would be an expanded "indication" model or a new "time limit" model. Under the indication model, abortion remained both illegal and punishable. In certain circumstances, however, called "indications," the state would refrain from punishing a woman who had an abortion or a doctor who performed an abortion. The existing law in West Germany followed the indication model, but it officially allowed for only one indication: the medical indication, under which abortion was allowed if the mother's

---

[13] This chapter draws on histories of abortion policy found in Gante 1991; Klein-Schonnefeld 1994; Maleck-Lewy 1994; and Kamenitsa 2001. Gante has the most extensive coverage of the internal politics of the political parties.

health was endangered. Various new indications were proposed, including most commonly the criminal indication (in cases of rape), the eugenic indication (when the fetus suffered a developmental defect), and the social emergency indication (when the woman was not able to cope with having a child, either financially or psychologically). Under all indication models, someone had to be designated to decide whether an indication was present or not. Most frequently, a medical doctor was given the right to make this decision, although some indications did not relate to medical health (Klein-Schonnefeld 1994: 117; Däubler-Gmelin and Faerber-Husemann 1987: 105–6).

The CDU certainly preferred the indications model to the other main possibility, the time limit model. This model legalized abortion during the first stages of pregnancy, generally during the first trimester. Under this model, the pregnant woman had the right to decide whether to have an abortion, as long as no more than three months had passed since conception. Particularly for committed Catholics in the CDU, the time limit model was completely untenable.

The political context for abortion reform offered the CDU a chance for a significant political victory. The parties in the governing coalition – the Social Democrats and the Free Democrats – were both open to liberalizing the law, but the FDP pushed for more far-reaching reforms. Many CDU politicians thought that if the CDU could convince enough Social Democratic parliamentarians to join the CDU in passing a modest reform based on an indication model, the CDU might be able to prevent what was viewed as a significantly worse outcome, abortion reform based on a time limit model. Furthermore, a CDU-SPD bill would have illustrated the tension between the governing coalition partners and therefore have been a significant political victory for the CDU. Because much of the SPD preferred an indication model, the possibility of compromise with the CDU was real (Gante 1991: 139). In 1971, the governing coalition's parliamentary majority was tiny, so convincing the partners to vote on opposite sides of an issue would have been a coup for the CDU and would possibly have set the stage for the collapse of the government.

While some leaders and sections of the CDU were open to the possibility of compromise legislation with the SPD, others in the party preferred a hard-line approach to abortion. Hardliners, notably the group surrounding former Family Minister and General Secretary Bruno Heck, viewed the possibility of compromise with the Social Democrats as selling out a core Christian Democratic value. In particular, these politicians were uncomfortable allowing abortion under the eugenic indication, i.e., if the fetus was known to not be developing normally. They argued that a country with the legacy of National Socialism could under no circumstances value handicapped life differently from nonhandicapped life. These politicians supported only a limited indication model that did not differ much from existing West German law.

The CDU began formulating its position on abortion reform following the *Stern* protest. In June 1971, the CDU's Parliamentary Working Group One, with responsibility for legal reform, began drawing up guidelines for the party's position (Gante 1991: 139). In December 1971, the CDU's National Executive Committee issued a position paper calling for an indication model that allowed the medical indication and a narrow criminal indication. In the spring 1972, Parliamentary Working Group One continued its discussion and agreed that the medical indication should include psychological illness, that the criminal indication should be included, and that the social indication should be excluded. The group failed to reach agreement on the health indication. New elections were called before further progress could be made (Gante 1991: 142).

During the early stages of the abortion debate, the CDU was experiencing a period of internal turmoil. As outlined previously, from 1969 to 1972, the CDU lacked both a stable leadership and a clear dominant coalition. Furthermore, the Women's Union – an internal party actor that was likely to take a lead role on abortion – changed leadership in 1971 and in any case was not yet a politicized internal party actor. During this time period, it was difficult for the CDU to act coherently on any issue, let alone one as difficult as abortion. Not surprisingly, the CDU failed to issue a proposal for abortion reform prior to the 1972 elections.

The SPD-FDP coalition was greatly strengthened by the 1972 elections. Moreover, the SPD had become more amenable to the time limit model. Prior to the election, the official government proposal had been an indication model, but after the election the SPD changed its position. The new government proposal was a time limit model. The chance of the CDU managing to pass abortion reform with the SPD was greatly diminished. A minority in the SPD still backed the indication model so the party submitted two different abortion bills (Gante 1991: 131–8).[14]

In 1973, the CDU gained both new, stable leadership and a new dominant coalition. However, the CDU still had difficulty formulating a coherent

---

[14] The SPD was also divided on abortion. Before the 1972 elections, the majority of the party supported an indication model. The tide was clearly shifting, however. By 1973 most of the party backed a time limit model while a minority remained in favor of an indication model.

abortion policy because the dominant coalition was itself divided. While the issue of abortion had by this time been raised within the Women's Union, the organization's activists disagreed. Some were willing to liberalize abortion law by expanding the indication model, and others were committed to an indication model permitting abortion only in cases of danger to the woman's health. Furthermore, other members of the dominant coalition were on opposite sides of the issue. The Social Committees are a thoroughly Catholic organization, and their members mostly opposed reform. The Youth Union, on the other hand, was relatively open to compromise. By the second round of the abortion debate, therefore, the CDU's dominant coalition was capable of acting cohesively on *some* issues, but not on abortion (Gante 1991: 138–46).

In 1973 the CDU submitted two bills on abortion reform. In agreement with the CSU, the CDU/CSU parliamentary caucus proposed an abortion reform that liberalized the indication model only slightly. Abortion was not punishable if the life or health of the mother was in danger. A subcase of this exception, the "child" indication, allowed abortion to remain unpunished if the fetus had a serious birth defect. Abortion within 12 weeks of conception was also allowed to go without punishment if the pregnancy was the result of rape or sexual assault. A three-person committee (consisting of two doctors and one nondoctor) was to decide whether these indications were present, and a three-day waiting period was required between a mandatory counseling session and the abortion procedure (Gante 1991: 155–6).

The other CDU bill, called the Heck proposal after the CDU's former Family Minister, allowed only for the medical indication. Abortion was punishable in all circumstances, except when the mother's health was in serious danger. The court was allowed to not apply the punishment if the woman had acted out of desperation (*Bedrängis*) (Gante 1991: 155–6). As an opposition party, the CDU ought to have been offering a clear alternative to the proposals of the governing coalition. Because the dominant coalition was divided, however, the CDU was unable to present a consistent counter-proposal to the SPD-FDP governing coalition.

The Bundestag passed the government's time limit model proposal in April 1974 by a vote of 247 to 233. This law was immediately challenged as unconstitutional by the CDU. In February 1975, the Federal Constitutional Court declared that the new law was incompatible with the Basic Law. The court not only dictated that abortion reform must be some kind of indication model, but also set down guiding principles for what indications would be permitted (Gante 1991: 157–79; Klein-Schonnefeld 1994; Kamenitsa 2001: 116–18) .

The Federal Constitutional Court (FCC) provided the following guidelines. The fetus must be protected at all times; therefore no time limit model is allowed. The law can show disapproval (*Missbilligung*) of abortion through some mechanism other than punishment, but it must provide actual protection for the fetus. In the extreme case, if protection cannot be assured in any other way, punishment is required. The law may not require continuation of pregnancy if the woman's health or life is in danger. Lawmakers may also allow abortion to go unpunished in cases of similar seriousness in their impact on the woman (Gante 1991: 174–5).

In the third round of discussion of abortion reform, the CDU again failed to submit a bill to the Bundestag. Because the FCC had provided guidelines for the indications, any bill would have to work within that framework. The governing SPD-FDP coalition aimed to pass a bill that was as liberal as the court decision would allow, while the CDU/CSU preferred a much more restrictive bill.

The bill proposed by the governing coalition allowed the medical, health, criminal, and social indications. A single doctor had the right to decide whether any of the allowable indications was present or not. The cut-off date for the criminal and social indications was set at 12 weeks. The health indication was permissible for the first 22 weeks of pregnancy. As with all other proposals, the medical indication was valid at all times. Under the SPD-FDP proposal, counseling about both sources of potential public and private assistance as well as the medical aspects of the procedure was required.

The CDU proposal also included medical, health, criminal, and social indications. The inclusion of a social indication was a clear change in the CDU position (Gante 1991: 191). While the CDU had been moving gradually toward allowing this indication, the final push seems to have come from the party's Baden-Württemberg regional organization (Gante 1991:190).

Under the CDU's proposal, the process required for a woman to obtain an abortion was different. The woman was required to visit a counseling center, where she could be advised about available assistance and about her responsibility to protect the life of the fetus. A mandatory three-day waiting period followed the counseling session. Then two doctors would decide whether the abortion should be allowed or not (Gante 1991: 192). At the time of this debate, the counseling centers were not yet in existence.

Although these bills were quite similar, the parliamentary caucuses of the parties failed to reach a compromise, primarily because the FDP refused to support a bill with additional restrictions on abortion. The SPD preferred to pass a bill with its coalition partner rather than with the opposition. The SPD-FDP bill passed in the spring of 1976 on a vote of 234 to 181 (Gante 1991: 199). The CDU decided not to submit its proposal to a vote, presumably because parliamentary leaders knew that the more conservative parliamentarians in the group around Heck would vote against it.

Although the CDU generally resisted change on abortion policy, this stance was not due to the actions of a dominant coalition with a clear position on the issue. During the early years of the abortion debate (1970–3), the CDU had little internal cohesion. The party changed chairs twice during this period and lost the national election in 1972. The parliamentary caucus submitted two abortion bills in 1973 because even this subunit of the party was unable to agree on a position.

From 1973 to 1976 a dominant coalition existed within the CDU, but it was divided on abortion. The Women's Union was itself internally split on what sort of reform would be most desirable (Annelies Klug; Renate Hellwig, personal interviews) and therefore this organization did not play an active role in pursuing a particular reform. The CDU was not only divided about whether to include the social indications. Many activists also opposed the health indication, which permitted abortion if the fetus was not developing normally. The question of whether women should be punished for abortions that did not have the relevant indications further split the party. These divisions did not line up with existing internal party actors. Rather, most internal party groups were divided on abortion and therefore ineffective.

ALTERNATIVE HYPOTHESES

Chapter 1 presented three rival hypotheses to explain CDU behavior on women's issues. The rival hypotheses are the essential Christian party theory, spatial voting theory, and classic catch-all party theory. The rest of this section briefly reviews these rival hypotheses and discusses their predictions about CDU behavior on women's issues in the 1970s.

The first hypothesis is that CDU behavior is driven by its Christian ideology. It predicts that the CDU will be unwilling to make major changes that conflict with this ideology for fear of losing its core support group. If they party feels sufficient electoral pressure, it may pass symbolic policy that is not in line with its Christian values. This hypothesis works relatively well in the 1970s, but works less well in later time periods.

The essential Christian party hypothesis predicts CDU behavior on abortion policy in the 1970s fairly well. Particularly because the CDU's Christian ideology is based on its Catholic history, we would expect the party to resist liberalization of the abortion law. This prediction is correct in that the CDU was for the most part trying to prevent or limit the extent of abortion reforms. The party's willingness in 1975 to support legislation with multiple indications – including the social indication – is somewhat puzzling for this hypothesis, but nonetheless, the overall behavior of the CDU on abortion was in keeping with its Christian ideology.

The CDU's Christian ideology would lead us to expect the party to have advocated work-family policy that kept mothers at home with their children and out of the labor force. The party advocated this policy in the 1970s. This hypothesis would not, however, predict serious internal party conflict over this issue, but the CDU experienced such conflict because some party leaders did not want to pay for this policy. Furthermore, this hypothesis would predict that the CDU would adjust to new demands with symbolic policy. The suggested payments to mothers do not constitute symbolic policy, however, because they involved real money. Once again, the Christian ideology hypothesis has generally predicted CDU behavior, but also raised some questions. The hypothesis would not have predicted such compromise on abortion nor would it have predicted an internal party fight over money for stay-at-home moms.

The second rival hypothesis from Chapter 1 is spatial voting theory. This hypothesis offers two types of predictions. First, if possible, parties will position themselves in such a way as to maximize the number of votes they receive. Second, particularly if vote maximization is unclear, the CDU will imitate the actions of the SPD in order to neutralize any advantage of the Social Democrats.

We can also use this approach to make more specific predictions about CDU behavior on abortion and work-family policy in the 1970s. The CDU was divided on whether to modernize its position on women's issues more generally. On abortion policy, the CDU responded to the SPD. Many politicians in the CDU wanted to be able to sign whatever law was eventually passed on abortion. To this end, the Bundestag caucus eventually submitted a bill that was extremely close to the SPD's original position. On abortion, the left-party-interaction hypothesis can explain CDU behavior in the 1970s.

On work-family policy, however, the CDU was not moving toward the SPD position. Both parties proposed changes in work-family policy in the 1970s, but the underlying visions were quite different. The SPD proposed (and eventually passed) extending maternity leave to six months and providing a payment of 750DM per month to the mother during this time. The implication of this policy was that mothers would return to work following the maternity leave. The CDU, however, advocated (and eventually implemented, after it returned to power) a much longer leave (up to three years). Furthermore, the money from the CDU policy was made available to *all* mothers, not just to mothers who were working prior to pregnancy. The SPD policy was based on a model of mothers working outside the home. The CDU policy in the 1970s was based on a model of mothers being paid for their work raising children while they remained at home. The CDU policy was an alternative rather than an imitation of the SPD policy. Like the essentialist Christian party hypothesis, this hypothesis also explains CDU behavior on abortion better than CDU behavior on work-family policy.

Kirchheimer's catch-all theory predicts that parties reaching out to new constituencies will do so by presenting abstract statements that appeal to many people. In order to prevent the party's core supporters from stopping this dilution of the party's position, the party will demobilize its membership. By weakening ties to members, the party's leaders can gain the necessary freedom to make the choices needed to be successful at the polls.

Catch-all theory predicts that the CDU would make fairly vague pronouncements on women's issues, whether on abortion or on work-family policy. Simultaneously, the CDU would demobilize its membership in order to gain the flexibility necessary to respond to changes in the electoral marketplace.

The CDU made a wide variety of pronouncements on women's issues throughout the 1970s, some of which were vague. The party's statements on work-family policy, however, were quite clear and detailed. Furthermore, contrary to catch-all theory's other prediction, the CDU actually mobilized membership. The CDU's membership dramatically increased over the course of the 1970s, at least partially because of the party's membership drives (Scarrow 1996: 67). Between 1969 and 1980 the CDU held twenty-three national level membership drives (Schönbohm 1985: 187). These efforts contributed to the astonishing growth in CDU membership. Membership in the CDU increased by 129 percent (Schönbohm 1985: 167). Furthermore, members took a more active role in shaping party policy than had previously been the case. On women's issues, the Women's Union became a politically engaged organization and a leader in developing the party's work-family policy.

The mobilization of membership within the CDU was at least partially the result of the party's corporatist structure. Because internal groups gain influence if their membership numbers are larger, group leaders had an incentive to recruit new members. Because the women in the Women's Union held a different vision from the SPD women, they had to get the CDU to carry out that vision. But their vision also diverged from the CDU's traditional vision, so they needed their party to change. The way to do this was through their representative within the party, the Women's Union. But the Women's Union would be more powerful if it could get more members and more active members. In order to succeed in its intraparty battle, the Women's Union wanted to mobilize membership, not demobilize it. More active internal organizations gained internal party influence.

The rival hypotheses may explain CDU policy making in a particular issue area, but to understand the party's behavior in multiple issue areas, we need to examine internal party dynamics. The theory of the corporatist catch-all party and internal party strategizing better explains the CDU's behavior in all issue areas.

CONCLUSION

Politics in West Germany were shifting dramatically in the late 1960s and early 1970s as many new actors joined the political scene. Scholars have studied the effect of this shift on the left of the political spectrum, but Christian Democrats also felt the magnitude of the change. The rise of the German's women's movement, in particular, contributed to the politicization of the CDU's women's auxiliary group within the party.

As the Women's Union became more active in internal party politics, it found coalition partners in the Youth Union and the Social Committees. By working together in a reform-oriented coalition, these groups were able to dominate the CDU's domestic policy making for most of the 1970s.

This reform coalition was not successful in shaping the party's abortion policy for a variety reasons. First, the groups were internally divided on abortion. Second, the abortion debate was already well under way by the time the three groups began working together in 1973. It was too late in the discussion for the coalition to do much on abortion.

During the 1970s, the dominant coalition of the Women's Union, the Youth Union and the Social Committees was able to control CDU work-family policy. Because the CDU was in the opposition, these groups could not get their policy preferences passed into law. However, they managed to get their chosen policy, child-raising money, anchored in a variety of party statutes and programs, despite the resistance of other party groups and the CDU's sister party, the CSU. These actions laid the foundation for actually passing the policies in the 1980s.

5

The Women's Union in the Dominant
Coalition, 1982–1989

The 1980s provide an excellent illustration of the power an internal organization of the CDU can have when it is in the dominant coalition. During most of this decade, the Women's Union and its allies, the Social Committees, could control much of CDU policy making. During the 1980s, the Women's Union persuaded the CDU to provide not only child-raising money, but also employment guarantees for parents returning to work. The dominant coalition was also able to prevent proposed policy change restricting abortion. The Women's Union furthermore convinced the CDU to adopt measures designed to increase women's participation in the party.

In the early 1980s, the CDU returned to power after having been in the opposition since 1969. The Christian Democrats were able to regain control of parliament when the FDP defected from its coalition with the SPD in 1982. The new governing coalition, consisting of the CDU, the CSU, and the FDP, was ratified by elections in 1983. This change of power was heralded and marketed as a "*Wende*," a turning point. Although the plan was to turn in a conservative direction, policy changes remained incremental, especially compared to the United States and Britain, two other countries also going through conservative turns during this period. Moreover, with regard to women's issues, the CDU not only did not move in a conservative direction; it generally accommodated women's demands.

This chapter begins by describing changes in the dominant coalition from 1979 to 1982. It then discusses the CDU's policy making during the 1980s on work-family policy, abortion policy and participation policy. The last section again reviews the alternative hypotheses and shows how they are less able to explain CDU policy making than the corporatist catch-all model.

CHANGE IN THE DOMINANT COALITION, 1979–1982

The Social Committees, the Women's Union, and the Youth Union had formed a dominant coalition within the CDU for much of the 1970s. These groups began cooperating in 1972, helped Helmut Kohl gain the position of party chair, and dominated the process of modernizing the CDU in terms of program and organization. This reform-oriented dominant coalition was able to control the CDU's actions because its leaders built up the party organization as a counterweight to the party's parliamentary caucus. The parliamentary caucus, under Carstens, was still controlled by national conservatives. However, because the CDU was in the opposition, the parliamentary caucus was not as important as it had been when the party was in government. The CDU used its time in the opposition to develop the extraparliamentary organization. The newly important party organization became much more important in terms of setting the CDU's agenda (Pridham 1977: 260–7; Clemens 1989: 253; Bösch 2002: 108–14).

The Conservative Interlude

From 1979 to 1982 the CDU experienced protracted internal turmoil. The old 1970s dominant coalition – the Social Committees, the Women's Union and the Youth Union – lost control of the direction of the party. Hard-line conservatives, led by Franz Josef Strauss and Alfred Dregger, were able to push Kohl to the side and temporarily seize control of the party. A series of events from the summer of 1978 to the summer of 1979 caused the existing dominant coalition to break down and allowed a new dominant coalition to take control. This new dominant coalition, led by Alfred Dregger (chair of the regional organization in Hesse) and Franz Josef Strauss (chair of the Bavarian CSU), controlled the direction of the CDU until the elections of 1980.[1]

Progressives, such as the 1970s dominant coalition, and conservatives, such as the dominant coalition of 1979–80, disagreed on many issues, but particularly on the better strategy for reentering government. Progressives favored a strategy of opening the Christian Democratic parties to cooperation with the FDP. They argued that this was the only strategy that had any hope of succeeding because the Christian Democrats were unlikely to

[1] This section draws largely on Kleinmann 1993 and Bösch 2002.

gain an absolute majority on their own. The CSU, and conservatives within the CDU, preferred a strategy of forming a majority by appealing to voters on the right and forming a governing majority without the FDP. They argued that the FDP was unlikely to desert the successful Social Democrats. These two internal party groupings disagreed over other issues as well. Progressives wanted to expand social benefits, particularly to families and working women. They were more accepting of the Social Democrats' foreign policy. Conservatives resisted expanding benefits because these policies were too costly. They also favored continuing with the traditional hard-line anti-Communist approach to East Germany.

The conservative nationalist alliance, led by Dregger and Strauss, had attempted to wrest control of the CDU from the dominant coalition following the election of 1976. This attempt failed, but the conservative nationalists tried again in 1978. The existing dominant coalition in the CDU was vulnerable in the summer of 1978. A scandal involving Hans Filbinger, the CDU Minister President of Baden-Württemberg, caused a huge loss of support.[2] Opinion polls showed that Kohl would lose dramatically to the SPD Chancellor, Helmut Schmidt.

Over the course of the year (summer 1978 to summer 1979), CDU conservatives made a series of attempts to oust the more progressive dominant coalition. In January 1979, Kurt Biedenkopf (Kohl's former General Secretary) proposed changing the leadership structure of the Christian Democrats to a trio including Kohl, Strauss (chair of the CSU), and a to-be-elected head of the parliamentary caucus (presumably Biedenkopf himself). Kohl was the head of the parliamentary caucus, and this attempt failed when Kohl refused to abandon that post, but it revealed which leaders of regional organizations could be swayed to work against Kohl. In January 1979, the CSU stated clearly that it did not accept Kohl as the Christian Democrats' Chancellor candidate. In May, CDU and CSU conservatives won the office of Bundespresident for Carstens, giving the conservatives another source of power (Kleinmann 1993: 427–33; Bösch 2002: 117–19).

---

[2] As a military judge during World War II, Filbinger had given the death penalty to soldiers accused of desertion, even in the final days of the war. These actions were condemned because they were viewed as remaining overly loyal to the National Socialists. Furthermore, Filbinger lied about his actions during the war. After each new death penalty case was revealed by the media, Filbinger claimed it was the last one. As subsequent death penalty cases emerged, however, Filbinger and the CDU continued to lose credibility. Filbinger finally resigned in August 1978. Kohl was injured by these events because the CDU overall dropped in opinion polls and Kohl was seen as partially responsible (Bösch 2002: 117).

The final key to the conservative takeover was Strauss's threat to campaign nationwide with the CSU unless he was chosen as the joint CDU/CSU Chancellor candidate. Normally, the CSU campaigns only in Bavaria and the CDU everywhere else. Then the two parties cooperate nationally. While the CSU would have been unlikely to beat the CDU overall in a national race, running CSU candidates would have split the Christian Democratic vote in many places, causing the SPD to win the election and CDU parliamentarians to lose their jobs. The Christian Democratic parties do not have a standard procedure for selecting a joint Chancellor candidate. Strauss was able to move this important decision-making process to the parliamentary caucus, the arena in which the existing dominant coalition was weakest. Once chosen as Chancellor candidate, Strauss and his conservative backers were able to control much of the rest of the activities of the CDU because during an election campaign the campaign officials have control of the party. Although the CDU General Secretary normally runs the campaign, Strauss refused to let Geissler, a leader of the former progressive dominant coalition, have influence over the campaign. Instead, Edmund Stoiber, the CSU General Secretary, ran the campaign (Kleinmann 1993: 434–40; Bösch 2002: 117–19.

Return to the Progressive Dominant Coalition

In the 1980 election the Christian Democrats suffered one of their worst losses in the history of the Federal Republic. This loss changed the balance of power within the Christian Democrats again. The conservative approach of attracting votes from the right and trying to form a majority without the FDP had failed dramatically. As a result, the progressive dominant coalition of the 1970s was able to reclaim control of the CDU. Kohl was elected parliamentary leader at the suggestion of Strauss (Kleinmann 1993: 442).

The dominant coalition of the 1980s had the same members as the dominant coalition of the 1970s, but it was not exactly the same. The most solid part of the 1970s dominant coalition had been the partnership between the Social Committees and the Youth Union. The Women's Union had been a member of the dominant coalition, but because its political agenda was not yet terribly clear, it had done less to shape the dominant coalition's policy agenda.

In the 1980s, the Women's Union replaced the Youth Union as the primary partner of the Social Committees. The Women's Union of the

1980s, furthermore, had a much clearer policy agenda of its own. Occasionally, this newly confident Women's Union had tension with the Social Committees, but for the most part, General Secretary Geissler (a leader of the Social Committees and a critical figure in formulating CDU women's policies) was able to smooth over difficulties. The Youth Union was a less reliable component of the dominant coalition because some conservative tendencies had started to emerge within the Youth Union.

This dominant coalition of the 1980s was stronger in the party organization than in parliament, but it also controlled several key ministries. Overall, it is easier for a dominant coalition to exercise power in the opposition, but control of ministries and the General Secretary position helped the "new" dominant coalition realize much of its policy agenda, even against the resistance of the conservative parliamentarians. The dominant coalition of the 1980s was able to compensate for its weaknesses in the parliamentary caucus by controlling both the party organization and the cabinet.

In the 1980s, the Women's Union exhibited strong cohesion on work-family policy, abortion, and quotas. Having worked over the course of the 1970s to develop their child-raising money package, the Women's Union was ready to defend that package in the 1980s. While there was a range of opinions within the Women's Union on abortion, the organization was united around the ideas of not punishing women for having abortion and not changing the existing law. On issues of participation, there was widespread agreement that the CDU should implement some measures to encourage women's participation, but that the party should not implement a required quota, such as existed in the Greens and the SPD. Because of its cohesion and its presence in the dominant coalition, the Women's Union was remarkably successful at getting the CDU to adopt its policy agenda in the 1980s.

POLICY MAKING ON WOMEN'S ISSUES: WORK-FAMILY POLICY IN THE 1980S

The story of German work-family policy during the 1980s is one of unequivocal and rather astonishing success for the CDU's Women's Union. Against considerable opposition, the Women's Union managed to bring significant change to a party ideologically committed to traditional values, values which in many cases included a strong belief that women had no business meddling in politics. And because the CDU happened to be in power at the time, it is the story of how a national policy came into being.

The moral of the story is twofold: First, the Women's Union's success, as in the 1970s, continued to hinge on the corporatist structure of the CDU and on the Women's Union's own privileged membership in the party's dominant coalition. Second, as we have seen elsewhere, and contrary to competing theoretical models, the dominant coalition managed to broaden the party's appeal primarily by mobilizing the membership of the relevant corporatist groups.

When the CDU returned to government in 1982, the existing work-family policy was based on the Social Democratic conception of work. For Social Democrats, employment is a critical component of citizenship. Therefore, mothers were expected to return to work as soon as possible after giving birth. The maternity leave passed by the SPD-FDP government in 1979 provided for six months off after delivery.[3] Mothers would receive 750DM per month and they were guaranteed to get their jobs back after the six months had elapsed. Because the Social Democratic vision was based on the attempt to make pregnancy and birth compatible with employment, mothers who were not working prior to pregnancy received no benefits and neither did fathers.

The new CDU vision of work-family policy, on the other hand, conceived of raising children as work, and therefore as an alternative to paid employment. This different conceptualization gave rise to different provisions in the law. While the SPD law paid benefits for only six months, the new CDU "child-raising vacation" provided benefits for ten months with provisions to extend the leave to up to three years. The CDU policy paid less money per month (600DM instead of 750DM), but it paid it over a longer period of time.[4] Because the CDU recognized raising children as work, the parent who stayed home with the children also received credit toward the pension plan as if she or he were earning 75 percent of the average national wage. Finally, because this leave was for *raising* children rather than *birthing* children, both fathers and mothers were eligible.

The female activists in the CDU's women's auxiliary organization, the Women's Union, had worked to develop this parental leave policy. This set of benefits reflected their views on how to negotiate the conflict between

---

[3] Mothers are required to take six weeks off before the birth and eight weeks afterwards. None of the parental leave benefits discussed here affects this maternity leave.

[4] After six months cash benefits are income tested. At first many benefited, but with inflation fewer benefited over time.

work and family. The women activists of the Women's Union had beliefs about combining work and family that centered around two main concepts: "*Wahlfreiheit*" and the three-phase-model. "*Wahlfreiheit*" translates as freedom of choice and simply implied that women (as well as men) should be able to combine work and family responsibilities as they liked. This concept was created in response to Social Democratic ideas that all women should work and traditional Christian Democratic ideas that all mothers should stay home. The three-phase-model described a progression for women that started with strong educational training and a career (phase one) that was to be followed by a more flexible period combining child raising and part-time work (phase two), then a return to a full-time job and a career in paid employment (phase three). The CDU's parental leave benefits were designed to maximize "*Wahlfreiheit*" and facilitate the three-phase model (Renate Diemers, personal interview).

The Women's Union was criticized for this plan from two directions. The SPD complained that the CDU's child-raising vacation would turn into a permanent vacation from paid employment for women. The SPD also noted that true "*Wahlfreiheit*" was an impossibility in the absence of the significant availability of child care, which the CDU did not yet support. Still, the Women's Union persevered with their model.

When we first tried to get pension credit for raising children, we got laughed at. They thought we were trying to put women back in the house. We wanted the opposite. We wanted the three-phase model. Good training, then raising the children, then back full time into the job. I still like it. (Renate Diemers, personal interview)

The Women's Union stuck with their policy despite these criticisms.

While the concepts of *Wahlfreiheit* and the three-phase model were criticized by the SPD, they were also originally rejected by the mainstream CDU because many in the party thought mothers should be at home full time without benefits. Opponents of the parental leave policy included the chair of the parliamentary caucus, Alfred Dregger, the party's Finance Minister, Gerhard Stoltenberg, and the party's auxiliary organization for middle class interests (*Mittelstandsvereinigung*) (Bärbel Sothmann, personal interview). The CDU's sister party in Bavaria, the CSU, also opposed the parental leave benefits. Opponents in the party further objected to the employment guarantee, which they felt would be overly burdensome for employers. Many also objected to the high costs of the benefits. West Germany was just recovering from the budget deficits of the late 1970s and these new benefits represented a significant expense. Finally, women's policies were seen as the domain of parties of the left, and many in the CDU felt that these issues were unimportant at best and would alienate conservative voters at worst (Heiner Geissler; Irmgard Karwatzki, personal interviews).

The dominant coalition was able to get the parental leave policy approved by the party despite this resistance. The Women's Union, the Social Committees, and the Youth Union had been working together since the mid-1970s to develop the CDU's parental leave policies and convince the party to adopt them. The proponents of the parental leave benefits were able to force their views through the party and subsequently through the parliament because they controlled the General Secretary's position, the Family Ministry, and the chairs of the Women's Union and the Social Committees.[5] This constellation of offices allowed the leaders of the dominant coalition to mobilize support for the policy in the party's extraparliamentary organization. The dominant coalition created widespread enthusiasm for the new policy, which put pressure on the CDU's more conservative parliamentary delegation.

Because representation of the various internal party groups in the party's decision-making bodies is relatively constant, no group can overrule the others by eliminating their representatives. Instead, one way party leaders can increase their influence over the party as a whole is by activating their membership. Particularly for groups such as the Women's Union, which cannot necessarily hope for large financial contributions from their constituencies, increasing activity and participation of members can increase the power of the group's leader vis-à-vis other CDU leaders. Mobilization of membership was one of the main strategies the dominant coalition used in getting the parental leave policy passed.

The dominant coalition focused its energies on the 1985 party congress to be held in Essen. The 1985 congress was devoted to women's issues. In preparation for the congress, the dominant coalition reached out to membership in the form of commissions and discussion.

We prepared the party congress for a year and a half. We had commissions that wrote out the Essener Leitsätze … The discussion process helped people in the party get used to the idea. (Heiner Geissler, personal interview)

---

[5] The Social Committees initially resisted the parental leave benefits. In fact, the Social Committees held its own Congress in 1981, titled "the Gentle Power of the Family," which emphasized the importance of mothers staying home with their children. Geissler was able to overcome the rift between the Social Committees and the Women's Union by inserting some pro-motherhood language into the women's program passed at the Essen party congress (Heiner Geissler; Irmgard Karwatzki, personal interviews).

In preparation for the 1985 party congress, Wex and Geissler mobilized support both within and outside the party. They organized a series of discussions at lower levels of the party to mobilize support for the parental leave policies and for changing the party's image of women more generally.

The party congress in Essen was the first step in creating support for the new parental leave policy. To focus such a large event on women's issues was quite controversial; this choice was seen as highly atypical for the CDU. In fact, prior to 1985, no other party had held a national party congress on women's issues. Some members of the Presidium resisted the idea of a women's party congress, arguing that women's issues were insufficiently important for a national party congress.

The conservatives, like Dregger and Stoltenberg, didn't want to do the party congress. It was foreign to CDU politics up to that point. They were black [Christian Democratic] and saw women's politics as Green. (Heiner Geissler, personal interview)

Ultimately, however, party congresses are the responsibility of the General Secretary. As an important actor in the dominant coalition, Heiner Geissler, the CDU's General Secretary, was able to use the party congress to support the goals of the dominant coalition.

Because the main topic of the party congress was women's issues, many local CDU branches felt obligated to send female delegates. These female delegates were more likely to agree with the suggestions of their auxiliary organization, the Women's Union, or at least to have been previously exposed to the relevant issues through the earlier discussions. Geissler and the leadership of the Women's Union seem to have discouraged delegates that they knew disagreed with their program (Irmgard Karwatzki, personal interview).

The party congress in Essen was also a chance for the CDU to reach out beyond existing members. The party invited 500 prominent women, many from outside the party, to attend the congress in Essen and discuss the party's "New Partnership" program. Rita Süssmuth, chair of the Women's Union from 1986 to 2001, became significantly more involved with the CDU when she was tapped to help organize the party congress (Rita Süssmuth, personal interview).[6] Several other future CDU leaders had their first contact with the party through the Essen party congress (Maria Böhmer; Kristel Bendig, personal interviews).

---

[6] Helga Wex died in 1986. She was replaced by Rita Süssmuth.

The party congress at Essen was great. There was lots of open, engaged discussion. No one could believe this was the CDU. It showed people that the CDU wasn't as repressed as they thought. (Stephan Walter, personal interview)

The dominant coalition used the party congress to mobilize support for its policy preferences on several issues. The main event of the congress was to pass a program paper called "A New Partnership between Man and Woman" (CDU National Party Congress 1985). This program was the dominant coalition's wide-ranging call to action on women's issues. It included statements calling for equality for women at work, in the family, and in politics. It also supported affirmative action programs in industry and academia, institutionalized funding for women's shelters, and recognized the contributions of the women's movement. The parental leave provisions were one of the main policy centerpieces of this program.

As hoped for, the party congress did approve "A New Partnership between Man and Woman" including the sections on the new parental leave policy. Geissler hoped that once the parental leave policies were approved by the party congress, he could use the official statement of the party organization to pressure the CDU's representatives in the Bundestag.

Getting the child-raising money and the pension credit was difficult because they cost money. I saw we were going to have trouble with the [CDU-led] government ... Because I was the General Secretary, I spoke in the Presidium in favor of the women's party congress. There was resistance, but Kohl supported the idea. (Heiner Geissler, personal interview)

Despite the opposition of the CDU's parliamentary leader, Alfred Dregger, the party congress had generated sufficient support for the parental leave policy to be approved by the Bundestag. Geissler and Wex had used the publicity surrounding the party congress to draw attention to the parental leave policies. If the CDU parliamentary caucus had refused to support these policies, the party would have risked losing support with the electorate because it would have been seen as divided and as not keeping its promises. The Bundestag approved the parental leave package early in 1986.

The CDU's actions on work-family policy cannot be characterized as party leadership demobilizing party membership. Instead, some party leaders *mobilized* portions of the membership that agreed with the leaders' political agenda. Getting "their" members more involved in the internal workings of the party increased the power of certain leaders to push their agenda through the party against the resistance of other leaders. Membership mobilization was designed to increase the influence of the dominant coalition, which included the Women's Union. Leaders of internal groups can use mobilized members as an instrument to further their agenda against the wishes of other leaders.

The CDU approved the parental leave policies of the 1980s because of the actions of the dominant coalition. The Women's Union worked with the Social Committees and the Youth Union to generate grassroots level interest in these policies, both within the CDU and in society more generally. The dominant coalition was able to use its power in the party organization and the cabinet to overpower a somewhat reluctant CDU parliamentary caucus.

POLICY MAKING ON WOMEN'S ISSUES: ABORTION POLICY IN THE 1980S

In contrast to the 1970s, by the 1980s the dominant coalition was unified on abortion. This unity – combined with the dominant coalition's control of important party offices – allowed the dominant coalition to fend off a serious internal party challenge. In the 1970s, the governing SPD-FDP coalition had passed abortion reform allowing abortion under certain conditions (health, medical, criminal, social emergency – see Chapter 4). Some actors within the CDU hoped to be able to restrict abortion once the Christian Democrats returned to power. The Women's Union, along with other reform-oriented groups in the CDU, opposed such change. Because the reformers made up the dominant coalition, they were able to fend off the challenge mounted by conservatives within the party.[7]

The CDU had vigorously opposed the abortion legislation passed in 1976 by the SPD-FDP governing coalition. This law allowed abortion in four situations: 1) the medical indication (if pregnancy and/or delivery would endanger the life and health of the mother), 2) the health indication (if the fetus was not developing normally), 3) the criminal indication (if the pregnancy was the result of rape), and 4) the social emergency indication (if the pregnant woman was psychologically and/or financially unable to cope with having a child). The CDU had been especially against the social emergency indication and the health indication. Under the 1976 law, a single doctor determined whether any of these indications were present.

---

[7] Much of the information in this section is drawn from Däubler-Gmelin and Faerber-Husemann (1987). The abortion discussions of the 1980s also demonstrate the incentives for organizing an internal party group. Pro-life activists within the CDU formed two groups in 1986, *Vereinigung Lebensrecht* and *Christdemokraten für das Leben* (Däubler-Gmelin and Faerber-Husemann 1987: 186). By the late 1980s these groups were important actors in the abortion discussion.

This doctor was also allowed to perform the abortion. Abortions for which any of these indications was present were covered by medical insurance (see Chapter 4; Gante 1991; Klein-Schonnefeld 1994).

There was pressure to change the abortion law because the CDU had opposed the law when it was passed in 1976. Many in the dominant coalition, however, had changed their views since then. The Women's Union and the Social Committees both favored maintaining the status quo. All major Christian Democratic women's organizations, including the Women's Unions of the CDU and the CSU and the Group of Women (the female Christian Democratic representatives in the Bundestag), opposed changing the law or increasing the difficulty of getting an abortion (*Stuttgarter Nachrichten* Feb 7, 1984; *Stuttgarter Zeitung* Feb 7, 1984; *Frankfurter Rundschau* Feb 20, 1984; BT-Plenarprotokoll 10/69 page 4968, May 1984). This position represented a change from the 1970s, when the Christian Democratic women's groups had been quite conservative. Even in Rhineland-Palatinate, a quite conservative *Land*, six out of the seven Christian Democratic women in the *Landtag* opposed their *Land*-level party's proposal to restrict abortion (*Süddeutsche Zeitung*, June 27, 1985). Between the mid-1970s and the mid-1980s, many female Christian Democrats had come to accept the social liberal reforms that they had once opposed (Däubler-Gmelin and Faerber-Husemann 1987: 17).

Important leaders of the Social Committees also advocated keeping the status quo, even though the Social Committees were predominantly Catholic. Both Heiner Geissler, the CDU's General Secretary, and Norbert Blüm, leader of the Social Committees, chair of the CDU in North Rhine-Westphalia, and Labor Minister, favored programs such as the conservatively oriented Mother and Child Foundation that provided money to pregnant women who decided not to have abortions rather than changing the law (*General Anzeiger* April 28, 1983). However, according to Jochen Schulz, a staff member at the national office of the Social Committees, the organization did not favor increasing restrictions.

Paragraph 218 is a hard topic. You can't really make laws to change people's minds. That was hard to clarify to our membership, which is more Catholic and wanted to protect life. We worked with Geissler on the compromise idea that we first had to change the social conditions to make it easier for people to keep their children. (Jochen Schulz, personal interview)

The Social Committees and other Christian Democrats who supported the existing law preferred to reduce the number of abortions by offering increased benefits to parents rather than through punishment.

Pressure to restrict abortion came from Christian Democratic regional leaders in federal states where the Christian Democrats governed alone. Unlike regional leaders from states where the CDU governed in coalition with the pro-choice FDP, these leaders could pursue pro-life change without risking alienating the FDP. Christian Democrats in southern, predominantly Catholic *Länder* (such as Baden-Württemberg, Rhineland-Palatinate, and Bavaria) were especially likely to push for pro-life reforms.

Abortion was a difficult topic for the CDU because not only was the party internally divided, it was also torn between its coalition partners. The CSU, the party's sister party in Bavaria, was strongly pro-life. On the other hand, the Christian Democrats were governing in coalition with the FDP, which was pro-choice. The coalition could not pass reform without the FDP's support.

Because the governing coalition was so internally divided and because abortion reform had been so difficult to pass in the 1970s, pro-life groups agreed that changing the law itself would probably be impossible (Juristen-Vereinigung Lebensrecht e. V., Nr. 1 1985: 5). Instead, these groups focused on two methods of limiting abortion access that did not require a full-blown legal change: curtailing or eliminating insurance funding for abortions and increasing the difficulty of the required counseling process.

The dominant coalition managed to fend off two attempts to pass more restrictive abortion policy in the 1980s. The first challenge to existing abortion policy occurred in 1984/85, when conservative Christian Democratic parliamentarians proposed legislation to increase the difficulty in obtaining an abortion by eliminating some of the medical insurance funding. In the Bundestag, a group of 80 Christian Democratic parliamentarians supported a bill proposed by the Parliamentary Speaker on Family Issues, Hermann Kroll-Schlüter. The *Land* Rhineland-Palatinate submitted a similar proposal to the Bundesrat. Even though these proposals received significant media attention, they had little chance of actually passing.[8] Despite the involvement of Kroll-Schlüter, party leaders easily ignored this challenge by backbenchers in parliament.

---

[8] See Däubler-Gmelin and Faerber-Husemann (1987) for thorough coverage of the attempt to restrict insurance financing for abortions. Rather than restricting access to abortion through a legal change, the dominant coalition favored policy changes that would encourage women to decide against abortion. The most prominent policy change was the creation of the Mother and Child Foundation, which was created to give money and support to women considering an abortion. Whether this approach would actually work was somewhat doubtful because many women were aborting for nonfinancial reasons. For more on the Mother and Child Foundation, see Däubler-Gmelin and Faerber-Husemann (1987: 115–18).

The second more serious attempt to restrict abortion was in response to the Green Party's campaign promise to legalize abortion. Rather than putting pressure on the CDU to move to the center on abortion reform, pressure from the left provoked a reaction from the more conservative sections of the CDU, which attempted to restrict abortion access.

The dominant coalition preferred not to restrict abortion both because many in the dominant coalition thought punishment would not help reduce the number of abortions and because they thought this position would lose votes for the CDU. Sticking to the relatively more progressive position, however, meant resisting increasing pressure from other quarters of the party. For example, in 1986 a local party organization (*Kreisverband Gütersloh*) brought a proposal to the national party congress to restrict abortion (CDU National Party Congress 1986). Heiner Geissler feared that such a discussion would lead the CDU to take on a more conservative position on abortion. He was able to postpone the discussion until after the elections but only by promising to devote an entire upcoming party congress to the topic (*Süddeutsche Zeitung*, October 8, 1986).

The presence of the two new pro-life groups, Christian Democrats for Life (*Christdemokraten für das Leben* or CdL) and the Right to Life Association (*Vereinigung Lebensrecht*) increased the internal pressure within the CDU to act on abortion reform. The CDU responded to this pressure after the 1987 election by asking the FPD to approve a section on the coalition agreement on restricting access to abortion by making the counseling process more difficult. The FDP agreed to these restrictions in exchange for concessions on some internal security issues (*Der Spiegel*, March 9, 1987). Because of increased internal pressure, the CDU was more interested in abortion reform in 1987 than it had been in 1983. In 1983 the CDU had not asked the pro-choice FDP to act on abortion in the coalition agreement. In 1987 after pro-life groups became active within the party, the CDU was willing to commit to changing policy – and to agree to other policy concessions with its coalition partner to do so.

The new written coalition agreement adopted by the CDU, the CSU, and the FDP contained the following measures. Counseling centers would only receive government certification and funding under the following circumstances: 1) when the counseling was directed toward preserving the life of the fetus; 2) when the counseling centers distributed money from the Mother and Child Foundation; 3) when the physicians involved in counseling and determining the presence of an allowed indication had undergone special training in protecting unborn life; 4) when doctors register the abortions (*Frankfurter Rundschau*, March 5, 1987). By changing the counseling process, these measures would have made it more difficult to get an abortion.

The dominant coalition used a variety of tactics to resist abortion reform. Heiner Geissler once again used his position as General Secretary of the party to influence the agenda of party congresses. Geissler had scheduled a national party congress on abortion for the fall of 1987 after the election had taken place. When the CDU was plagued by an unrelated scandal, however, Geissler again postponed the abortion congress until June 1988. Geissler changed the party congress agenda to protect Kohl and the reformist dominant coalition from the wrath of the pro-life delegates at a time when they might have been vulnerable for other reasons. He also added several other topics to the agenda in order to water down the impact of any congress resolutions (*Der Spiegel*, April 25, 1988).

Leaders of the dominant coalition also held Ministries that were critical in passing abortion legislation. These Ministers worked to block abortion reform. Rita Süssmuth, Minister of Families, Women, and Health and also chair of the Women's Union, was charged with drafting the legislative proposal on abortion reform. The guidelines in the coalition agreement were not yet a proposal for legislation, which must be more specific. Süssmuth delayed drafting the legislation for almost a year until the pressure to act on abortion lessened.

Another leader in the dominant coalition, Norbert Blüm, was Minister of Labor. Pro-life groups within the CDU, such as Christian Democrats for Life, the regional organization in Baden-Württemberg, and the CSU, continued to pressure the party to stop health insurance funding for abortion. Changes in insurance funding, however, had to be overseen by the Labor Ministry. Norbert Blüm, Labor Minister and chair of the Social Committees, refused to consider changing the insurance rules (*Der Spiegel*, December 14, 1987). Without his support, pro-life groups could not change the insurance funding. Because the dominant coalition controlled two Ministries important in abortion policies, it was able to stymie reform efforts.

Finally in June 1988, the dominant coalition stopped abortion reform entirely. Geissler had added several other topics to the agenda of the June 1988 party congress (which was supposed to be devoted to abortion) in order to water down the impact of any congressional resolutions. In early June, Süssmuth's counseling proposal was finally brought before the cabinet. Kohl planned to have the support of the cabinet for a relatively liberal proposal secured, in order to present the party congress with a *fait accompli (Der Spiegel*, June 13, 1988). Instead, the CSU refused to support the counseling law, and it was tabled indefinitely. Although conservative CDU members were angry at the party congress, it was too late to influence the reform process. By controlling the 1980s abortion debates, the dominant coalition was thus able to prevent change on abortion policy, even though pro-life reforms had been written into the governing coalition agreement.

The 1980s abortion debates represented a victory for the reform-oriented dominant coalition within the CDU. It was a victory with a cost, however, because new actors emerged out of these debates. The lawyers' group, *Vereinigung Lebensrecht*, and most critically the group Christian Democrats for Life did not manage to get their policy preferences implemented by the CDU, but they were recognized as important actors on the abortion issue. This recognition did not extend to granting these groups representation in the party's general policy-making bodies, in the manner of the Women's Union. However, it ensured them an important role in future CDU commissions on abortion. The CdL would prove to be an especially important actor in CDU policy making on abortion in the 1990s.

POLICY MAKING ON WOMEN'S ISSUES: PARTICIPATION POLICY IN THE 1980s

The third case study of policy making in the 1980s, participation policy, again illustrates the strength of the dominant coalition. The Women's Union and the Social Committees were able to make significant changes to the internal party statutes to increase women's participation in the party. In this case, the dominant coalition chose not to mobilize membership because its own members were divided on the possibility of a quota.

Quotas or other mechanisms to influence women's participation in the CDU differ from the other two issue areas discussed in this book because they are an internal CDU issue only. This difference has several implications. First, the process for adopting a quota is different. Both abortion policy and family policy ultimately go through the Bundestag. Quotas do not. A quota requires a change in the party statutes. The CDU can change its party statutes through a vote by the party congress.[9] The second

---

[9] A change in the party statutes requires an absolute majority of those eligible to vote. Potential quotas that are anchored in the party statutes would need to be approved by the national party congress by an absolute majority of the eligible delegates.

implication is that because quotas are an internal CDU matter, the other parties have no say on them. Even the CDU's sister party, the CSU, has no direct control over the CDU's policies on quotas.

The primary impetus for increasing female participation was electoral pressure. The CDU did not recover its lost "Women's Bonus" in the 1983 election even though female membership had increased dramatically in the 1970s. Leadership was still overwhelmingly male, and some party leaders thought presenting a more female leadership team would help win women's votes (Maria Böhmer, personal interview).

The CDU also came under pressure to increase female participation because both parties on the left – the Greens and the SPD – adopted quotas during the 1980s. In 1985, the Greens implemented a 50 percent quota, which is still in place. At least half of the candidates from the Green Party have to be female. The Greens have a "zipper" system of strict female-male alternation on party lists. Furthermore, the number one candidate must always be a woman (Green Party Statutes, Women's Statutes, Part I).

In 1988 the SPD also implemented a quota stating that each gender should hold at least 40 percent of the seats (SPD Statutes, paragraph 11). The SPD quota has been phased in gradually. Although the SPD has regularly missed its stated goal, the party has also steadily increased female representation. The increased number of women representatives from the left-wing parties showed that the quotas were working and put pressure on the CDU to do some something comparable (Kolinsky 1991; Matland and Studlar 1996; McKay 2004; Davidson-Schmich 2006).[10]

When both parties of the left, the Greens and the SPD, implemented women's quotas in the 1980s and significantly increased the number of women in their leadership, the CDU's lack of female leaders became more embarrassing. As one leader in the Women's Union put it:

What really helped us [on participation] was the Greens getting into the Bundestag with lots of women. The SPD also had a quota early and they had more women. (Renate Diemers, personal interview)

With both parties on the left increasing their number of female leaders and female voters, many Christian Democrats became interested in some mechanism to increase female participation in their party.

Two of the auxiliary organizations in the dominant coalition, the Women's Union and the Social Committees, wanted the CDU to implement

---

[10] For more on the different processes by which the SPD and the CDU approached quotas, see Leslie and Wiliarty (2009).

policies to increase women's participation. The new leader of the Women's Union, Rita Süssmuth, was particularly interested in encouraging women's participation in the CDU and believed that quotas would facilitate this goal. Furthermore, Süssmuth wanted to increase the power of the Women's Union within the party. The quota was one possible avenue for doing so.

The second auxiliary organization in the dominant coalition, the Social Committees, also favored implementing some kind of mechanism to increase women's participation. The Social Committees and the Women's Union had been working together since the mid-1970s.

The Social Committees participated in the CDU's quota debate [in the 1980s]. We had our people in the CDU National Executive Committee work on it and other decision-making bodies too. There were a few people in the Social Committees opposed to the quota, but not many. It was clear we were for it. (Jochen Schulz, personal interview)

Because the two organizations had such a reliable partnership, an increase in influence for the Women's Union was seen as likely to benefit the Social Committees as well. Furthermore, the Social Committees are strongly represented on the CDU's decision-making bodies through the existing system of internal corporatism, and this representation was not in jeopardy.

While the Women's Union and the Social Committees consistently backed a wide range of policies to increase women's participation, the Youth Union was only willing to support participation mechanisms that would also increase the participation of young people. The Youth Union had worked with the Women's Union and the Social Committees in the dominant coalition of the 1970s, but it was a less important member of the dominant coalition in the 1980s. Furthermore, the CDU sometimes viewed youths and women as rivals for the same positions. Because both women and youths were regarded as inexperienced, the CDU sometimes gave a position on an important committee to either a woman or a young person, but not both. Therefore, if the mechanism in question clearly helped only women, the Youth Union opposed it. However, some participation mechanisms, such as allowing internal party primaries, were seen as potentially benefiting both young people and women because the mechanisms circumvented the seniority system. The Youth Union supported proposals that contained mechanisms like this.

Although many in the CDU opposed implementing mechanisms to increase female participation, there was no focal organization for this resistance. No regional organization or auxiliary organization was committed to opposing these measures *as an organization*. While individual CDU activists opposed measures to increase women's participation, they were not concentrated in a particular CDU organization.

The dominant coalition made three attempts in the 1980s to get the CDU to adopt measures to increase women's participation. The first attempt – an effort to involve the Youth Union in participation policy making – failed because the CDU was unwilling to adopt internal primaries. The next two attempts, however, saw the party adopt increasingly rigorous measures to increase women's involvement and influence in the party.

The dominant coalition was well positioned to succeed on participation policy. Because participation policy is a CDU level policy, the critical arena for passing participation policy is the party congress. The Bundestag is not involved. This arrangement was advantageous for the dominant coalition of the 1980s because this alliance was stronger in the party organization than in the Bundestag.

The dominant coalition's power extended to the National Executive Committee and the position of General Secretary. The CDU's National Executive Committee is a critical filtering mechanism for party congresses. The National Executive Committee (NEC) sorts through the various proposals made prior to the party congress. The NEC generally makes a recommendation either to approve or reject each proposal. Furthermore, the NEC can combine several proposals on similar topics and write its own proposal. This technique allows the NEC to control which compromises are made. Because the dominant coalition had a lot of influence in the NEC, it was likely to get its policies passed at the party congress. Furthermore, Geissler, a key member of the dominant coalition, was also the party's General Secretary, and was responsible for organizing and running the party congress.

Despite this strength in the party organization, the dominant coalition failed in its first attempt at addressing participation policy because it reached too far. Its proposal at the party congress in Essen would not just have increased women's participation; it would have dramatically rearranged the distribution of power within the party. Party congress delegates approved nearly the entire proposal (see the previous discussion of work-family policy) except for a section on participation, line 35. Line 35 read as follows:

(1) We need more than token women in politics. The national, regional, and municipal governments need to try harder to get

women in leadership positions. Both men and women are responsible for women's participation.

(2) The party executive must work out suggestions for increasing
women's participation.

(3) The General Secretary must report regularly on women's participation and all party sub-organizations must participate in creating
this report.

(4) The process for internal party nominations shall be changed as was
suggested in 1975: the party members will vote prior to the decision
on a candidate for a constituency. Members must be able to vote by
mail. (CDU National Party Congress 1985)

While the first three sections of this proposal deal with women's participation, the fourth section does not. Section 4 of line 35 would have
changed the procedure used to select candidates for the CDU's party lists
by instituting internal party primaries. This provision was apparently
added as a way of gaining the support of the Youth Union, which favored
internal primaries. It is not clear that internal party primaries would have
helped increase female participation in the CDU.

The majority of the CDU party congress was not willing to approve
internal primaries and as a result, the entire paragraph on women's
participation was defeated (CDU National Party Congress 1985). The
regional organizations control most of the selection procedure for the
candidate lists. Changing to a system of internal party primaries would
have meant a significant loss of power for the party's regional organizations. Pleas from the delegates to separate the internal primaries section
from the other provisions were denied by the party congress leadership
(CDU National Party Congress 1985). This is a case of the dominant
coalition reaching the limits of what it could accomplish. Even in the
context of a national party congress in which the dominant coalition
wielded its maximum amount of power, it could not force through such
a major re-alignment of internal party power.

Although the dominant coalition was not able to pass internal party
primaries, it was strong enough to keep the discussion of how to increase
women's participation open. The regional organization Westfalen-Lippe
proposed an amendment to the new statement on women's policies that
mandated future consideration of improved measures to advance political
equality. Westfalen-Lippe had very active and cooperative organizations
of the Women's Union and the Social Committees (Renate Diemers,
personal interview). The Women's Union had well-placed activists both

in the party congress amendment commission (Renate Hellwig) and running the debate (Leni Fischer). They helped pass the Westfalen-Lippe proposal.

The dominant coalition's second attempt at participation policy focused exclusively on women and was successful. The chair of the Women's Union, Rita Süssmuth, had made participation policy one of her top priorities. Under Süssmuth's guidance, the Women's Union wrote a new proposal for increasing women's participation for the 1986 party congress in Mainz. A slightly modified version of the Women's Union proposal was presented to the party congress by the NEC.[11] Because the dominant coalition controlled both the National Executive Committee and, through Geissler, the workings of the party congress, the participation policy was approved easily by the party congress. The revised proposal received near unanimous support (CDU National Party Congress 1986).

The CDU's participation policy of 1986 had three critical components. First, it set the goal of having the percentage of women in offices and positions equal the percentage of female CDU members. Second, it mandated an annual report on women's participation at the national level and recommended a report at other levels of the party. Third, it stated that when selecting candidates "women should be placed so that they have a chance of winning" (CDU National Party Congress 1986). The National Executive Committees of the CDU and the Women's Union were to work together to formulate a concrete plan to reach these goals.

The dominant coalition continued to pass increasingly stringent participation policy at the party congress in Wiesbaden in 1988. This policy went further than the Mainz proposal on all three critical components. The Wiesbaden policy recommended that as a first step toward achieving the goal of having the percentage of female office holders equal the percentage of female members, the CDU ensure that the percentage of women nominated for offices be at least the percentage of women in membership. The Wiesbaden policy required a report on women's participation at *all* levels of the party, not just the national level. Finally, the Wiesbaden policy added the requirement that all committees of the CDU consult with the

---

[11] The Women's Union's proposal was rewritten by the National Executive Committee to be both clearer and somewhat weaker. For example, although a primary goal of the participation policy was to set a target percentage for women in CDU leadership positions, the Women's Union's proposal did not specify the percentage. The version presented by the Women's Union could be interpreted as setting the goal at the percentage of women in the population. The version presented by the NEC set the goal as the percentage of women party members.

Women's Union during the process of candidate selection. Overall the Wiesbaden policy on women's participation was not as strong as policies adopted by parties of the left, but it was significantly stronger than the policy adopted in 1986 in Mainz. Furthermore, it contained nearly all of the suggestions of the Women's Union (CDU National Party Congress 1988).

The Wiesbaden policy was passed despite increasing objections within the CDU and within the Women's Union itself. The stipulation that female office holders equal female membership was a step toward a quota, which many in the party (and the Women's Union) opposed. The dissent within the Women's Union was especially problematic. Irmgard Karwatzki, chair of the largest regional level Women's Union (North Rhine-Westphalia), opposed a strict women's quota:

In Wiesbaden, we had the first disagreement about participation. Süssmuth already wanted a quota. I was against the quota. There hadn't been any public fights yet. If I had gone public, I would have had everyone on my side. (Irmgard Karwatzki, personal interview)

As Karwatzki noted, a detailed, open discussion of women's participation policy would likely have generated significant disagreement within the party congress. The dominant coalition therefore changed tactics. Instead of making a standard party congress proposal, the dominant coalition presented its participation policy as an "initiative proposal."

Initiative proposals differ from a standard party congress proposal in that initiative proposals are not generally distributed prior to the party congress. Initiative proposals can be brought before the party congress if 30 delegates have signed on in support of them (CDU Statutes). While in theory, initiative proposals exist so that delegates can make a suggestion on the spot, in practice, party leadership sometimes uses initiative proposals to circumvent discussion.

We can see from this example that the dominant coalition does not always mobilize its supporters in order to pass policy. If its supporters are divided, as in this case, it makes more sense not to activate membership. Understanding this dynamic, the dominant coalition successfully passed participation policy using an initiative proposal at the party congress in 1988. By using its representatives in the party organization, the dominant coalition was able to control the debate. For example, Dr. Helmut Linssen led the discussion of the participation policy. Linssen favored instituting this policy and he could arrange the speakers' list so that the most powerful and convincing proponents of the policy (Helmut Kohl and Norbert Blüm) spoke at the end of the debate. Despite a small number of votes against it, the policy passed easily.

The analysis of women's participation policy in 1980s West Germany thus allows one to draw several conclusions: First, as we have seen before, a strong alliance can pass significant reforms even against a resisting party. The Women's Union and the Social Committees worked together on this issue. While the benefits of participation policy to the Women's Union are clear, the Social Committees consistently backed women's participation policy, even though these policies would not directly benefit the Social Committees. The Social Committees continuously supported participation policy because they had been working with the Women's Union for so long that increasing women's power in the party was regarded as also helping the Social Committees. This example illustrates the advantages of a dominant coalition that exists over time over a cobbled coalition that does not.

Second, working through some kind of organized group is critical to realizing a policy agenda in the CDU. While it was clear that resistance to women's participation policy existed in the CDU, those opposed to the policy had no organizational home. Regional organizations and auxiliary organizations either favored women's participation policy or were divided on the issue. Thus, those opposed to the policies were unable to mount a serious challenge.

Third, the organization of a corporatist catch-all party does not mean that groups always mobilize their membership in order to pass policy. In the case of women's participation policy, the Women's Union could get its agenda approved without mobilizing its membership. Mobilization is only necessary when the policy in question is in danger of not passing.

In fact, as will be seen in the next chapter, mobilizing the membership of the Women's Union to support participation policy was a complicated undertaking because many of the members of this organization opposed the policy. This idea points to another implication of this analysis: Groups within the CDU will be more effective when they are clearly united behind a particular policy.

Finally, this analysis shows the limits of a dominant coalition. While the dominant coalition of the 1980s was able to accomplish a great deal, it was defeated on the issue of internal party primaries. In this case, the dominant coalition was trying to lessen the power of the regional organizations through a vote by the party congress. Not surprisingly, the *Länder* refused to go along with a policy that would limit their influence.

ALTERNATIVE HYPOTHESES

None of the rival hypotheses under consideration can explain the CDU's 1980s women's policies as instructively as the corporatist catch-all model. The essentialist ideology hypothesis fares particularly poorly during this decade. Whereas this hypothesis seems to hold to some extent during the 1970s (categorical resistance to abortion, policies that encourage women to stay out of the workforce), in the 1980s, (Catholic) Christian ideology has ever-diminishing influence on the CDU's policy making with regard to women's issues. As we have seen, the 1980s CDU passes a work-family policy that helps mothers combine family responsibilities with paid employment outside the home. The party also supports policies to encourage more women to participate in politics. Even on abortion policy, the CDU makes peace with a liberalized set of rules enacted by their opponents, despite having pledged to repeal this law during the 1987 election campaign.

The spatial voting theory hypothesis, being in many respects an opposite of the essentialist hypothesis, fares accordingly better. This model expects the CDU to behave in whatever way will produce the best result in the electoral marketplace. If it is unclear what policy will win the most votes, then this hypothesis expects the CDU to imitate the SPD in order to neutralize that party's growing advantage with female voters. On some level, one might suggest that each of the CDU's policies during the 1980s moves closer to its SPD counterpart, but this simple observation glosses over important differences between the policy results that can only be appreciated when one considers the process that brought them about. Spatial voting theory's strongest case would be the abortion policy, where the CDU forsakes its own previous agenda to adopt that of its opponent. In a similar way, the CDU's participation policies can be understood as a watered down version of the SPD's quotas. On work family policy, however, we see something different. The CDU's policy here is more than a compromise between Catholic/Christian ideology and the contingencies of the electoral marketplace, even though it involves elements of both. The CDU's 1980s work-family policy is original, and it is original because it includes new perspectives – the perspectives of Christian Democratic women. It is not the case that the CDU is grudgingly acquiescing; it is energetically carving out a new political space. This is a behavior that the spatial voting theory does not account for.

The same policy area, work-family policy, also poses the greatest difficulty for the classical catch-all model. When leaders (intent on winning elections) want to take a catch-all party in a new direction, they will supposedly have to demobilize party members, who may be more committed to ideology than to winning. In the 1980s we do see the CDU leadership outflanking membership with respect to participation policies. The leaders want to appeal to women voters, and they know that the membership at large will not support them, so they resort to a parliamentary tactic that leaves the membership out of the mix. The story of work-family policy, by contrast, is one where membership is selectively mobilized precisely as a way to propel the CDU in a new direction.

From the perspective of any of the rival hypotheses, the CDU's 1980s work-family policy is a conundrum: It runs counter to the party's traditional ideology, it involves more than merely minimizing the differences between the party and its successful rival, and it happens with the enthusiastic participation of large segments of the party membership. To understand what is going on we need to look inside the party in order to appreciate how its corporatist organization creates opportunities for change from below as well as above.

CONCLUSION

On one level, when we look at the case studies from the 1980s we might want to mark each of them as a success for the Women's Union. If we stop there, however, we miss revealing and intriguing distinctions. On abortion policy, success means protecting a threatened status quo. On participation policy, success means making moderate gains against the inclinations of the party membership. On work-family policy, success means energizing the party to take the country in a new direction. To some extent, the difference in these outcomes is related to the degree to which the party's corporatist structure comes to the fore in each case. Contrasting these successes therefore allows us to formulate hypotheses about the conditions under which a corporatist catch-all party can promote a previously marginalized group to a leading role.

What the cases have in common is that the Women's Union was in the party's dominant coalition, and that the party itself was in the government. What sets the cases apart, primarily, is the degree to which the Women's Union itself has a clear and unified agenda. The clearest success is the work-family policy, and that is also the area in which membership was most active. Opinions within the Women's Union on abortion policy are less unified, except that there is a consensus that there should be no punishment for women who chose an abortion. There is common ground, but with respect to policy, it is formulated as a shared resistance to change rather than as the political will to introduce specific new policy. On participation policy, there is unity within the dominant coalition, but growing division within the Women's Union itself. The combined efforts of the Social Committees and the Women's Union are sufficient to pass increasingly rigorous participation policy, but in this policy area, leadership does not act to mobilize members because doing so would be potentially counterproductive. As we will see in the next chapter, in order to get more progress on participation policy, the leaders of the Women's Union were forced to engage in an extensive dialogue with their members in order to get membership on board. By that time, however, the partnership with the Social Committees had collapsed and the Women's Union was acting from a much more difficult position, outside the dominant coalition.

6

Looking Eastward

The Women's Union and Cobbled Coalitions, 1989–1998

In the 1990s the power of the Women's Union waned because the organization was no longer part of the dominant coalition. From its weaker internal position, the Women's Union was able to make some gains, but the reforms were limited compared with those of the 1980s, even though women's issues were arguably more a part of mainstream German society than they had been in the 1980s.

Once the Women's Union was no longer in the dominant coalition, it was forced to work through "cobbled coalitions" to get its preferred reforms adopted by the CDU. A cobbled coalition is an ad hoc alliance formed only for a short period of time around a single issue or policy. Cobbled coalitions can achieve one-time successes, but they cannot mount a long-lasting campaign. The reforms passed by a cobbled coalition are also likely to be more limited than those enacted by a dominant coalition. Cobbled coalitions are possible in a corporatist catch-all party partly because minority elites in such parties are not completely excluded from the decision-making process.

The 1990s Women's Union did have the advantage of being able to work with a new, often sympathetic, group – easterners from the former German Democratic Republic. Working with this new alliance partner, the Women's Union successfully ensured CDU backing for a policy mandating child care spots for all children aged three to six (Kindergarten). On the other hand, the party balked at providing funding for those Kindergarten spots. The eastern CDU and sections of the Women's Union also cooperated with the opposition parties and the FDP to pass legislation liberalizing access to abortion. The Women's Union was unable to gain thorough backing of the eastern CDU on participation policy, however. On this issue, the Women's Union was only able to convince the CDU to pass policy that was largely symbolic.

This chapter consists of five sections. The first section describes the change in the dominant coalition at the end of the 1980s and briefly outlines the actors and goals of the new dominant coalition. The next three sections examine CDU policy making on work-family policy, abortion policy, and participation policy respectively. Finally, the last section investigates the ability of the alternative hypotheses to explain CDU behavior on women's issues in the 1990s.

THE DOMINANT COALITION CHANGES

A Failed Internal Coup and German Unification

The position of the Women's Union was refashioned by two events in 1989 – the fall of the Berlin wall and a more obscure development within the CDU. In the summer of 1989, just a few short months before the events that would transform Helmut Kohl from a plodding politician to the father of German unity, members of the CDU's dominant coalition sought to oust Kohl from the party leadership. This attempt failed partly because the leaders of the dominant coalition were not able to agree about who would replace Kohl and partly because they underestimated the level of support that Kohl enjoyed within the CDU. Following the failed coup, Kohl removed many leaders of the former dominant coalition from their party positions, and a new dominant coalition emerged.

In the spring of 1989, Kohl appeared particularly vulnerable. The government's reforms in such areas as tax policy and health insurance had proved extremely unpopular. The CDU had lost a series of elections at the *Land* level, and the far-right Republican Party was growing in popularity. In April, *Der Spiegel* published a poll showing that only 36 percent of those asked would vote for the CDU/CSU if elections were held the following Sunday, one of the lowest CDU scores ever (*Der Spiegel*, April 24, 1989). The same survey asked respondents who was better qualified to be Chancellor, Helmut Kohl or Lothar Späth, the Christian Democratic Minister President of Baden-Württemberg. Seventy-three percent of respondents chose Späth and only 27 percent chose Kohl.

The leaders of the dominant coalition opposing Kohl included Heiner Geissler, Rita Süssmuth, Ernst Albrecht, and Norbert Blüm. These leaders not only blamed Kohl for many of the CDU's troubles, but also preferred that the party move to the left in an attempt to win votes in the center of the electorate. They were joined by Lothar Späth, who had enjoyed extraordinary electoral success in Baden-Württemberg and was also critical of Kohl. In the spring and early summer of 1989, this group of CDU leaders was considering an attempt to remove Kohl from the position of CDU chairman at the party's national congress in September 1989 (Bösch 2002: 131).

While the attempt to dislodge Kohl attracted a significant amount of media attention and Kohl was clearly vulnerable, the initiative ultimately failed for two reasons. First, the conspirators were unable to agree on a replacement for Kohl. Neither Geissler nor Blüm was popular enough. Süssmuth was the most popular politician in West Germany at the time (*Der Spiegel*, April 24, 1989), but much of her support came from outside the CDU, and no one thought the CDU was ready for a woman as party chair. Späth was also very popular, and he was from Baden-Württemberg, a populous and well-off southern *Land*. The leaders of the dominant coalition wanted the CDU to move to the left, however, while Späth's politics were more ambiguous. Particularly on issues of abortion and immigration, Späth had more in common with conservatives in the party. The CDU's poor showing in Baden-Württemberg in the European elections in June 1989 was also viewed as evidence that Späth's support was less strong than originally believed (*Der Spiegel*, August 7, 1989). The dominant coalition did not have a leader clearly ready to take the helm of the party.

The second reason for the failure of the coup attempt was the organizational strength of Helmut Kohl. Although Kohl's popularity in the electorate was low, most CDU activists remained loyal to him (Bösch 2002: 132). Kohl had created a number of internal party positions, filling them with supporters (*Der Spiegel*, September 4, 1989). Furthermore, Kohl had maintained excellent ties to many of the leaders of the CDU's regional organizations (Chandler 1993: 133).

Finally, Kohl acted quickly and removed Geissler as his General Secretary before the conspirators had a chance to decide on a replacement. At the party congress in Bremen in September 1989, where they had planned to stage their coup, the conspirators did not have a candidate to run against Kohl in the election to party chair. While the party congress delegates voiced serious misgivings over Kohl's treatment of Geissler, they reelected Kohl as party chair with a vote of 77 percent (CDU National Party Congress 1989). This score was less than Kohl had received previously, but still a strong vote of confidence. Volker Rühe, Kohl's choice for the new General Secretary, was elected with a comfortable (if not impressive) 84 percent (CDU National Party Congress 1989).

Most of the (now former) dominant coalition continued to hold power within the CDU, but they were no longer as influential in policy making (Bösch 2002: 133). Geissler was elected to the CDU's Presidium, where he maintained some of his ability to criticize Kohl, but no longer had the power of the General Secretary's office to act on his agenda. Süssmuth, Blüm, and Albrecht were also all reelected to the Presidium. Lothar Späth did not fare so well. Späth's role in the attempt to oust Kohl spelled the end of his ambitions as a national level politician. In 1991 he was forced to resign as Minister President of Baden-Württemberg because of an unrelated scandal (Prinzing 2006).[1] The members of the former dominant coalition continued to be able to voice their opinions, as would be expected in a corporatist catch-all party. However, they no longer had access to positions of power within the party that would allow them to enact their agenda relatively easily.

The situation of the Women's Union within the CDU was affected by a second development in 1989 besides the failed coup – the fall of the Berlin wall. German unification brought an entirely new set of actors into the CDU. The Christian Democratic Union merged with the eastern Christian Democratic Union that had been allowed to exist in East Germany under communism.[2] The creation of a new, larger party meant that existing CDU groups that were unable to expand to the eastern *Länder* were weakened. These groups included all the regional organizations as well as the Social Committees. The new *Länder* in the east had their own regional organizations. While it might have been expected that the Social Committees would attract a significant following in the formerly Communist east, where people had been encouraged to identify as workers, eastern membership in the Social Committees remained very low (Schmidt 1997: 143). The principal reason is that the Social Committees are a strongly Catholic organization and the eastern *Länder* are almost entirely Protestant or atheist. In contrast to the Social Committees, the Women's Union benefited from unification because all female members of the CDU are automatically enrolled in the Women's Union.

Eastern Germans, including those in the CDU, differed in several ways from Germans in the west. After forty years of a Communist regime, people in the east were less religious than in the west. Furthermore, Catholicism, one of the foundations of German Christian Democracy, had never been

---

[1] Späth found success in eastern Germany as head of Jenaoptik. In 1998, Kohl recruited Späth to be head of a working group on "Future and Innovation" as part of the 1998 national elections.

[2] For more on the CDU in the former East Germany see Ute Schmidt (1997).

very widespread in the eastern territories, which had been mostly Protestant. Finally, gender roles in eastern German were quite different from their western counterparts. Most women in East Germany had been employed full time and were used to an extensive system of public day care. Furthermore, abortion had been legal in East Germany since 1972.[3] Bringing the eastern Germans into the western CDU, therefore, meant bringing in a large number of members and politicians who had quite different backgrounds and ideas from Christian Democrats in the west (Chandler 1993; Kolinsky 1998).

Under these changed conditions, forming a dominant coalition became increasingly complicated (Clemens 1993). Because there were more internal groups, it was easier for Helmut Kohl, the party chair, to play them off against each other. Thus, while the new dominant coalition was made up of business and nationalist groups within the CDU and excluded the Women's Union, the Women's Union was not shut out from CDU policy making altogether.

For the Women's Union, German unification brought both challenges and opportunities. On the one hand, unification cemented the power of Helmut Kohl, who had excluded the Women's Union from the dominant coalition. On the other hand, the eastern CDU was sympathetic to the Women's Union's positions on abortion and child care. Furthermore, although easterners did not form an official auxiliary organization, they were recognized as an important group and gained representation on most CDU decision-making bodies.[4] The new Minister for Women and Youth, Angela Merkel, was also from East Germany. In the 1990s, the Women's Union had the most policy success when it was able to forge a cobbled coalition with eastern Germans.

The New Dominant Coalition of the 1990s

After unification, the CDU went through a period of internal turmoil and increased power for Chancellor Kohl. After the failed attempt to take

---

[3] There is an extensive literature on the differences on women's roles and experiences in East and West Germany both prior to and following unification. For some examples, see Ferree 1993; Meyer and Schulze 1998; Trzcinski 1998; Young 1999; Miethe 1999. Also interesting is the catalog from the exhibition "Ungleiche Schwestern? Frauen in Ost- und Westdeutschland" published by the Haus der Geschichte der Bundesrepublik Deutschland. Much of this literature is devoted to showing that East German women were the "losers of unification." East German women have suffered higher rates of unemployment than East German men. Their work-family benefits have declined and obtaining an abortion is more difficult than prior to unification.

[4] For more details on representing easterners in the CDU, see Chapter 7.

over the party leadership in 1989, Kohl was careful to place people loyal to him in important positions whenever possible (Langguth 2001: 54). This was particularly true of his new General Secretary, Volker Rühe, and Rühe's later successor Peter Hintze. Because of unification, the CDU also increased the size of the National Executive Committee and the National Party Congress, which made it more difficult for these bodies to act coherently (Bösch 2002: 134). Furthermore, because of generational turnover in the West and a series of scandals in the East, the *Land*-level leadership in both halves of the newly united Germany fluctuated dramatically in the early 1990s (Bösch 2002: 138–42). These developments made it harder to form a cohesive dominant coalition.

The dominant coalition that eventually emerged was made up of actors and groups within the CDU with neo-liberal and conservative-nationalist orientations. The party was moving in a more market-oriented direction (Bösch 2002: 60). Important internal groups in the CDU's dominant coalition in the 1990s included the regional organizations of two major *Länder*, Hesse and Baden-Württemberg, the business and industry association (*Wirtschaftsrat*) and the refugee association (*Union der Vertriebenen und Flüchtlinge*). After a change in leadership in 1994, the Youth Union (*Junge Union*) also began working with the dominant coalition (Schroeder 1998). Important leaders of the new dominant coalition included Wolfgang Schäuble from Baden-Württemberg, the new chair of the parliamentary caucus; Manfred Kanther from Hesse, Minister of the Interior; and Volker Rühe from Hamburg, the CDU's new General Secretary. The CSU, led by Edmund Stoiber and Theo Waigel, also worked more closely with this dominant coalition than with that of the 1980s.

The new dominant coalition pursued policies such as cutbacks in welfare benefits, immigration restrictions, and efforts to increase Germany's influence in international politics. It worked to slow the CDU's recognition of existing borders with the Czech Republic and Poland and to gain approval for sending the *Bundeswehr* to out-of-area conflicts. The dominant coalition in the 1990s also pursued employer-friendly legislation such as smaller payments for sick leave and pension reform, as well as policies to make it easier for companies to fire workers.

The dominant coalition of the 1990s opposed the positions of the Women's Union on most women's issues. Because the new, neo-liberal dominant coalition sought to curb state spending, it preferred not to increase payments for parents staying home to raise their children or to expand publicly financed child care. While the northern actors in the dominant coalition were more ambivalent on the issue of abortion, their southern allies in Bavaria and Baden-Württemberg sought to limit access to abortion. Finally, the new dominant coalition opposed a women's participation quota for a variety of reasons. Quotas were at odds with liberal ideology, and increasing the power of the Women's Union was not something the new dominant coalition wanted to do. Most of these actors were men, so a strong women's quota threatened their own internal party positions. With the new dominant coalition in charge it was much more difficult for the Women's Union to make headway on its policy agenda.

POLICY MAKING ON WOMEN'S ISSUES: WORK-FAMILY POLICY IN THE 1990S

The Women's Union's attempts to pass work-family policy in the 1990s are an excellent illustration of the workings of a cobbled coalition. In the 1980s, as a part of the dominant coalition, the Women's Union helped pass a major, expensive, reform to work-family policy, the implementation of child-raising money (paid parental leave). In the 1990s from outside of the dominant coalition, most of the Women's Union's proposals met with defeat. The one policy that passed – the right to a Kindergarten spot – was hustled through on the coattails of the unification treaty. This relative success was mitigated by the fact that the party failed to fund it adequately.

Unlike in the United States, Kindergarten in Germany is not the first year of school. German Kindergarten is child care for children aged three to six, equivalent to preschool in the United States. For younger children there is very little day care available (Kreyenfeld and Hank 2000). Passing the Kindergarten law was a first step toward increasing the amount of available child care.[5]

In many ways the context for policies to help working mothers had improved in the 1990s and it should have been easier to pass this type of

---

[5] Even once children enter the school system, the problem for parents is not solved because school hours in Germany are short and irregular. While the implementation of the Kindergarten law has been uneven, the result has nonetheless been a significant increase in the number of Kindergarten spots in the West. Many of these spots are part time, however.

reform. Previously, many in the CDU had opposed providing child care because of a belief that children received the best care from their mothers. The Women's Union was one of the few internal groups to favor part-time child care and child care for single parents. CDU politicians were more explicit than politicians in other parties in their opposition to child care for children under the age of three on the grounds that child care for young children was detrimental to the child's health. This view is not specific to the CDU, however, but is widely held in Germany and supports Esping-Andersen's classification of Germany as having a corporatist welfare state regime (Esping-Andersen 1990; 1999).

By the 1990s, however, three demographic changes had made the need for child care more pressing. While Germany's female labor force participation was still low by international standards, it had increased significantly. In West Germany, 46 percent of women worked in 1970. By 1980 women's employment rate had risen to 50 percent and by 1990 it was 59 percent (Bundesministerium für Familie, Senioren, Frauen und Jugend 1998: 53). Germany also had increasing numbers of both single parents and only children. Even traditional conservatives agreed that Kindergartens should be available for single parents, and child psychologists argued that only children needed to spend time in Kindergarten in order to develop healthy relationships with peers. All of these changes made the CDU more amenable to the idea of child care outside the family (Maria Böhmer, personal interview).

German unification also made the possibility of increased child care seem more palatable to westerners. German unification merged the society of West Germany, which had very little child care, with that of East Germany, where an extensive public child care system was the norm (Wagner, Hank, and Tillmann 1995). As Annelies Klug, former business manager of the Women's Union, explains, the addition of the eastern *Länder*, where nearly all children attended Kindergarten, made the argument that this form of child care damaged children untenable:

The addition of the East helped [pass the Kindergarten law] because people saw that it was possible to send children to Kindergarten. In this question, unification was quite good. It brought us further. You couldn't question whether putting children in Kindergarten is sensible because that would have depressed all the women in the East, and we couldn't do that. (Annelies Klug, personal interview)

Furthermore, as will be seen in the following, the process of unification created policy openings for pro-Kindergarten groups. In the context of unification, when nearly all things from East Germany were denigrated, it was important to find something positive to rescue from the East. The widespread system of child care was one possibility.[6]

Finally, the Women's Union itself was more unified on the question of extrafamilial child care in the 1990s than it had been in the 1980s. While the organization had been fairly conservative on child care in the 1970s, the Women's Union became more open to care away from families in the 1980s, and committed to expanding child care options in the 1990s. As reported by Hanne Pollmann, the chair of the German Women's Council (*Deutscher Frauenrat*, a nonpartisan lobbying group on women's issues):

> At first, the Women's Union opposed child care away from the mother because the organization was still very old-fashioned. Then in 1987, one [unidentified] older woman changed her opinion, and she swung the rest of the Women's Union along with her. She argued that it wasn't in keeping with the times not to have child care, especially since there were so many single mothers. (Hanne Pollmann, personal interview)

In the 1980s the Women's Union stopped blocking demands for increased all-day child care in the German Women's Council. In the late 1980s and early 1990s, the Women's Union began advocating on behalf of the Kindergarten law.

The Women's Union worked to mobilize the CDU's parliamentary groups for women on the Kindergarten issue. By soliciting cooperation from the *Gruppe der Frauen* (Group of Women – all female Christian Democratic parliamentarians) and the *Arbeitsgruppe Frauen und Familien* (Parliamentary Working Group for Women and Families), the Women's Union pushed to get the necessary parliamentary organizations on board (Birgit Lüders, personal interview).

The Women's Union was assisted in its efforts by the Social Committees. In the late 1980s, the business manager of the Women's Union, Ingrid Sehrbrock, had had close ties to the Social Committees. According to staff members at the national office of the Social Committees, she was able to

---

[6] The Kindergarten law was ultimately effective at increasing the number of child care spots for children aged three to six in West Germany. Coverage rates went from 74.4 percent in 1994 to 90.2 percent in the West (excluding Berlin), though many of these spots were part time. For the same time period coverage rates in East Germany (excluding East Berlin) went from 96.6 percent in 1994 to 105.1 percent in 2002. The increase in coverage in the East was caused by the dramatic decline of the birth rate in East Germany, however. The absolute number of Kindergarten spots actually decreased (Leitner, Ostner, and Schmitt 2008: 192–3).

explain to the Social Committees why they should support the Women's Union on the issue of child care (Bernhard Breuer; Jochen Schulz, personal interviews).

The support of the Social Committees in the 1990s, however, was less valuable than it had been in the 1980s because the Social Committees had become significantly weaker. Norbert Blüm, former head of the Social Committees, had remained Labor Minister and was affiliated with the Social Committees, but he was no longer the chair of the organization. The Social Committees were further weakened by infighting, loss of membership, and inadequate leadership (Schroeder 1998: 182–8). Under Norbert Blüm in the 1980s the Social Committees had frequently been successful in influencing CDU policy making. In the 1990s, under Ulf Fink and Rainer Eppelmann, the Social Committees had little effect on the CDU's decision-making process. The Women's Union's former ally was less valuable in the 1990s.

The Women's Union also worked with several regional organizations. The new eastern *Länder* sought to preserve their extensive child care networks and supported the Kindergarten law, though they sometimes thought it inadequate. In the west, the CDU *Land* organization in Rhineland-Palatinate has a long tradition of working with the Women's Union and supporting its policies. The Social Minister in Rhineland-Palatinate ensured that the Kindergarten law was implemented in Rhineland-Palatinate, the first western *Land* to adopt the policy (Maria Böhmer; Heiner Geissler, personal interviews).

The dominant coalition in the 1990s, consisting of neo-liberals and nationalist-oriented groups and politicians, opposed the Kindergarten law. Financial conservatives, such as Finance Minister Theodor Waigel, were watching the budget. Local-level CDU politicians feared that they would be forced to pay for the Kindergartens. In postunification Germany, funds were short for everything, and child care was not a high priority of the dominant coalition. The open disagreement within the CDU most frequently focused on whether Kindergartens were affordable, but at least some of the time, politicians were using lack of affordability to argue against providing child care that they opposed for ideological reasons (Beate Hesse, personal interview).

Because the Women's Union was not in the dominant coalition, its attempts to pass policy on child care were unlikely to succeed directly. Fortunately for the activists in the Women's Union, another opportunity presented itself: German unification provided an opening to activists within the CDU for passing child care policy.

A long-time policy analyst for the CDU on women's issues, Udo Kollenberg, played a critical role in linking the Kindergarten law to German unification. As a civil servant at the Women's Ministry, Kollenberg had worked closely with both Helga Wex and Rita Süssmuth. Kollenberg proposed that language on women's policies be inserted into the unification treaty.

> With the unification treaty, there was nothing about women. So I wrote a letter formulating language that could be in there and sent it to the people in the East and the West who had to sign the treaty. Then the letters were in there during the final negotiations. Everyone was opposed at first. But Kohl said, we can't really be against that. If it gets out that we voted against this we're finished. We [at the Ministry] also had to call the German Women's Council and other lobby groups and get them to push a bit. (Udo Kollenberg, personal interview)

Kollenberg not only had language on women's issues inserted into the treaty. He ensured that if the CDU had rejected adding this language to the treaty, it would have been well publicized by the lobbying groups (Udo Kollenberg; Stephan Walter, personal interviews).

The resulting section of the unification treaty on "Families and Women" (chapter VII, Article 31) contained a variety of provisions designed to improve gender equality. The treaty obligated the national government to help pay for child care in the eastern *Länder* until June 30, 1991 at a cost of one billion marks (*Süddeutsche Zeitung*, May 18, 1991). It further required lawmakers to take into account the different positions of men and women regarding paid employment and to set up laws to make combining family and career possible.

This section of the treaty also contained regulations for reforming the differing abortion laws in East and West Germany. It required that the new abortion law provide for social benefits better than those available in either part of Germany at the time of unification. While the Kindergarten law was not explicitly mentioned, the language of the treaty clearly implied that it was to be one of these benefits.

The treaty thus created a critical link between abortion reform and increased provision of child care. The need for a new abortion law created serious internal difficulties for the CDU and the CSU. Over the course of 1991, a variety of internal party commissions worked to develop a unified Christian Democratic position.[7] The requirement that abortion reform include increased social benefits gave the Women's Union an opportunity

---

[7] See the following section of this chapter for details.

to push through the Kindergarten law. As one Women's Union leader, also a member of parliament, explained:

> In connection with paragraph 218 we [the Women's Union] got our break. One reason for having an abortion is if there isn't any child care. So we couldn't have abortion be illegal, but leave all these other problems. (Renate Diemers, personal interview)

Both the Women's Union and women from the eastern *Länder* were represented on the abortion policy commissions. They worked to integrate social measures, including the Kindergarten law, into the CDU/CSU abortion proposal. On September 20, 1991, the Union agreed to a new abortion proposal, which included the right to a Kindergarten spot (*Süddeutsche Zeitung*, September 20, 1991).[8]

Although the cobbled coalition was able to attach the Kindergarten law to abortion legislation passed in the wake of unification, it was not strong enough to ensure that this legislation was enacted. The dominant coalition, including Finance Minister Theodor Waigel (CSU), preferred not to spend money on child care. Waigel quickly cut the funding to only 10 percent of the originally planned expenditures (*Der Spiegel*, September 23, 1991). Waigel refused to fund Kindergartens at the national level and forced the financing dilemma onto the *Land* and municipality levels. The implementation of the Kindergarten law was slowed dramatically by lengthy disagreements about how to fund the new Kindergartens. While the number of available Kindergarten spots increased significantly over the course of the 1990s, many of these spots were for half-day care.

From outside the dominant coalition, the Women's Union was not able to control the CDU's agenda on women's issues. Unification provided the Women's Union with both new alliance partners in the form of eastern sections of the party and a shock that opened opportunities for new child care policy. With these advantages the Women's Union was able to get the CDU to commit to the Kindergarten law, but working from outside the dominant coalition, it was not able to secure funding for the new policy.

---

[8] The Bundestag passed the Kindergarten law in the summer of 1992 as part of an abortion reform law. The abortion law was supported by the SPD, the FDP, and progressive CDU parliamentarians. The section of the law regulating abortion was eventually struck down by the Federal Constitutional Court, but the court also ruled that the accompanying social measures, including the Kindergarten law, were valid.

POLICY MAKING ON WOMEN'S ISSUES: ABORTION POLICY

The Women's Union had little influence over the CDU's stance on abortion in the 1990s. Working from outside the dominant coalition, the Women's Union's only chance to influence abortion policy would have been through some kind of cobbled coalition with another internal party actor. However, like most other organizations within the CDU, the Women's Union itself was also divided on abortion. Many western Germans in the Women's Union would have been happy with the West German status quo, while some easterners – and Rita Süssmuth, chair of the Women's Union – hoped for liberalization if not legalization. While some in the organization, and especially Süssmuth, were active on abortion reform, the Women's Union itself had little effect on policy.[9]

Unification had brought abortion to the political agenda and the CDU had to act on the issue. Abortion had been legal in East Germany since 1973 (Klein-Schonnefeld 1994: 117). In West Germany, however, abortion was only permitted under certain well-defined circumstances, as specified by the 1976 reform. The West German law allowed abortion only in cases of rape, medical danger to the mother, fetal deformity, or "social emergency."[10] Only a doctor could decide whether the necessary circumstances were present. Finding a compromise acceptable in the east and the west was one of the most difficult challenges of unification. When it appeared that the entire unification process might collapse because of the abortion law, the unification committee decided not to decide. Under the terms of the unification treaty the eastern and western *Länder* would maintain their separate laws until December 31, 1992 and the Bundestag was charged with writing a compromise law by that date (Ferree et. al 2002: 41).

Abortion was a more difficult issue for the CDU than for any other party (Neidhardt 1996: 79). The party had already been divided in the 1980s, and this disagreement worsened in the 1990s. In the course of German unification, the CDU in eastern Germany and western Germany merged to

---

[9] There is a large literature on the postunification abortion reform in Germany. Some of the most useful sources include Czarnowski (1994); Klein-Schonnefeld (1994); Mushaben (1997); Kamenitsa (2001); and Ferree et. al. (2002).

[10] What constituted a social emergency was quite vague. The vast majority of abortions in West Germany were performed under this indication. Doctors frequently decided based on whether a woman earned enough money to support an additional child and whether she was psychologically able to raise the child (Däubler-Gmelin and Faerber-Husemann 1987).

become a single party. The East-West split in the Women's Union ran through the entire party (indeed, the entire German population) with (many) easterners preferring a more liberal abortion law than (most) westerners (Banaszak 1998; Rattinger 1994). Unification increased the voices within the CDU in favor of liberalizing the West German law. Over the course of the abortion debate in the 1980s, however, pro-life groups affiliated with the CDU also had become stronger and more vocal. These groups saw unification as a chance to implement an abortion law that was stricter than the old West German version. In the 1990s, then, the CDU had more activists on both sides of the abortion issue, as compared to the 1980s.

The ability of the Women's Union to influence the CDU's actions on abortion was limited. The Women's Union did not have access to offices within the party that would have allowed the organization to shape the abortion debate. Furthermore, the Women's Union was internally divided on the abortion question. The chair of the Women's Union, Rita Süssmuth, favored liberalizing abortion, but most members of the Women's Union did not back her proposal. Furthermore, Irmgard Karwatzki, the chair of the largest *Land* organization of the Women's Union, strongly favored keeping the old West German law.[11]

The CDU formed two commissions on abortion in the spring of 1991, one for the party and one for the parliamentary caucus. These commissions worked to develop a position acceptable to as much of the CDU as possible. The ability of the dominant coalition to control internal party policy on abortion can be seen in the choices to chair these two commissions.

Despite its internal tension, the Women's Union attempted to exert some influence over the CDU's abortion debate by nominating Süssmuth to chair the CDU's commission on abortion to be formed in the spring of 1991 (Sehrbrock 1990). As President of the Bundestag, former Minister of Women's Affairs and chair of the Women's Union, Süssmuth was the CDU's highest-ranking female politician. She was also known as successful at working with the opposition parties. Süssmuth, however, was openly in favor of liberalizing access for abortion. For this reason, she was never a serious contender for chairing the party commission. The CDU's General Secretary, Volker Rühe chose Hannelore Rönsch, Minister for Families and Seniors to chair the Commission.[12] Rönsch was a conservative

---

[11] For more on the disagreement between Süssmuth and Karwatzki, see Keller-Kühne (1998: 76–82).

[12] Angela Merkel, at that time Minister for Women and Youth, was appointed deputy chair of the joint party commission.

member of parliament from Hesse, who opposed liberalizing abortion. The desires of the Women's Union had no effect on this choice.

Christian Democrats formed a second commission on abortion, based in the Bundestag and also titled "Commission to Protect Unborn Life." Maria Michalk, a woman from the eastern CDU with a strong pro-life position on abortion, chaired the parliamentary commission. These Commissions produced nearly identical proposals, which significantly shaped the CDU's draft of the abortion law that was presented in fall 1991. The dominant coalition, which was pro-life and included General Secretary Volker Rühe, was able to select leaders of the commissions to guide the party according to its own wishes.[13]

As a member of the CDU party Commission to Protect Unborn Life, Süssmuth was able to voice the position of the pro-reform group. This allowance of internal dissent would be expected for a corporatist catch-all party. At a hearing on April 25 and 26, 1991, Süssmuth presented her third-way proposal. The discussion at this meeting was quite acrimonious, and Süssmuth was not treated well by her fellow party members. She was interrupted as she spoke and yelled at as she was leaving (*Katholische Nachrichten Agentur*, April 27, 1991). While those in the dominant coalition could not keep Süssmuth from presenting her ideas, she had little influence over the proposal ultimately approved by the Christian Democrats. Despite this incident, there was a great deal of free discussion within the CDU on the abortion issue and some genuine efforts to find a compromise (Helga Roesgen, personal interview).

The Women's Union issued a position paper on abortion in July 1991. This statement adopted the medical and psycho-social indications that had previously been developed by the two CDU/CSU Commissions on abortion reform. The Women's Union approved of mandatory counseling. In terms of one of the key questions – who was responsible for deciding whether an indication was present in a particular case – the Women's Union proposal was vague. It stated that the decision was to be made by the pregnant woman and the gynecologist (Frauen Union 1991). (*Leitsätze der Frauen-Union zur Neuregelung des §218 StGB 1991*). Most of the abortion proposals gave the right of decision either to the woman *or* the

---

[13] For more on the development of the CDU position on abortion over the course of 1991 see CDU-Bundesgeschäftsstelle (1991). Information presented here is also drawn from the minutes of the meetings of the "Commission to Protect Unborn Life" from March 21, 1991; May 23, 1991; May 29, 1991 and June 5, 1991 (See CDU-Bundesgeschäftsstelle 1991); and the reports from the two hearings held at the Konrad Adenauer Foundation on April 25–6, 1991 and November 28–9, 1991 (Konrad-Adenauer-Stiftung 1991; 1992).

doctor. By listing both, the Women's Union avoided a clear decision, because it was internally divided. While the Women's Union position paper seemed to advocate the indication model over the time limit model, even this stance was not entirely clear. The Women's Union was too internally divided to act coherently on abortion.

The two Christian Democratic Commissions ultimately produced what was called the Rönsch bill. This proposal, like Süssmuth's, called for mandatory counseling. Unlike the third-way proposal, however, the Rönsch bill remained essentially an indications model. It provided for two indications, medical and psycho-social. The three indications from the West German law – criminal, eugenic, and social emergency – were subsumed under the psycho-social indication. Critically, the decision of whether abortion was permitted in a particular case continued to rest with the doctor. The Rönsch bill was backed by the majority of the CDU/CSU parliamentary caucus.[14]

Although Süssmuth and other liberalizers within the CDU had little influence over their party's bill, they played an important role in the parliamentary maneuverings that shaped the legislation eventually passed in June 1992. After the parliamentary caucuses submitted their proposals to the conference committee in the fall of 1991, there was initially little progress on abortion. Then female parliamentarians from the SPD and FDP began working together to draft a consensus bill that would receive cross-party support. They were later joined by parliamentarians of Alliance 90/Greens. This cross-party bill, called the Group Resolution (*Gruppenantrag*) was based on the time limit model and permitted abortion during the first trimester of pregnancy. The compromises among parliamentarians from different parties related primarily to the type of counseling that would be required for women seeking an abortion. The compromise proposal required counseling, but did not force the woman to divulge her reason for wanting an abortion (*Der Spiegel*, May 11, 1992; Czarnowski 1994; Mushaben 1997; Kamenitsa 2001; Ferree et. al. 2002: 40–3).[15]

The parliamentarians working on the Group Resolution gained the support of some moderate Christian Democratic parliamentarians by

---

[14] Hard-line conservatives supported the more restrictive Werner bill, which realized the demands of the Christian Democrats for Life. This bill permitted abortion only in cases where the mother's life or health was endangered. This restrictive bill initially had the support of over 90 Christian Democratic parliamentarians, but in September 1991, only 46 were willing to vote for it (Czarnowski 1994).

[15] For an alternative view of the abortion policy-making process, see Young (1998).

adding the provision that the stated goal of the counseling be protecting the life of the fetus. The Group Resolution additionally required a three-day waiting period between counseling and the medical procedure. For the organizers of the Group Resolution, having some Christian Democrats endorse their legislation allowed them to portray their bill as a genuine cross-party compromise, with some support from all democratic parties.

On June 25, 1992, the Bundestag debated and voted on the seven proposals for abortion legislation. In an unusual procedure, the Bundestag agreed that the first bill that received a majority of votes would be passed and debate would cease. Ultimately, however, the parliamentarians discussed and voted on all seven bills in a session that lasted from 8 o'clock in the morning until 1 o'clock the following night. The Group Resolution, which was ultimately approved, was discussed and voted on last. It passed with the support of 357 in favor, 284 against, and 16 abstentions.[16] Those in favor included 32 parliamentarians from the CDU/CSU, 73 from the FDP, 233 from the SPD, 10 from the PDS/Left List, 6 from Alliance 90/Greens and 2 independents (Czarnowski 1994). Of the 32 Christian Democrats voting for the Group Resolution, 19 were from the eastern *Länder* (Mushaben 1997: 78).

This legislation was not the last word, however. Conservative Christian Democratic politicians, including 249 parliamentarians and the government of Bavaria, immediately challenged the new law as unconstitutional (Czarnowski 1994). On May 28, 1993, the Federal Constitutional Court struck down the new law and issued a ruling with detailed guidelines for meeting the constitutionality test.

The Court declared abortion illegal, but not punishable (*rechtswidrig aber straffrei*). Most observers at the time focused on the continued illegality of abortion and certainly this ruling implied less access to abortion in the former East Germany (Mushaben 1997: 81). However, the court's decision was a major shift in German abortion law. It effectively sanctioned the time limit model, giving women, rather than doctors, the right to decide whether a woman could have an abortion. Although abortion was still officially illegal, women could now decide for themselves about abortion without having to get approval from a doctor. The ruling also specified that nonindicated abortions need not be funded by health insurance (Mushaben 1995: 92).

---

[16] The most notable of the abstentions was Angela Merkel, the future Chancellor and future chair of the CDU. She was torn between her desire for a relatively liberal abortion law and her desire to advance in the party.

After initial discussion of six proposals in February, the CDU/CSU, the FDP, and the SPD found a compromise reform, which was approved on June 29, 1995 with 486 yeas, 145 nays, and 21 abstentions (Mushaben 1997: 82). These negotiations were much simpler than the earlier round. The new law closely followed the court ruling, in some cases using the exact language of the decision.

As just discussed, the new law declared abortion illegal, but not punishable if the woman attended a mandatory counseling session. When the abortion was necessary for medical reasons or the pregnancy was the result of rape, then the procedure would be covered by the national health insurance.[17] Otherwise, women had to pay for the abortion themselves, but additional provisions in the law provided financial payments for low-income women. Some categories of women, such as students, welfare recipients, and foreigners, also receive medical coverage for abortions in all cases (Mushaben 1997). While the social emergency indicator was eliminated in the new legislation, any woman who had undergone counseling could now get an abortion. The law stated that the counseling was to be both directed at the goal of preserving life and open to any result. In reality, much counseling has been purely *pro forma*.

The Women's Union played little part in bringing about this outcome. It was difficult to influence CDU policy from outside of the dominant coalition. Furthermore, the Women's Union was divided. The organization's chair was more interested in liberalizing reform than most of the members of the Women's Union. Consequently Süssmuth could not mobilize membership to support her, and members could not count on Süssmuth to lead the organization in a way that would suit them. The Women's Union pushed to have Süssmuth selected as a leader of one of the party's commissions on abortion, but this effort was blocked by the dominant coalition.

Süssmuth and others within the CDU, particularly parliamentarians from the eastern *Länder*, were able to influence the legislation passed by the Bundestag in 1992 by working with the opposition parties and the FPD. Many of the provisions about abortion counseling described in Süssmuth's original "third-way" proposal ended up in both the 1992 legislation that was overturned by the Court and the 1995 legislation

---

[17] After significant debate, the law ultimately passed by the Bundestag subsumed the embryopathic indication under the medical indication. Criminal indications (abortion in the case of rape) had to be determined within the first trimester. Medical indications could be determined at any time (Mushaben 1997: 83).

that is still valid in Germany today (Rita Süssmuth, personal interview). The only way for the Women's Union to influence abortion policy in the 1990s was through the ad hoc policy-making process possible with a cobbled coalition.[18]

POLICY MAKING ON WOMEN'S ISSUES: PARTICIPATION POLICY IN THE 1990S

Participation policy in the 1990s provides another illustration of the limited influence available to groups outside of the dominant coalition. The leadership of the Women's Union initially attempted to slip reform on participation through the party congress while delegates were not paying attention. When that strategy failed, the leadership of the Women's Union turned to an extensive mobilization campaign to convince membership that a women's quota was necessary. They were supported in their efforts by the Social Committees and the CDU's new General Secretary, Peter Hintze. Eastern Christian Democrats, however, were more reluctant in their support of a quota. The Women's Union pressured the CDU to confront the possibility of participation policy four times in the 1990s, but it was not strong enough to get the party to adopt its policy preference, a quota. Instead, the CDU adopted a much weaker measure to support women's participation, the quorum.

Although the decision to establish a quota for women's participation depends only on the CDU, the party has been influenced by the actions of other parties. Both the Greens and the SPD had implemented women's quotas in the 1980s. These parties subsequently increased the percentage of women in their leadership and the amount of electoral support they received from women. The CDU, therefore, felt pressure to respond (Kolinsky 1991; Matland and Studlar 1996; Davidson-Schmich 2006).[19]

Table 6.1 shows the number of female members of the Bundestag in each party from 1987 to today. The SPD introduced its quota in 1988 and

---

[18] After the 1994 elections, the CDU had only a slim majority, small enough that the governing coalition could not pass legislation without the support of female Christian Democrats from the former East Germany. The refusal of these women to vote in favor of a stricter abortion law contributed to the CDU's readiness to compromise on the legislation that was ultimately passed (Bärbel Sothmann, personal interview).

[19] The literature on gender quotas is enormous. Some of the best studies for both theorizing and cross-national analysis include Lovenduski 2005; Dahlerup 2006; Kittilson 2006; Krook 2009. For work on quotas in Germany in particular, see Kolinsky 1991, 1993; McKay 2004; Kamenitsa and Geissel 2005; Davidson-Schmich 2006; von Wahl 2006.

TABLE 6.1 *Number of Female Members of the Bundestag (Percentage of Women in Party Caucus)*

	CDU/CSU	CDU	CSU	SPD	FDP	Greens	PDS (Linke in 2005)	Total
1987–1990	18 (8%)	15 (9%)	3 (6%)	31 (16%)	6 (13%)	25 (57%)	–	80 (15%)
1990–1994	44 (14%)	39 (15%)	5 (10%)	65 (27%)	16 (20%)	3 (38%)	8 (47%)	136 (21%)
1994–1998	41 (14%)	35 (14%)	6 (12%)	86 (34%)	8 (17%)	29 (59%)	13 (43%)	177 (26%)
1998–2002	45 (18%)	39 (20%)	6 (13%)	105 (35%)	9 (20%)	27 (57%)	21 (60%)	207 (31%)
2002–2005	57 (23%)	43 (23%)	12 (21%)	95 (38%)	10 (21%)	32 (58%)	2 (100%)	195 (32%)
2005–2009	44 (20%)	38 (21%)	7 (15%)	80 (36%)	15 (25%)	29 (57%)	26 (46%)	193 (31%)

Information calculated from Ritter and Niehuss (1991); Frauen-Union der CSU (1997); Schindler (1999); Von Schwartzenberg (2002); McKay (2004); Statistisches Bundesamt (2005).

the effect can clearly be seen as the percentage of female parliamentarians rises from 16 percent in 1987 to 36 percent today (nearly reaching the party's quota of 40 percent). When the CDU and CSU percentages are viewed together, it appears that there has been a gradual increase over time with setbacks in 1994 and 2005. When the CDU and CSU results are viewed separately, however, the effect of the CDU quota (introduced in 1996) is much clearer. The CDU elects a higher percentage of women after 1996 and maintains its greater representation of women even after a poor overall electoral result in 2005. The women of the CSU – without a gender quota – do not fare as well.

The desire of the leadership of the Women's Union to act on participation policy crystallized in the course of the 1994 Bundestag election campaign. The party lists – available several months before the election – made it clear that regardless of the election results, the number of women in the CDU's Bundestag caucus would actually decline (Kristel Bendig, personal interview). The prediction was viewed as particularly unfortunate because the CDU was already faring poorly with young female voters and it was thought that female candidates and female representatives would be more likely to attract female voters.

In response to this situation, the Women's Union submitted a proposal to the February 1994 party congress that the party take action to ensure that the resolutions from Mainz and Wiesbaden were being implemented (CDU National Party Congress, February 1994). The resolutions of Mainz and Wiesbaden called for the CDU to nominate women to party offices at the same percentage that they were in party membership. Although Süssmuth played down the impact of the Women's Union proposal, it also called for one third of the CDU's candidates to be female, both for internal office and for the next Bundestag election. This addition clearly went beyond the regulations from Mainz and Wiesbaden both in terms of the higher percentage of women and in terms of being a mandate rather than a suggested goal (CDU National Party Congress, February 1994). Some of the leadership of the Women's Union believed the softer recommendations of Mainz and Wiesbaden would not be effective and that the party needed a stricter quota (Maria Böhmer, personal interview).

With this first attempt, Süssmuth and the leadership of the Women's Union were continuing their strategy from the 1980s by attempting to pass policy over the heads of membership. That strategy had worked in the late 1980s, but this time it did not. Tamara Zieschang, chair of the Association of Christian Democratic Students, was a member of the amendment commission and she noticed the proposal. Zieschang quickly arranged for delegate Nicole Bonnie to speak against the "hidden quota." This speech, purposely delivered by a relatively unpracticed young woman, quickly gained the attention of the party congress delegates (Tamara Zieschang, personal interview). This exposure maneuver succeeded, and Süssmuth's proposal was changed to one that only required further discussion at the next party congress. Even this promise of future discussion was approved only when Kohl himself intervened, a fairly rare occurrence at party congresses.

The amendment approved by party congress delegates in February 1994 charged the CDU's National Executive Committee with the task of developing procedures for internal party elections that would fulfill the guidelines passed by the party at the party congresses in Mainz in 1986 and Wiesbaden in 1988. The new procedures were to be prepared for discussion by June 30, 1994 and ready for delegates to vote on at the 1994 fall party congress. The amendment also called for one-third of the candidates selected for the 1998 national elections to be female (CDU National Party Congress, February 1994). None of these measures was permanent except for the requirement to discuss participation policy again in the fall.

Over the summer of 1994, the Women's Union changed tactics. Instead of trying to circumvent a divided or even antagonistic membership, the leadership of the Women's Union began to persuade and mobilize membership in favor of a women's quota. They did this through a series of meetings at all levels of the Women's Union and the CDU. As reported by Kristel Bendig, the business manager of the Women's Union:

Then we went to all the *Länder* to talk about why we needed the change. I was part of this. There were unending speeches and discussions. (Kristel Bendig, personal interview)

The issue of women's participation in the CDU was also covered extensively in *Frau und Politik*, the magazine of the Women's Union (Kristel Bendig, personal interview). Although they often encountered hostility, the activists of the Women's Union helped spread the quota discussion throughout the CDU.

Between February 1994 and the next national party congress in November 1994, a working group headed by General Secretary Peter Hintze developed a concrete proposal for an internal party quota. Hintze presented this proposal to the CDU's Presidium on October 26, 1994 and to the party's National Executive Committee on November 7, 1994 (*Süddeutsche Zeitung*, October 28, 1994; *Frankfurter Allgemeine Zeitung*, November 1, 1994).

On October 16, 1994 the CDU narrowly won the national election and was able to maintain its hold on the government. The party's already-poor showing with young women continued to worsen. As predicted, the number of female CDU members of parliament decreased from 44 to 41 (Hoecker 1995: 137).

At the party congress in November 1994, Süssmuth and Hintze would have preferred approving a women's quota. Taking into account the resistance from the dominant coalition, however, they proposed only that the national party congress *discuss* a women's quota in 1995 (*Frankfurter Allgemeine Zeitung*, November 19, 1994). Many delegates were angered that Kohl was pressuring them to support the quota proposal, while he himself had not met the goal of having one-third of his cabinet be women. The Presidium and the National Executive Committee had also failed to meet the quota. The debate on the proposal was lengthy with many speakers voicing opposition. The proposal was ultimately approved by 416 delegates in favor against 361 opposed (CDU National Party Congress, November 1994). Because this proposal only mandated further discussion, a simple majority was sufficient. This result would not have been enough support for a statute change, however.

The proposal approved by the delegates in November 1994 called for the CDU to develop procedures for increasing women's participation in the party, which would be voted on at the next national party congress.[20] This proposal also contained guidelines for the procedures, including that the goal should be to have at least one-third of candidates be female and that existing procedures to ensure adequate regional balance be extended to women. The proposal also encouraged intensive discussion about women's participation at all levels of the party (CDU National Party Congress, November 1994). This proposal differed from previous suggestions, in that it required a vote on a statute change at the next party congress. Many opponents of a women's quota preferred not to have to vote on it because voting down a quota would make the CDU appear unfriendly to women (Irmgard Karwatzski, personal interview).

Without being part of the dominant coalition, the Women's Union was managing to nudge participation policy along, especially with the help of the General Secretary. Because they had been unable to pass participation policy *without* membership involvement, the leadership of the Women's

---

[20] In fact, in an overly optimistic prediction, the proposal mandated that "this procedure will be made a party statute at the 7th CDU party congress" (CDU National Party Congress, November 1994).

Union provoked a difficult internal party debate as a way to pass partic-ipation policy *with* membership involvement. Between November 1994 and October 1995 (the next national party congress), the party engaged in extensive internal discussion about the women's quota at all levels of the party (Helga Roesgen, personal interview). The Women's Union partici-pated in these discussions and was particularly active in promoting the quota in the eastern *Länder*. Rather than circumventing or disempowering membership, in the mid-1990s the CDU engaged in significant member-ship mobilization on this issue.

Even so, the Women's Union was not powerful enough to push the quota through against the opposition of the dominant coalition. In July 1995, Hintze presented details of the women's quota to the National Executive Committee. Leaders of the dominant coalition, including Wolfgang Schäuble, the CDU's parliamentary chair, and Manfred Kanther, Minister of the Interior and chair of the CDU in Hesse, successfully opposed the proposal and postponed discussion (*Süddeutsche Zeitung*, July 6, 1995). Schäuble acknowledged, however, that given the resolution of November 1994, the party would have to pass something. At a second meeting at the end of August, the National Executive Committee approved a revised proposal that had been drafted by a working group of supporters and opponents of the quota (*tageszeitung*, August 29, 1995). Two members of the NEC voted against even this weakened formulation (*Süddeutsche Zeitung*, August 29, 1995), and the end of September, the dominant coali-tion had weakened the proposal still further (*FOCUS*, September 30, 1995).

The proposal submitted to the party congress in October 1995 provided for two significant changes in how the CDU selects candidates. Ballots for internal party elections would only be considered valid if at least one-third of the chosen candidates were female. Party lists would be required to have a woman in every third slot in the list. The proposal also contained a variety of other less rigid measures, such as recommending more vigorous recruitment of female activists (CDU National Party Congress, October 1995).

The dominant coalition was able to arrange the agenda of the party congress so that the chances of the quota proposal being defeated were greatly increased. As a statute change, the quota proposal required an absolute majority of all delegates (not just all delegates voting). With 1,000 delegates to the national party congress, 501 would have to vote in favor of the quota for it to pass. The vote on the quota was scheduled for the last day of the party congress. This choice was controversial. General Secretary Hintze had wanted to hold the quota vote on the second day of the party congress, when all delegates would be present. Schäuble, however, wanted his agenda on the second day, and he prevailed with Kohl even though the organization of the party congress was supposed to be the prerogative of the General Secretary (*Associated Press Germany*, October 18, 1995). The choice to put the quota discussion on the last day of the national party congress contributed to the ultimate defeat of the quota (Kristel Bendig; Heiner Geissler; Irmgard Karwatzki, personal interviews). According to Irmgard Karwatzki, chair of the Women's Union in North Rhine-Westphalia:

In Karlsruhe many delegates left before the vote on the quota because they didn't want to be on record as voting either for it or against it. So some delegates were missing when the vote was taken. (Irmgard Karwatzki, personal interview)

The CDU party congress rejected the quota proposal by a very narrow margin. The proposal received 496 votes in favor, five fewer than the 501 that would have been sufficient for approval. Because the vote on the quota was taken on the last day of the party congress, many of the delegates had already departed. The dominant coalition had successfully arranged a party congress agenda that contributed to the defeat of the proposed gender quota.

Helmut Kohl regarded the rejection of the quota as a personal defeat and initially promised to bring the same proposal to a vote the following year. Over the summer of 1996, however, a working group rewrote the quota proposal and renamed the policy a "quorum." This new policy was significantly weaker than the one the CDU had rejected in October 1995. Individual ballots were not required to have selected a certain number of women to be considered valid. If an internal party election resulted in fewer than one-third female winners, then the election was to be declared invalid and held a second time. The results of the second election were valid, however, regardless of how many women won. In terms of party lists, the new proposal only required that women be "sufficiently" represented among CDU candidates, without stipulating a percentage. The ideas about how to structure this weaker participation mechanism stemmed from Manfred Kanther (Irmgard Krawatzki, personal interview). The party congress voted on this proposal without discussion. Because the new proposal was so weak, former opponents of the quota had little trouble supporting it. It was approved with 609 in favor and 297 opposed (CDU National Party Congress, October 1996). Süssmuth and the Women's Union regarded it as a defeat even though it has subsequently turned out that the quorum has boosted women's representation.

Working from outside the dominant coalition, the Women's Union made only marginal progress on participation policy in the 1990s.

Despite the cooperation of the General Secretary and even the Chancellor and party chair, Helmut Kohl, the efforts of the Women's Union to get the CDU to adopt a quota for women failed. The dominant coalition, led by the parliamentary leader, Wolfgang Schäuble, and the Minister of the Interior, Manfred Kanther, defeated the women's quota through a combination of weakening successive proposals and manipulating the voting at the national party congress (Bärbel Sothmann, personal interview).[21] These latter actors controlled the CDU's policy making on women's participation and successfully fended off the attempts of the Women's Union to implement a quota.

The Women's Union worked hard to mobilize its membership in favor of a women's quota. Efforts to form a cobbled coalition failed, however. The actor that supported the Women's Union in its quest for a quota, the Social Committees, was too weak to be effective. Eastern Germans, who had acted as partners for cobbled coalitions on work-family policy and abortion policy, were at best ambivalent and at worst opposed to the idea of a women's quota. The Women's Union was too weak to convince the CDU to act on participation policy. The continued pressure of the Women's Union on the issue of women's participation did contribute to the CDU's approval of the weakened instrument of the quorum.

ALTERNATIVE HYPOTHESES

Although theories based on essentialist ideology, strategic interaction with (or emulation of) parties of the left, and more traditional ideas about catch-all parties can help us understand some aspects of the CDU's response to women's' issues, we see again that we need to take the CDU's internal organization into account if we want to understand the party's behavior. Because the CDU is a corporatist catch-all party, the new balance of power among the party's internal interest groups had a critical effect on the party's policy making.

The essentialist ideology hypothesis predicts that the CDU would remain true to its ideological roots as a Christian, predominantly Catholic party. According to this hypothesis, the CDU would do little to change its policies toward women in response to societal change, even in the face of an electoral challenge. If the CDU's actions in the 1980s already

---

[21] As chair of the CDU's regional organization in Hesse, Kanther introduced a weak quota, which he hoped would serve as a model for a national-level policy (*Frankfurter Allgemeine Zeitung*, January 28, 1996; February 4, 1996).

called this hypothesis into question, developments in the 1990s were especially problematic. Despite long-standing beliefs that young children were best cared for in the home, the CDU approved legislation mandating day care spots for all children aged three to six. Even more surprising, the CDU signed a law giving women the right to decide for themselves whether or not to have an abortion. While ideology clearly played a role – the CDU took smaller steps in these policy areas than parties of the left and waited longer to do so – it is also clear that CDU actions reflected much more than just traditional Christian Democratic doctrine.

The spatial voting theory hypothesis predicts that the CDU would imitate the party of the left. This hypothesis expects the CDU to liberalize abortion policy, institute a women's quota, and implement policies to help women combine work and family. In the 1990s, the CDU liberalized abortion policy and provided more day care, but it voted down an internal party quota for women, even though both the Green Party and the Social Democrats had already established women's quotas in the 1980s. Furthermore, this hypothesis cannot explain why the CDU acted to liberalize abortion in the 1990s when it had chosen not to do so in the 1980s. Although there were definitely interactions with the policies of the parties on the left and the CDU was certainly trying to win elections, much CDU behavior cannot be explained by the spatial voting theory hypothesis.

The third rival hypothesis, catch-all party theory, predicts that the CDU would respond to new societal demands with vague policy pronouncements. The theory further predicts that the CDU would demobilize membership, if possible, in order to prevent members from pushing the party into an electorally disadvantageous position. This theory does not accurately describe the CDU's behavior on women's issues in the 1990s. On both participation policy and abortion policy the CDU engaged in prolonged internal debates. The party leadership requested and received extensive input on the quota proposal in particular. The resulting policies were quite detailed, not vague pronouncements.

None of these theories can explain CDU behavior in the 1990s. The alternative model presented here – with its emphasis on party organization and internal party alliances – better explains CDU policy making on women's issues.

CONCLUSION

This chapter has illustrated the more limited ability of the Women's Union to pass reforms from outside the dominant coalition. Because this auxiliary organization was not at the center of CDU policy making in the 1990s, the Women's Union was unable to mount a long-term successful campaign for its policy objectives. The reforms that the Women's Union pushed through were modest in comparison with its achievements in the 1980s when it still belonged to the dominant coalition.

The successes of the Women's Union in the 1990s were limited in all three areas under investigation. On work-family policy, the Women's Union helped convince the CDU to approve legislation mandating a Kindergarten spot for all children aged three through six. This change was not the result of efforts to convince internal party actors who opposed child care to change their minds. Instead, the Kindergarten law was approved because a Women's Ministry staff member inserted language into the unification treaty. The Women's Union also made sure their supporters kept an eye on this section of the treaty. This cobbled coalition was not strong enough, however, to procure funding for the new Kindergartens or to pass other legislation desired by the Women's Union, such as an increase in child-raising money. In this case the Women's Union was mobilized and had an alliance partner for a successful cobbled coalition.

The Women's Union was unable to influence CDU policy making on abortion because in addition to being outside the dominant coalition, it was internally divided. Politicians within the CDU interested in liberalizing abortion access had little effect on their party's position. Although Süssmuth was the CDU's highest-ranking and most well-known female politician, she was not chosen to chair either of the Christian Democratic Commissions that developed the party's stance on abortion. Instead, the dominant coalition ensured that less prominent, but strongly pro-life politicians took these positions. While checked within the CDU, abortion liberalizers, primarily women and easterners, were able to influence the 1992 abortion reform by working outside the party, with the opposition.

The Women's Union elicited only modest reforms on participation policy, even though this was perhaps the organization's most important goal during the 1990s. On this issue, a cobbled coalition with the easterners was not possible because many easterners rejected the idea of a quota or other measures to increase female participation in the CDU. Although the Women's Union had the support of the Social Committees, that auxiliary organization was crippled by inadequate leadership, internal strife, and declining membership. The sustained pressure of the Women's Union certainly contributed to the CDU's actions on participation policy. Despite being quite mobilized, however, in the absence of a stronger ally, the Women's Union managed only to convince the CDU to implement the symbolic "quorum."

The internal dynamics of a political party are a critical influence over that party's policy making. In the 1980s, when the Women's Union was in the dominant coalition, it was a key group in deciding on the party's policies. In the 1990s, however, the Women's Union had lost most of its influence over the CDU. During this period, the organization could pass only limited, one-time reforms. This loss of power within the CDU for the Women's Union had an important effect on the CDU's policy making on women's issues. Ironically, at a time when the positions of the Women's Union had become more mainstream in German society, the Women's Union was less able to get the CDU to go along with these positions.

7

The Rise of Angela Merkel

Policy and Personnel Decisions of the CDU in Unified Germany[1]

Thus far, this book has argued that the corporatist catch-all party structure shapes the CDU's approach to policy making. This chapter contends that internal party organization has also had an important effect on the selection of party leadership. A corporatist catch-all party demands a diverse leadership team. Because leadership positions within the party are inherently limited, any single person who can fill more than one internal minority slot will be highly desirable. This person's presence on the leadership team frees up another slot for a different member of the party elite.

Angela Merkel, the chair of the Christian Democratic Union (CDU), was elected Chancellor of Germany in 2005, the first woman to hold this position. The logic at work in the leadership selection process in a corporatist catch-all party can help explain the rise of Angela Merkel. At first glance Merkel, a female Protestant from the East, appears to be a poor match for the CDU, a party known for its roots in Catholic southern Germany and for its conservative ideology regarding women. Merkel's rise to power can only be understood by studying the internal party dynamics of the CDU and Merkel's leadership approach.

The CDU's corporatist catch-all party structure contributed to Merkel's initial rise to prominence. Because Merkel could be viewed as representing several internal party groups, she was a frequent choice when the CDU was selecting its leadership team. Once in office, however, Merkel proved to be a surprisingly competent politician. Her ability to make the most out of a

---

[1] An earlier (shorter) version of this chapter was published as Wiliarty (2008a.)

particular position also contributed to her quick advancement within the party. Without understanding the CDU's internal dynamics and Merkel's own leadership ability, Merkel's rise to the Chancellorship is inexplicable.

This chapter develops an explanation based on the CDU's internal dynamics and Merkel's leadership approach, the two factors responsible for her quick rise through the party. While the previous three chapters examined the CDU's policy choices over time, this chapter illustrates the contribution of the party's organization to the career of a particular politician. This shift in dependent variable necessitates a different analytical approach. To examine how the corporatist catch-all party contributes to personnel choices, the chapter investigates five critical moments in Merkel's career. Four of these moments demonstrate Merkel's success in advancing through the party hierarchy. In 1991 she became Minister for Women and Youth. In 1998 she became CDU General Secretary. In 2000 Merkel was chosen as chair of the CDU. Finally, in 2005 she became the CDU's candidate for Chancellor. The chapter also examines one failed case of advancement. In 2002 Merkel wanted to run for Chancellor, but the CDU and its sister party in Bavaria, the Christian Social Union (CSU), chose Edmund Stoiber, leader of the CSU, instead. For each of these moments, this chapter analyzes the role of the corporatist catch-all party structure and Merkel's own leadership approach. The chapter also briefly looks at developments in two of the three policy areas since 1998, work-family policy and participation policy. There have been no significant changes in abortion policy since the mid-1990s.

The structure of a corporatist catch-all party requires internal representation of a broad variety of internal party groups. As a female Protestant from the former East Germany, Merkel alone fulfilled three important internal party quotas. This fact made her a particularly desirable choice whenever internal decision-making bodies were being constituted. Protestant women have always been in short supply for the CDU. Internal party documents beginning in the 1950s are filled with suggestions for party committees that list several particular people and then note that the committee also needs a Protestant woman (Bösch 2001: 307). Merkel could not only be this missing Protestant woman, but she fulfilled the unofficial eastern quota as well.[2]

---

[2] When Germany unified in 1990, the West CDU merged with the East CDU, a smaller party that had supported the East German Communist party. The CDU made a variety of internal changes designed to integrate the two parties and to make sure that the easterners were well represented within the CDU (Bösch 2002: 134–5). The CDU did not end up forming an

LEADERSHIP IN A CORPORATIST CATCH-ALL PARTY

The second factor in explaining Merkel's rise to the top is her approach to leadership. She is a master of the party manager approach, which is particularly suited to the CDU (Clemens 1994; Clemens 1998; Ansell and Fish 1999). A corporatist catch-all party like the CDU tends to have a polycentric elite (Helms 2000). A party manager does a good job balancing internal groups against each other.

In the CDU, there are alternative paths to leadership. An obvious one would be to become the leader of an internal party suborganization. This approach almost certainly yields representation near the top. But an overly strong affiliation with a particular political tendency within the party makes achieving the position of party chair unlikely, because at the very top leaders need to appeal to all the internal party groups. Adenauer, who was not closely linked with one wing of the party, also used the party manager approach, as did Helmut Kohl (Clemens 1998; Bösch 2001: 59). Merkel has often been considered Kohl's protégé and she observed him using this approach. Merkel, like Kohl, is known for her tendency to avoid commitment to a particular policy direction until the last possible moment. At times this approach looks like indecision, but it also allows a party leader to remain connected to the various internal party groups as long as possible.

Whether through natural inclination or study of Helmut Kohl, Merkel has the right approach to leading the CDU. She did not seem to have any difficulty implementing this approach to leadership even as a woman. Party managers can have either gender. This approach is good for the party chair, but it is also effective in other positions. It would probably work for a Minister President balancing rival groups within his or her *Land*. Merkel used it effectively as Women's Minister and as Environmental Minister. In both cases, once in office, she was able to rally many groups to her cause because she did not alienate people by committing to a single internal party direction.

internal suborganization to represent eastern interests. If easterners had formed such a group, it would likely have been able to exert a greater influence over the national level of the party (Bösch 2002: 142). However, a variety of factors mitigated against such a development. Certainly the federal structure of the West CDU meant it was much more likely for each *Land* in the East to create its own regional party. Furthermore, the fact that many of the East CDU's members had links to the old regime meant that they were regarded as tainted, so much of the existing party elite was deemed ineligible for a further career in politics.

CASE STUDIES

This section examines five critical moments in Angela Merkel's career. It shows how the combination of the corporatist catch-all party structure and Merkel's leadership approach worked to advance Merkel's career.

Minister of Women and Youth: The Power of the Triple Quota

The corporatist catch-all party structure generates a need for the CDU to fulfill its internal quotas. People who meet the appropriate criteria may be able to advance quickly through the party hierarchy, especially if they fulfill more than one quota. In the context of unification, simply fulfilling a quota was often sufficient to gain a position within the party.

After the fall of the Berlin wall, Merkel, who had been working as a physicist at the Academy of Science, joined one of the new political parties in East Germany, *Demokratischer Aufbruch* (Boysen 2005: 95). She ended up working in the press office of Lothar de Maizière, the first freely elected Prime Minister of East Germany (Boysen 2005: 122). In December 1990 she was directly elected to the Bundestag. Following the election, Kohl chose Merkel as his Minister for Women and Youth.

It is surprising that someone with no political experience could become a cabinet member in just over a year's time. Some of Merkel's quick rise to power can be traced to the circumstances surrounding unification. As a corporatist catch-all party, the CDU represents important societal groups in its leadership. With the advent of unification, the party felt the need to bring some East Germans into positions that were at least symbolically important. This need created a variety of challenges, however. First, despite the euphoria of unification, politicians from West Germany were not eager to relinquish their jobs to easterners. Second, the background of many easterners proved problematic. Estimates are that over 400,000 people – approximately one in twenty-five adults – had worked in some capacity for the Stasi, the East German security police (Jarausch 1994: 35). People with links to the Stasi or to the old regime were regarded as tainted and therefore not eligible for high office in unified Germany. Those who were not tainted, however, often lacked sufficient experience to be qualified for high posts. Easterners who appeared to be innocent of a Stasi connection and who seemed minimally politically competent could advance quickly.

Kohl chose three East Germans for cabinet positions, none of them very important Ministries. Günther Krause became Minister of Transportation.

Rainer Ortleb was chosen for the Ministry of Education and Science. Merkel became Minister for Women and Youth. Of these three, only Merkel lasted the entire legislative period. Krause had to step down following a series of scandals. Ortleb resigned when the strains of attempting to adapt to life in western-style politics led to alcohol abuse and depression (Yoder 1999: 110–11). Merkel completed her term and went on to become Environmental Minister from 1994 to 1998. The CDU's internal structure generated the need for easterners to fill cabinet positions, but not all of these politicians were skilled enough to stay in office. In other words, Merkel (and people like Merkel) were more likely to get a chance at some kind of internal party office. However, once in office, her future depended on her own abilities.

Finding an eastern woman who was a possibility for a cabinet post was particularly lucky for Kohl because symbolically he needed women as well as easterners. Kohl considered nominating another eastern woman, Sabine Bergmann-Pohl, President of the Volkskammer, but changed his selection to Merkel following advice from Lothar de Maiziére and Günther Krause (Boysen 2005: 139–40). Merkel was both eastern and female. Furthermore, she was a Protestant, another under-represented group within the CDU. At the time of her advancement into the cabinet, much was made of her "triple quota" status (Schley 2005: 32).[3] Because Kohl had plucked her from relative obscurity, he could also expect her to remain loyal to him, which she did until the major campaign financing scandal broke in 1999.

After she was appointed Minister of Women and Youth, Merkel proved to be quite competent. Staying in power depends on a politician's abilities. Women and Youth is not a powerful Ministry and Merkel was unlikely to make a major splash in the position. Furthermore, because of the real differences between women in East Germany and women in West Germany, there was some chance that a political misstep could damage Merkel's political career (Stock 2005: 68).[4] Neither her predecessor, Ursula Lehr, nor her successor, Claudia Nolte, was at all successful at the Ministry. Both were chosen partially because they fulfilled internal party quotas, but they did not prove to be politically savvy.

Unlike the other easterners chosen for cabinet positions in 1990 and also unlike her predecessor and successor at the Women's Ministry,

---

[3] Actually Merkel fulfilled a *fourth* "quota" because of her youth.
[4] See Chapter 6 for more on the differences between East and West German women.

Merkel was successful in her position. According to one of her colleagues at the Ministry, Merkel viewed the position as a chance for her to prove herself (Udo Kollenberg, personal interview). She focused on issues such as preserving funding for East Germany's extensive child care network. In 1991, she successfully rounded up interim funding for East German Kindergartens to keep them going until a longer-term solution could be found (*Süddeutsche Zeitung*, September 11, 1991). She guided through a new law on equal rights (Schley 2005: 33). On abortion, one of the most politically difficult issues during her tenure at the Ministry, Merkel steered a moderate course (Kamenitsa 2001: 123–4; Boysen 2005: 156). She did not clearly have any great interest in women's issues prior to her Ministry post, but she was eager to perform well there in order to advance her career. The same Ministry colleague remarked "Angela Merkel could have been assigned to the Bat Ministry of the United Nations and she would have made something out of it" (Udo Kollenberg, personal interview). The CDU's internal dynamic helped Merkel acquire her position. Once in office, her own talent for politics allowed her to make a success of it.

General Secretary: The Advantages of the Internal Minority

The case study of the selection of Merkel for General Secretary also illustrates the advantages of being an internal minority in a corporatist catch-all party. Because a corporatist catch-all party demands a diverse leadership team, some internal party elites are eliminated from consideration for certain positions, depending on the composition of the already-existing leadership. For example, a committee with five members cannot consist of five Catholics, or five people from Berlin, or five men. When a new person is being considered for a leadership position, existing elites must take into account how the new addition will change the composition of the leadership group. While the General Secretary is a single position – and therefore not part of an obvious team – for the sake of creating balance, the General Secretary is often considered together with the position of party chair and also as part of the group of the chair's deputies.

Angela Merkel was appointed CDU General Secretary in the wake of the CDU's electoral defeat on September 27, 1998. This defeat marked a major turning point for a party that had been in office since 1982, and it resulted in a great deal of internal party shuffling. Furthermore, Helmut Kohl, party chair since 1973, resigned following the lost election. The loss of government offices and the loss of its long-time leader contributed to a moment marked by both turmoil and opportunity.[5]

Kohl announced in his resignation speech that he would like his heir apparent, Wolfgang Schäuble, to become the new party chair (Bösch 2002: 147). Schäuble was already the leader of the CDU/CSU caucus in the Bundestag and was widely respected within the CDU. Indeed, the CDU had no other leader of Schäuble's stature and despite some grumbling about Kohl's method, there was no opposition to Schäuble's taking over the party chair position. The party chair has the sole right to nominate a General Secretary for approval by the CDU's governing bodies and on October 22, Schäuble announced Merkel as his choice for the position (*Associated Press Germany*, October 22, 1998). The National Party Congress approved Schäuble as party chair and Merkel as General Secretary on November 7, 1998.

While the CDU's statutes are clear that the party chair has the right to nominate any person he or she chooses for General Secretary, structural forces within the party worked against some candidates Schäuble might have preferred and worked in favor of Merkel. One of Schäuble's closest confidantes, Hans-Peter Repnik, would have been a good candidate for the General Secretary position. However, both Schäuble and Repnik are from South Baden, and that would have given that region too much representation in the CDU leadership (*Frankfurter Allgemeine Zeitung*, October 1, 1998).

Two other possible candidates, Friedrich Merz and Volker Rühe, took themselves out of the running for General Secretary for reasons unrelated to the corporatist catch-all party structure. On October 1, 1998, the Süddeutsche Zeitung reported that Schäuble had apparently chosen Friedrich Merz as the party's new General Secretary (*Süddeutsche Zeitung*, October 1, 1998). Merz was a financial expert with parliamentary experience. He is from North Rhine-Westphalia, the largest and most important *Land*. And, at 42 years old, he was young enough for the CDU to claim him as a sign of renewal. However, Merz was not eager for the job, preferring to remain active in the parliamentary party. Volker Rühe would have been another logical choice. Although closer to Schäuble in age, he is from Hamburg in the north and could have provided regional representation. Additionally, Schäuble clearly wanted Rühe to have an important position in the CDU leadership. Because Hamburg is a small *Land*, Rühe

---

[5] See Wiliarty (2008b) for more information on how "unusual times" can help women advance in politics.

might risk not being elected if he ran for one of the vice chair positions, while he would be guaranteed election as General Secretary (*Frankfurter Allgemeine Zeitung*, October 16, 1998). But Rühe had been already been General Secretary under Kohl from 1990–92 and felt that taking the position again would be a step backwards for his career (Bösch 2002: 195). Merz and Rühe were potentially good candidates for General Secretary who signaled that they did not want the position for reasons unrelated to the argument at hand.

The implications of the corporatist catch-all party structure are well understood by actors within the party. While these initially more likely candidates were being eliminated, some actors within the CDU were pressuring for other factors to be taken into account with the appointment of the General Secretary. The CDU regional party in Saxony was quite vocal in suggesting that the new General Secretary be from the former East Germany (*Associated Press Germany*, September 30, 1998). The CDU General Secretary is responsible for running election campaigns. In both 1994 and 1998 the CDU had fared poorly in the eastern *Länder*. The former General Secretary, Peter Hintze, had run campaigns condemning the PDS, the ex-Communist party, and implying that the SPD would work together with the PDS. These campaigns were unsuccessful, however, and the CDU was losing support in the East. The idea that an easterner might run more effective campaigns in the East was compelling so that made this argument more convincing. Part of the point of a diverse leadership team is to be sure that important views are heard on the party's decision-making bodies.

The corporatist catch-all party structure increased the pressure to have someone from the East in a relatively high position within the leadership, but just being from the East was insufficient. The Saxony CDU's proposal of Arnold Vaatz, former Environmental Minister of Saxony and first-time Member of the Bundestag, was not realistic. Vaatz was too unknown and inexperienced. Indeed, the only politician from the East who could have been considered a credible General Secretary was Merkel (*Süddeutsche Zeitung*, October 16, 1998).

Female activists within the party also saw the leadership shuffle as an opportunity to increase female representation within the upper echelons of the CDU. Rita Süssmuth, former president of the Bundestag and chair of the Women's Union, was pressuring for a female General Secretary (*Stern*, October 8, 1998).[6] Süssmuth pointed out that the CDU, with just over

---

[6] Petra Roth, mayor of Frankfurt and another prominent CDU woman, also called for more women in the new CDU leadership (*Süddeutsche Zeitung*, October 12, 1998).

18 percent, had the lowest percentage of women of any party in the Bundestag. The party was not following its own internal gender "quorum." Furthermore, electoral losses among women had been particularly severe. For only the second time in its history, the CDU had done worse in 1998 with female voters than with male voters (Molitor and Neu 1999: 254). The CDU only found above average support among women over 60 (Molitor and Neu 1999: 256). Süssmuth herself was too old and had too much history to be considered for General Secretary. The CDU's outgoing Women's Minister, Claudia Nolte, was widely regarded as incompetent. Once again, Merkel was the only woman really suited for the General Secretary position.

While Merkel fit the bill in terms of being an easterner and also being female, she was turning out to be successful at winning elections and one of the primary responsibilities of the General Secretary is coordinating election campaigns. Northern Germany (Hamburg, Bremen, Schleswig-Holstein, Lower Saxony, Mecklenberg-Vorpommern) has 61 directly elected seats in the Bundestag. From the 1994 election to the 1998 election, the CDU went from holding 34 of seats to holding only 6 (Feist and Hoffman 1999: 237). One of the remaining seats was Merkel's. Furthermore, the CDU fared relatively well (or relatively less badly) in Merkel's home region, Mecklenberg-Vorpommern (where she is the head of this regional party). The CDU's result in Mecklenberg-Vorpommern was 29 percent, behind only Saxony (where the CDU is best anchored in the East). CDU also did not drop as much in Mecklenberg-Vorpommern as most places in the East. These results for Mecklenberg-Vorpommern were credited to Merkel as having done a good job organizing her home region (Feist and Hoffman 1999: 238).[7]

Schäuble nominated Merkel as his General Secretary and this choice was approved by CDU's National Party Congress in November 1998. Clearly, though, Schäuble's choice was shaped by the dynamics of the CDU's corporatist catch-all party structure. Merkel advance was aided because of criteria unrelated to her merit (being female and from the East), while her rivals were eliminated due to potential regional overrepresentation.

---

[7] While the credit cannot all go to Merkel, the CDU did do very well in the seven *Land* level elections during her tenure as General Secretary between October 1998 and October 1999 (Helms 2000: 421). In both Hesse and Saarland, the CDU enjoyed surprising victories and was able to take over the governing coalition in the *Landtag*. The CDU also led the SPD by 18 percent in elections to the European Parliament (Helms 2000: 421). Certainly Merkel must have been pleased by these results.

Party Chair: The Party Manager Approach Succeeds

An analysis of Merkel's ascension to the party chair shows again some of the ways in which the corporatist catch-all party structure can work to favor internal party minorities. We see again how other actors were deemed ineligible for the position of party chair because of the composition of existing leadership. This case study shows Merkel's use of the party manager approach (and also shows her one deviation from that approach). Merkel was able to obtain the position of party chair partly because she did not stick her neck out to campaign for it and partly because she had maintained a good relationship with many sections of the CDU. She also used the powers of the General Secretary position to orchestrate a context that increased her chances of being chosen.

In April 2000 Merkel was officially elected chair of the CDU at the national party congress in Leipzig. The position of chair became available when Schäuble resigned on February 16, 2000, because he was implicated in the campaign finance scandal that reverberated through the CDU in late 1999 and early 2000. Schäuble's resignation left two positions vacant: party chair and leader of the parliamentary group. In the wake of Schäuble's departure, there was widespread agreement on two points. First, the positions should be held by different people (because no one of Schäuble's stature was available to fill both of them). Second, Friedrich Merz quickly emerged as the consensus choice for the parliamentary leadership position (Stock 2005: 142–3). Filling the party chair position was significantly more controversial. Factors linked to both the party's internal structure and Merkel's leadership approach led to her emergence as the sole candidate by late March 2000.

The party structure of the CDU influenced the choice of a new party chair in at least three ways. First, as a corporatist catch-all party and a federal party, the CDU has strong tendencies toward a polycentric elite (Helms 2000: 421). CDU Minister Presidents, leaders of CDU *Land* organizations, and leaders of CDU suborganizations all provide potential people for the position of party chair. Rüttgers, Rühe, Vogel, Biedenkopf, and Merkel were all potential candidates for the party chair position. The multiplicity of candidates did not necessarily work in favor or against Merkel.

Given the CDU's internal structure, the party strives to maintain some kind of balance at the top. While perfect balance need not be achieved, there is a clear precedent of having a diverse leadership team. This structure worked in Merkel's favor for two reasons. First, the choice of Merz as parliamentary leader meant the party already had someone at the top from the important *Land* of North Rhine-Westphalia. One of Merkel's primary rivals for the chair, Jürgen Rüttgers, was thus effectively eliminated because he was also from North Rhine-Westphalia (*Associated Press Germany*, February 16, 2000). Having both Merz and Rüttgers at the top would overrepresent that region.

The second reason the internal structure worked in Merkel's favor is she was unlikely to have the same problem as Rüttgers. There were no other women and no other Easterners in serious contention for the party chair. Two of Merkel's rivals were Minister Presidents in the eastern *Länder*, Bernhard Vogel and Kurt Biedenkopf. But they were both originally from the west and were not regarded as representative of eastern views. As the only Easterner and the only woman in the upper echelons of the party, Merkel would make the party leadership more diverse regardless of which position she took on.

While the internal party structure contributed to Merkel's gaining the chair of the CDU, her own actions in this regard were also critically important. Merkel did not create the party finance scandal, of course, but she did take advantage of the opportunity it presented. In December 1999 she placed an article in the *Frankfurter Allgemeine Zeitung* criticizing Kohl and calling on the party to break ties with him. Merkel was the first CDU leader to distance herself from Kohl (Langguth 2005: 200).[8] Her actions won her the loyalty of the party's grassroots activists who were thoroughly disgusted with Kohl. This action does not fit with the tenets of the party manager approach because Merkel was in the vanguard on this issue. However, her risk clearly paid off. Perhaps she understood the party finance scandal as a once in a lifetime opportunity and was willing to break with her usual method in order to take advantage of it.

Merkel also used her position as General Secretary to create an environment that would highlight her leadership ability. As General Secretary, Merkel took a leading role in calling a series of seven regional conferences for the early spring of 2000, ostensibly to discuss the finance scandal (Stock 2005: 144). The meetings, however, turned into a series of plebiscites on the future leadership of the party and Merkel emerged as the clear choice of the conference delegates (Langguth 2005: 204–5).

---

[8] Merkel had already written the article when she called Karl Feldmeyer, an editor at the *Frankfurter Allgemeine Zeitung*, to offer it to him. Within five minutes, she had faxed it to him. The article was clearly Merkel's initiative (Langguth 2005: 201).

During the critical weeks in February and March 2000, Merkel kept with the classic technique of the party manager: wait-and-see. Merkel's wait-it-out strategy served her brilliantly. As more and more internal party actors began advocating for Merkel as the new party chair, she remained cagey about whether she would run at all (Stock 2005: 143). By letting others in the party suggest her for the party chair, she avoided confrontation (Boysen 2005: 218). Had she openly declared her candidacy, she might have become a target for criticism. As it was, she did get some criticism, particularly from the CSU, but in the absence of a definitive candidacy, this remained somewhat superficial (*Neue Züricher Zeitung*, February 19, 2000). In the meantime, various actors in the party began openly asking her to run. Because Merkel had maintained ties to a variety of groups within the party, many internal party actors supported her. Also, she could be a reasonable compromise candidate or second choice for those internal party actors who did not prefer her. The combination of the corporatist catch-all party structure plus Merkel's approach to leadership (plus the surprise development of the party's financial scandal) helped her gain the position of party chair.

Chancellor Candidate in 2002 (failed)

The influence of the corporatist catch-all party seems to affect even positions filled by a single person such as party chair or General Secretary. Although these positions cannot be filled by a balanced leadership team, they are considered together with other party positions, such as the party chair's deputies and the leader of the parliamentary caucus, in an effort to provide a diverse leadership. This logic does not hold for the choice of Chancellor candidate, however. The selection of a Chancellor candidate depends more on the perception of the candidate's ability to win, support from within the party, and the relationship with the CDU's sister party, the CSU.

The importance of being an effective party manager does influence the selection of the Chancellor candidate. If the Christian Democrats do not hold the Chancellorship, then the choice of candidate is likely to be contentious, both because the CDU itself has a polycentric elite and because the Chancellor candidate represents both the CDU and the CSU. In this scenario, a successful party manager approach is critical. It is important for a potential Chancellor candidate to maintain ties across the party. It is also advantageous to refrain from openly declaring oneself to be running for Chancellor candidate. Open candidacies are likely to be the target of internal party criticism.[9] A successful approach, then, is one in which calls for the potential candidate to run for Chancellor emerge from across the party's internal political spectrum – without the potential candidate appearing to orchestrate these events.

Edmund Stoiber, chair of the CSU, and Merkel, chair of the CDU, both signaled their interest in running as the Christian Democratic Chancellor candidate for the 2002 elections. In mid-January 2002, Merkel yielded to Stoiber in the context of extreme internal party pressure for her to do so. This section will explain why Merkel's attempt to become the Chancellor candidate failed.

The CDU does not have clear selection procedures for choosing a Chancellor candidate. When an obvious candidate is not available, then the problem arises that the CDU has a sister party, the Christian Social Union (CSU), which exists only in Bavaria. Who should be the Chancellor candidate: The chair of the CDU or the chair of the CSU? This problem has come up before, as discussed in Chapter 4, but no decision-making procedure has been institutionalized (Bösch 2002: 155). The sister parties confronted this problem again in 2002.

As chair of the CDU, by far the larger party, Merkel had some advantages over her rival, Edmund Stoiber, chair of the CSU and Minister President of Bavaria. Merkel had a "clean hands" image, having been helped to prominence through her willingness to condemn Kohl's behavior in the party financing scandal. Furthermore, as General Secretary she had overseen a series of electoral victories at the *Land* level, evidence that she could oversee a good campaign.

As Minister President of Bavaria, Stoiber had a major advantage. Many CDU Chancellors have advanced to the national level after having proved themselves as leader of a *Land*. Minister Presidents are thought to make better Chancellor candidates (Langguth 2005: 226). While Bavarian origins are sometimes a disadvantage in the rest of Germany, Stoiber was well respected for his competence in security policy and economic policy. Throughout the fall and winter of 2001/2002, the question of who would be the Christian Democratic candidate heated up. Public opinion surveys showed clear evidence that Stoiber was more likely to beat Schröder, the sitting Chancellor (*Süddeutsche Zeitung*, January 7, 2002). A clear majority of CDU regional elites also backed Stoiber (*Agence France Press*, January 5, 2002).

---

[9] For an opposing view on the possible advantages of an early declaration of the desire to run for Chancellor see Bösch (2002: 155).

Internal party dynamics did not help Merkel in her quest for the Chancellor candidacy. She also did not use the party manager approach of waiting it out. Instead, Merkel actively pursued the chance to run for Chancellor. Merkel was more open about her candidacy than Stoiber was (Langguth 2005: 225). She was also stubborn about giving up even when the cards appeared stacked against her (Langguth 2005: 228). This approach may have been less successful than the technique of refusing to state whether she was running or not.

By early January 2002, it was clear that a significant majority of CDU Minister Presidents opposed Merkel's candidacy (Langguth 2005: 229). Merkel arranged for a secret breakfast meeting with Stoiber, at his home, for the two of them to decide who would be the candidate (Stock 2005: 174). Merkel announced later that day that Stoiber would run as the Christian Democratic Chancellor candidate. Stoiber lost to Gerhard Schröder in September 2002.

Merkel has often benefited from being a coveted outsider in a party that feels obligated to represent outsiders. The need to present a diverse leadership group even influenced the CDU's choices of General Secretary and party chair. Although these positions had to be filled with a single person, the CDU made efforts to present a balanced slate by considering other positions, such as vice chairs and parliamentary leadership. These efforts did not extend to the choice of a Chancellor candidate, however. Instead other factors, such as support from regional leaders (Langguth 2005: 227) and results of public opinion polls, mattered more in the selection of the candidate. In attempting to be selected as Christian Democratic Chancellor candidate, the party's internal structure did not help Merkel. Furthermore, she did not use the party manager approach to advance her cause.

Chancellor Candidate 2005

On May 22, 2005, the SPD lost a regional election to the CDU in North Rhine-Westphalia. North Rhine-Westphalia, the most populous of the *Länder*, had long been dominated by the Social Democrats and this loss was a serious blow. In an effort to discipline his own party and gain support for some of his reform proposals, Chancellor Gerhard Schröder called a motion of confidence and asked his party to vote against him in order to trigger new elections. Despite some doubts on the constitutionality of this maneuver, the SPD went along with it and new elections were planned for the fall. By late May, 2005, the CDU and the CSU had agreed on Merkel as the Christian Democratic Chancellor candidate.

What was different in 2005 when compared with 2002? As noted previously, the need for internal balancing does not apply to Chancellor candidates. However, Merkel's leadership within the CDU – and with regard to the CSU – had been strengthened in several ways since 2002. Some of the difference is surely that by 2005, Stoiber had already run against Schröder and lost. It was Merkel's turn to see if she could beat him. Another important difference is that the elections were called unexpectedly in 2005. Merkel's rivals had no time to generate support for themselves or opposition to her. These factors were not things that Merkel had control over.

On the other hand, Merkel had improved her position within the CDU – and in relation to the CSU – since 2002. In the wake of the 2002 electoral defeat, Merkel was able to take over the parliamentary party leadership from Friedrich Merz. It is rumored that she made Stoiber's support for this change a condition for her withdrawal from the earlier candidacy for Chancellor (Langguth 2005: 238). This position is critical because it implies leadership of both the CDU and the CSU. The CDU had also enjoyed additional success at the *Land* level, which continued to add to Merkel's credibility. Merkel was also able to have her choice for Bundespresident, Horst Köhler, emerge victorious, which contributed to her being chosen as Chancellor candidate (*tageszeitung*, June 1, 2004). Gaining support for Köhler involved getting the backing of the CSU as well as the CDU. In 2005, Merkel was also doing better in public opinion polls than Stoiber. Furthermore, the CDU regional leaders were backing her candidacy instead of his (*Der Spiegel*, October 23, 2004).

MERKEL IN POWER: THE SURPRISING ROLE OF GENDER

Merkel's ability to represent three internal groups and her wait-and-see approach to party management helped her quickly ascend the ladder of party power. How did Merkel's actions once in power, both as chair of the CDU and as Chancellor, affect policy making on the issues under consideration here? Did it matter that the party chair and then Chancellor was female? The changes in abortion policy since Merkel became chair of the CDU have been minor. The following sections examine gender quotas and work-family policy since 1998.

No Real Quota but a Girls Camp

As discussed in Chapter 6, the CDU does not have a gender quota, but it does have a rule the party calls a quorum. The CDU has generally fulfilled the quorum for high profile national offices, but the party has been less successful at doing so at the *Land* level and below. The *Länder* also show a great deal of variation in achieving a leadership that is one third female (Davidson-Schmich 2006: 216–17). Despite criticism of its lack of teeth, the quorum has certainly helped increase the number of women in leadership within the CDU even though the party has not reached its goal of one third (McKay 2004: 71). Leaders within the Women's Union also believe that the quorum has significantly increased the power of their organization (Elke Holzapfel, personal interview).

The quorum had been put in place initially for a five year trial period, which meant that the CDU had to address the question of whether or not to renew it. Even though withdrawing the quorum would have created quite a stir, it appeared in the summer of 2001 that there was no majority in the party for extending it (*Die Welt*, July 2, 2001). According to the business manager of the Women's Union, at the National Party Congress in December 2001 where the vote was to take place, the Women's Union helped arrange the speakers' list for the debate to highlight those speaking in favor of the quorum and in particular, to find men to advocate for the extension of the quorum (Claudia Hassenbach, personal interview). Merkel also pushed to renew the quorum (*Süddeutsche Zeitung*, December 5, 2001). It was extended indefinitely.

One criticism of gender quotas has been that they have increased the number of women in formal positions of power, but they have not been able to affect women's access to positions of informal power. A Chancellor or other leader has designated deputies and he or she must consult with them, but real decision making may take place in some other arena. Given that these informal channels of decision making have been a last bastion of male political power, it is ironic that they are often referred to as the "kitchen cabinet." Gender quotas can definitely change the percentage of women sitting in parliament or on a party's National Executive Committee, but they have not been as effective at increasing women's presence in the kitchen cabinet.

Having Merkel as chair of the CDU, however, has made a significant difference in the kind of access that women have to informal channels of political power. Somewhat jokingly called the "Girls Camp," her closest advisors during much of her first term as Chancellor were Beate Baumann, her office manager, and Eva Christiansen, her press secretary (Schley 2005: 55). This trio has determined who will have access to the Chancellor, assessed the political situation, and gone shopping together to decide what Merkel will wear for an audience with the Pope (*Stern*,

August 14, 2003). While it is true that Merkel's advisors are no longer solely female, Baumann and Christiansen are not the only women in the inner circle. Other close advisors include Annette Schavan, Minister for Education and Research, Hildegard Müller, former chair of the Young Union, and Ursula von der Leyen, Minister for Families, Seniors, Women, and Youth (Schley 2005: 55). The quorum is not forcing the CDU to have women occupy one third of all positions, but that may not matter when the Kanzlerin's kitchen cabinet is so heavily female.[10]

In leading up to the final case study, it is worth noting that both Hildegard Müller and Eva Christiansen had babies while working for Merkel. Both took time off and returned to political office.[11] Ursula Heinen, the chair of CDU/CSU's parliamentary women's caucus, also has young children. These advisors are not just *Powerfrauen*. These are *Powermüttis*.

Germany's New Parental Leave Policy

The final case study examines a major change in Germany's parental leave law. The new law was passed in 2006 and went into effect January 1, 2007. The Social Democratic-Green coalition had made a number of changes to the parental leave law as it existed in the mid-1990s. By 1998, when the Christian Democrats left national office, parents (either mothers or fathers) were entitled to three years of leave with an employment guarantee. For the first two years, the parent on leave also received an income-tested benefit of up to 300 euros a month. This policy package was clearly in line with the values of a Christian Democratic or corporatist welfare state regime (Esping-Andersen 1990, Bussemaker and van Kersbergen 1999).

The Social Democratic-Green coalition made a number of changes in parental leave policy when it was in office from 1998 to 2005. The law passed under this coalition gave parents a choice of 12 months of parental leave paid at 450 euros a month or 24 months of leave paid 300 euros a month. Everyone received the money for 6 months and after that it was means-tested. The leave was made more flexible in a variety of ways. Parents could take leave simultaneously; parents could work up to 30 hours a week (instead of only 19 under the previous policy); and parents

---

[10] That is not to claim that Merkel has no male advisors. She certainly does: Volker Kauder, Matthias Graf von Kielmannsegg, Peter Hintze, and Willi Hausmann to name a few (Schley 2005: 57–8). The point is that she *does* have an unusually high number of close informal female advisors.

[11] Müller subsequently left to work for an employers' organization.

could put off some of the leave until any time up to the child's eighth birthday. The leave had mixed goals: promoting flexibility; encouraging shorter leave times, especially for mothers, but also reducing the number of leave-takers. The income-limits were initially raised in 2000 and then significantly reduced in 2004 (Leitner, Ostner, and Schmitt 2008: 196). The Social Democratic-Green policy had elements of both Social Democratic and Christian Democratic welfare state regimes.

The new parental leave law, passed in 2007 by the Christian Democratic-Social Democratic coalition, explicitly acknowledges and encourages women's labor force participation. The new law allows one parent to stay home for 12 months and be paid at 67 percent of his or her previous salary. Monthly payments are capped at 1800 euros (Bundesministerium für Familie, Senioren, Frauen und Jugend 2006). The move to wage replacement rather than flat rate payments marks a paradigm shift in parental leave policy. This change acknowledges the importance of women's incomes and women's careers. Furthermore, if the other parent, generally the father, also takes time off, then he can receive an additional two months, also at 67 percent wage replacement. Everyone is eligible for a monthly payment of 300 euros, but any additional payments are linked to a prior relationship with the work force. It is estimated that this new policy will cost 4 billion euros a year (*Frankfurter Rundschau*, April 22, 2006).

Parental leave policies such as this one, which emphasize wage replacement and a connection to the labor force, are much more commonly seen in countries that are considered Social Democratic welfare state regimes (Esping-Anderson 1990). Furthermore, this type of policy is generally passed by Social Democratic parties. Christian Democratic parties have favored longer leaves at much lower monthly payments that tend to motivate women to stay home with their children rather than to engage in paid labor.

Although this policy was originally formulated by the SPD and was part of the Social Democrats' electoral campaign, since the Christian Democrats and the Social Democrats signed their coalition agreement in 2005, parental leave policy has been the prestige project of the Christian Democratic Family Minister, Ursula von der Leyen. Von der Leyen took enormous political heat for her proposal. The bonus father months in particular were severely criticized (*Der Spiegel*, April 13, 2006; *tageszeitung*, April 27, 2006). The left wing of the SPD accused von der Leyen of being insufficiently socially minded because under the new policy benefits are linked to income (*Der Spiegel*, April 13, 2006). This means that wealthier families will receive higher monthly payments than less well-off families. Some Christian Democrats attacked the new policy because it aims at supporting working mothers, not housewives (*ddp*, March 12, 2006). These Christian Democrats view von der Leyen (correctly) as trying to change the party's image of the family. Even though this began as an SPD policy, it is now very clearly the domain of the CDU and of Ursula von der Leyen in particular.

There are several reasons that parental leave reform became a priority in the 2005 legislative period. As has been pointed out elsewhere, the extent to which this reform represents a paradigmatic shift means that approaches such as comparative social policy or historical institutionalism, which tend to focus on continuity, will be less able to explain recent reforms in German family policy (von Wahl 2008). Instead, political leadership was a crucial factor in passing these reforms.

According to senior Ministry officials, the successive leaders of the Family Ministry, Renate Schmidt (SPD) and Ursula von der Leyen (CDU), were both critical to the passage of the new parental leave law (Malte Ristau-Winkler; Eva Maria Welskop-Deffaa, personal interviews). Both women moved their respective parties in the direction of supporting the reform. For the SPD, this meant moving away from the 1968 critical vision of the family, which saw the family as an institution that oppressed women. For the CDU, the change meant acknowledging that many mothers worked outside the home. For both parties, the combination of the new parental leave law and the expansion of child care for children under three meant accepting that young children would be cared for outside of the family (Malte Ristau-Winkler, personal interview).[12] That Ursula von der Leyen followed Renate Schmidt in office – and that the two Ministers found common ground – meant that the reforms begun under the Red-Green coalition could continue under the Grand Coalition after the 2005 election (Malte Ristau-Winkler, personal interview).

The Family Ministry took additional actions to facilitate the passage of the reforms. Particularly through the preparation of the Seventh Family

---

[12] In its efforts to pass the new law, the Family Ministry generally stressed comparisons with France and Sweden, countries with higher fertility rates, higher test scores for children, greater maternal satisfaction, and countries which are favored vacation destinations for Germans. Comparisons with East Germany were generally downplayed because the quality of child care under the German Democratic Republic was viewed as low (Malte Ristau-Winkler, personal interview). Within the Women's Union, however, conversations between women from the East and women from the West were helpful in convincing the westerners that the new policy was a good idea (Elke Holzapfel, personal interview).

Report, the Ministry held wide-ranging discussions with relevant societal actors about possible reforms. Through these discussions, it was discovered that there was significant support for the proposed reforms. For example, even though the *Familienbund der Katholiken* opposed the new parental leave money, the other two major Catholic groups (the *Zentralkomitee der deutschen Katholiken* and the *Katholische Frauenverbände*) both supported it, as did Bishop Wolfgang Huber, the Chairman of the Council of the Evangelical Church in Germany (Eva Maria Welskop-Deffaa, personal interview). In preparing the legislation for the parental leave money and the child care expansion, the Family Ministry was also able to secure the support of the business community, important actors within the political parties (such as Roland Koch), and the backing of the Finance Ministry (Malte Ristau-Winkler, personal interview). Therefore, although the quite severe criticism from Joachim Meisner, Archbishop of Cologne, and Walter Mixa, Bishop of Augsburg, received a great deal of media attention, the reforms were supported by important religious and economic actors. The Ministry's preparations also revealed the extreme dissatisfaction of German mothers (especially working mothers) when compared with other mothers in Europe (Malte Ristau-Winkler, personal interview).

Ursula von der Leyen herself also played a critical role in getting the reforms enacted. As a working mother of seven children, von der Leyen represented a new vision for the CDU. Von der Leyen has consistently been the second most popular politician in Germany, behind Chancellor Merkel. She has enormous support in German society, as do her reforms. She was able to take a lead role and is definitely the person most associated with these new policies. She has also proved to be an astute politician, able to win a variety of supporters from within and outside of the CDU.

In keeping with her party manager approach to leadership, Merkel herself did not lead the charge on the new parental leave policy. In fact, several newspapers noted Merkel's lack of participation throughout most of the debate (*Associated Press Germany*, April 19, 2006). Merkel allowed most of the arguing over the new law to happen before she made any comment at all. The debate began seriously in early January 2006 and Merkel took her first public stand in April (*Stuttgarter Nachrichten*, April 20, 2006). Even then, she did not comment on her preference regarding the father months, the most controversial section of the new law. Later, once a compromise on the father months was nearly reached, Merkel came out strongly in support of her Family Minister. The new parental leave policy was approved by the Bundestag in fall 2006. The new and controversial law that radically reshaped a policy area was passed with apparently little input from the Chancellor. Of course, Merkel selected von der Leyen as Minister in the first place and von der Leyen's plans for parental leave policy were well known. In typical party manager style, Merkel managed to stay above the fray of internal party controversy.

CONCLUSION

Merkel's achievements should not be labeled a fluke or a coincidence (Thompson and Lennartz 2006). It also does not seem appropriate to call Merkel an "honorary man" (Mushaben 2006). Her rise in power has been at least partially *because* of her gender, and not in spite of it. Furthermore, she has brought significant numbers of women to power with her and she is passing important policies with a feminist slant. Certainly the women's movement has had an important influence in reframing ideas about gender and power in Germany. Gender quotas and other instruments for party competition over women's votes have also helped reshape the political environment (Ferree 2006). While these explanations can help us understand why *some* woman might be able to rise to the position of German Chancellor, however, they cannot help us explain why that woman would be a Christian Democrat. The CDU and the SPD seem to have embarked on a type of arms race to see who can do and spend the most on family policy. But to understand the *CDU's* participation in this arms race, we need to understand the party's internal party dynamics and Merkel's leadership approach.

In corporatist catch-all parties where a diverse leadership team matters, it can be extremely helpful for individual leaders to represent one or more marginal groups. Opportunities for Angela Merkel repeatedly opened up because the CDU needed to represent either women or easterners in the upper echelons of the party. Furthermore, leaders from marginal groups are much less likely to be "blocked" because their group is already represented in the party's leadership. The corporatist catch-all party structure can facilitate the ability of internal minorities to rise to power.

Second, the advantages of representing marginal groups do not extend all the way to the top. Somewhat surprisingly, Merkel's marginal status was helpful even in attaining offices that must be filled by a single person, such as the General Secretary position or the party chair. However, when it came to the chance to run for Chancellor, Merkel's marginality did not help her and possibly hurt her. For this position, popularity among the electorate and CDU elites, and internal party power were the factors that mattered most.

In terms of leadership approach, there are two important insights for scholars of women and politics in particular. First, while having more women in politics and in particular more female role models are certainly noble goals, we should not lose sight of the fact that men can also act as role models and mentors for women. Kohl regarded Merkel as his protégé and helped advance her career. While his habit of referring to her as "the girl" was not particularly empowering, it did not seem to affect her ability to advance through the ranks of the CDU, nor her ability to eventually break with her former mentor.

Finally, this research points to the need for further research into Merkel's actions on "women's issues." Prior to becoming Minister for Women and Youth, Merkel had shown no particular interest in women's issues. Yet she correctly perceived her time at the Ministry as a stepping stone to higher office. As Women's Minister she acted to preserve some of the child care available in East Germany. As Chancellor she oversaw a paradigmatic change in parental leave policy. Merkel's Family Minister, Ursula von der Leyen, sparked a new debate with her proposal for a tripling of the available child care for children under the age of three. Merkel has been a moderating influence on abortion and she oversaw the permanent extension of the CDU's gender quorum. While Merkel claims not to be a feminist, feminist activists may welcome many of Merkel's policy reforms. Certainly Christian Democratic women believe that she is helping them achieve their policy goals (personal interview, Doris Pack).

8

Christian Democracy with and without Corporatism

Policy Making on Women's Issues in Austria, Italy, and the Netherlands

This book has argued that the German CDU's response to women was defined primarily by party organization and internal alliances. I tested this argument by pitting it against rival hypotheses in explaining CDU policies toward women over a thirty-year period. This chapter adds a comparison across countries to the comparisons across time and policy. Like the German CDU, Christian Democratic parties in Austria, the Netherlands and Italy have confronted new demands from women over the past thirty years. Like the German CDU, the Austrian People's Party (ÖVP) is a corporatist catch-all party in which women are represented. The Dutch Christian Democratic Party, the CDA, has only a weakly developed corporatist catch-all party structure. It is not as well developed as the CDU's or the ÖVP's. Furthermore, the women's organization of the CDA is a weak actor within the party without the power to select its own leadership. The Italian Christian Democratic Party can be regarded as a corporatist catch-all party because it did ensure representation of its internal factions. Despite some debate on the question, newer scholarship concludes that these factions were linked to policy directions. The Italian Party (the DC) had a women's organization, called the Women's Movement, but it was not a powerful player within the party.

As our central hypothesis would lead us to expect, the particular vision of Christian Democratic women has made substantially less headway in Italy and the Netherlands than it has in either Germany or Austria. Both the German and Austrian parties have quota-like mechanisms, though neither has a hard-core quota. The Italian and Dutch Christian Democrats did not go beyond vague recommendations to get more women into political office. Both Germany and Austria have long, paid parental leaves. Parental leaves in Italy and the Netherlands are much shorter and in the Dutch case, unpaid. For abortion policy, the policy outcome is more complicated because nonparty actors have often been highly influential. Despite these differential outcomes, however, Christian Democratic women's organizations were important actors in both Germany and Austria. In Italy and the Netherlands, they were not.

The chapter examines each country in turn. Each section gives an overview of the party system and the internal organization of the Christian Democratic Party in particular, before analyzing how policies in each of the three policy areas were passed.[1]

AUSTRIA

For most of the postwar period, Austria had two large political parties, the Social Democrats (SPÖ) and the Austrian People's Party (Christian Democrats, ÖVP), as well as a smaller third party, the Freedom Party (FPÖ). While both the Social Democrats and the People's Party have governed alone and in coalition with the Freedom Party, the most frequent coalition arrangement has been a grand coalition of the Social Democrats and the People's Party governing together. After a conservative interlude from 2000 to 2007, when Austria was governed by the Christian Democrats and the Freedom Party, the Grand Coalition of Social Democrats and Christian Democrats re-formed in January 2007.

Like the CDU, the ÖVP is a corporatist catch-all party. The Austrian People's Party has both regional suborganizations and functional suborganizations. The regional suborganizations are based on the Austrian federal states, also called *Länder* (Müller 1997: 266). Regional suborganizations have been increasingly powerful since the 1980s, particularly in those *Länder* where the People's Party dominated the regional government (Müller 1997: 275).

The original three functional suborganizations, called the Leagues (*Bünde*), are the Austrian League of Workers and Employees, the Austrian Farmers' League, and the Austrian Business League. These three suborganizations are exceptionally powerful within the party. In fact, the People's Party was founded by representatives of the three original Leagues (Pelinka and Rosenberger 2003: 145). The original three Leagues

---

[1] In these shadow case studies, I do not investigate the question of dominant versus cobbled coalitions.

have enormous power over personnel and policy decisions. The Leagues also have the traditional right of filling a certain number of slots on the party's electoral lists and in other decision-making arenas within the party. While it is possible to join the People's Party directly, nearly all members first join one of the three Leagues (Müller and Steininger 1994: 88). In the 1970s, three other suborganizations, the Austrian Women's Movement, the Austrian Senior Citizens' League and the Young People's Party, were given formally equal status to the original three Leagues. In reality, however, the original three Leagues remain much more powerful than the three newcomers.

In comparison with the CDU, representation of women within the Austrian People's Party is more complicated. Like the CDU, the Austrian People's Party's women's organization, the Austrian Women's Movement, represents all women within the party. However, the three main Leagues each also have a suborganization for women and the groups within the Leagues have significant power over policy making. Depending on the issue, the various suborganizations for women may cooperate or be in conflict with each other.[2]

Austria legalized abortion during the first trimester in 1974. While this legislation was passed by a coalition consisting of the SPÖ and the FPÖ, after an initial failed attempt to repeal the law, objections from the ÖVP have been minimal. The Austrian Women's Movement, along with the ÖVP's internal organization for youth, was a critical actor in convincing the party to be more open to liberalizing reform on abortion. Both the Austrian Women's Movement and the women's suborganization of the League of Workers and Employees shaped the new child care leave policy passed in 2001. The Austrian Women's Movement pushed for the expansion of eligibility so that this benefit would cover housewives as well as employees. They also helped override internal objections that the policy was too expensive while the women of the League of Workers and Employees got the earnings limit while on leave raised. The ÖVP did not adopt a formal gender quota, but the Women's Movement did succeed in having a quota added to the party's Basic Program, a document used in electoral campaigns. This is a stronger position than Christian Democrats in either Italy or the Netherlands achieved. On all three issues, then, the Austrian Women's Movement played an important role in shaping party policy.

---

[2] Information about the Austrian Women's Movement is drawn from Rosenberger (1990) as well as sources cited here.

Abortion

On the abortion issue, the Austrian Women's Movement was a moderating force on the ÖVP's position. The party started from a quite conservative standpoint. The Austrian Women's Movement pushed the ÖVP to liberalize its position on abortion, laying the groundwork for an eventual peaceful settlement on the issue.

From 1938 to 1945 Austria was part of the Third Reich. During this time period, abortion was legal to save the life of the mother or for eugenic reasons (Köpl 2001: 18). After the war, the Nazi-formulated eugenic indication was removed and abortion law reverted back to the 1934 law, which allowed abortion only for medical emergencies. Legally, this law was a grey zone because it did not adequately clarify medical emergency (Mesner 1994: 34). Furthermore, in the immediate postwar period, the occupying army committed large numbers of rapes. Abortion was generally permitted for a pregnancy resulting from rape, though this practice does not seem to have been set down as policy and in these cases a medical indication was often given as justifying the abortion (Mesner 1994: 40–4).

The Austrian parliament passed abortion reform in 1974. The new law legalized abortion during the first trimester provided the pregnant woman consented to the procedure, consulted with a doctor, and the abortion was performed by a doctor (Lehner 1994: 5). After the first trimester, abortion is not punishable (even though it is still illegal) if the mother's life or health is in danger, if the child is likely to be born with serious birth defects, or if the woman is under 14 years of age (Lehner 1994: 5).

The new law was soon challenged through a political instrument known as a People's Initiative. With a People's Initiative, organizers can force parliament to consider a bill if they gather 100,000 signatures within one week (Köpl 2001). Antiabortion forces quickly gathered more than the requisite number of signatures, but the parliament refused to change the law. Since that time, abortion has been nearly a nonissue in Austria.[3]

---

[3] Abortion is not covered by the national health insurance, however. Abortions are also not available in many state-run hospitals, especially those in regions governed by the Christian Democrats. While lack of funding and lack of availability definitely act as constraints on a woman seeking an abortion, nonetheless, the procedure is readily available in Vienna. In a country the size of Austria, the lack of abortion clinics in the countryside is certainly a drawback, but not a major difficulty. Indeed, women have traveled from Germany to Austria in order to obtain abortions. While exact figures are not available, there is consensus that the abortion rate in Austria is high when compared to the international average (Lehner 1994: 8). The Austrians had a debate about RU-486 in the 1990s, but their liberal abortion law remains in place and is not the subject of serious controversy.

During the 1960s there was a fair amount of discussion of abortion reform. A proposal to allow consideration of social and economic factors when deciding the legality of abortion failed when the coalition government that was investigating the issue fell in 1966 (Köpl 2001: 21). From 1966 to 1970 the Austrian People's Party governed alone. The ÖVP proposed a more restrictive abortion law, but then tabled it when it became clear that the parties needed more time for internal discussion (Mesner 1994: 168).

The ÖVP began to shift its position in the early 1970s. In 1970 the political situation in Austria changed completely when the Social Democratic Party (SPÖ) won the elections. The SPÖ had an absolute majority and was therefore able to govern alone for the first time since World War II. This shift in the political power dynamics opened the door to much more sweeping change on the abortion issue. The SPÖ initially proposed a bill that would allow for abortions without punishment for social reasons, as well as medical and eugenic ones, in other words, a greatly expanded indications model (Köpl 2001: 22). In a context of a society that was secularizing and interested in more liberal positions on moral issues, even the Austrian People's Party and the Catholic Church signaled interested in liberalizing access to abortion (Mesner 1994: 183). At first it appeared that some kind of compromise among all three major parties was possible and indeed likely. Before any action could be taken, however, forces on the left mobilized in favor of a more far-reaching reform.

In the fall of 1971 a new organization, the *Aktionskomitee für die Abschaffung des §144* (Action Committee for the Repeal of §144), began advocating in favor of full decriminalization (Köpl 2001: 22). Formerly, the SPÖ approached the issue of abortion reform as a matter of social justice. Even when it was illegal, the well-off could get access to abortion, whereas poorer women could not. Reform, therefore, was about class equality. For the *Aktionskomitee*, however, abortion reform was about women's emancipation. The women's organization of the SPÖ quickly incorporated this change of viewpoint and began advocating for it within the party (Köpl 2001: 23).

At the national party conference in 1972, the SPÖ changed from supporting an expanded indications model to supporting the time limit model. Both the *Aktionskomitee* and the SPÖ's women's organization favored a more liberal approach to abortion reform than party leaders had initially proposed. Many local and regional groups had written Christian Broda, the Social Democratic Minister of Justice, to support the time limit model and declare their intentions to offer an amendment at the party's national conference (Mesner 1994: 194). Given the extent of the internal party conflict, the SPÖ leaders signed on to the time limit model. With an absolute majority in parliament, the SPÖ quickly formulated a bill, which passed in 1974 (implemented 1975). This legislation withstood both a constitutional challenge in Austria's Supreme Court and the People's Initiative just discussed. It remains the law of the land.

Because the SPÖ was governing alone at the time of this debate, most of the actions that resulted in legal change occurred within or in relation to the Social Democratic Party. However, the Austrian People's Party was also undergoing internal change on the issue of abortion. In the context of the electoral defeat of 1970, the People's Party was rethinking its position on a variety of issues. Party leaders believed that following the moral course of the Catholic Church was no longer a path that would successfully win elections. The Christian Democrats signed on to legislation changing the crimes of homosexuality and adultery from felonies to misdemeanors, openly breaking with the church on these issues (Mesner 1994: 181).

The women's organization of the ÖVP was a key actor in getting the party to shift its position on abortion (Mesner 1994: 187). Particularly the Viennese branch of this organization and its leader, Marga Hubinek, worked to get the People's Party to shift its position to allow for backing a more liberal abortion reform. Both the women's organization and the party's youth organization agitated on behalf of supporting the SPÖ government's original proposal (an expanded indications model) (Mesner 1994: 198). A group of young women, primarily students, within the ÖVP's women's organization was particularly active in changing the party's position.

The ÖVP began to shift its position even prior to elections in 1971, but its electoral loss certainly sped up the party's willingness to be open to abortion reform (Mesner 1994: 198). Urged on by the women's organization, the party signaled its willingness to sign on to eugenic and ethical (rape) indications as well as being willing to take other "conflict situations" into account. This change represented a significant shift in the party's position since its own proposal of 1968 and the internal party organizations for women and youth were the main instigators of the change.[4]

---

[4] The party's new position fell short of recognizing a social indication. The Christian Democrats continued clearly to reject any form of time limit model (Mesner 1994: 199).

This analysis shows the importance of women's organizations in shaping both the Social Democratic and the Christian Democratic positions on abortion in the early 1970s. Furthermore, in the Austrian People's Party, the women's organization had a critical influence over the party's position on abortion, moving the party in a more liberal direction. The original impetus for liberalizing abortion came from the new women's movement in Austrian society. But these ideas were mediated and shaped by the ÖVP's internal party organization for women as the party reformed its own position.

Parental Leave

Changes in the parental leave policy in Austria reveal the power of both the Austrian Women's Movement and the women of the League of Workers and Employees to shape the policy of the ÖVP. In 2001 the Austrian government adopted new laws to address the work-family conflict. This new package, which went into effect on January 1, 2002, represented a significant departure from the former policy. The former laws were called parental leave benefits and the new laws are called child care benefits.

One of the most significant changes is that the old parental leave law was only for people in the labor force. Everyone who has a child receives the new child care benefits, regardless of employment status. The length of the benefit has also been extended. The former parental leave benefit of 24 months was extended to 36 months. One aspect of the benefit that did not change is that parents only receive the full benefit if each parent takes 6 months of leave. If only one parent takes the leave, the time is shortened by 6 months (formerly to 18 months, now to 30 months). Notably, the job protection aspect of the benefit was not extended. Workers on leave still only receive job protection for 24 months (Lutz 2004).

The new law also increases the financial benefit. The new child care benefit provides for 14.53 euros per day, which is 6.3 percent higher than the parental leave money (Lutz 2004). The parental leave money had not been increased since 1995. More significantly, the new law also raises the maximum amount that people on leave are allowed to earn through working. Under the parental leave policy, people on parental leave could only earn about 3,600 euros a year. Under the child care benefit, those on leave can earn up to 14,600 euros a year. The purpose of increasing the maximum allowed earnings was to help leave-takers maintain a connection with their workplace.

The new child care benefit was the product of a new governing coalition. In 2000 the Austrian People's Party formed a government with the Freedom Party. For the first time in 30 years the Social Democrats were not in the governing coalition. More significantly, it marked the first time the Freedom Party entered the government since it repositioned itself as a right-wing populist party in the 1980s (Pelinka 1998: 77). Both parties in the new coalition had made the child care benefit a centerpiece of the electoral campaign.[5]

Both the People's Party and the Freedom Party supported the child care leave policy despite some internal disagreement. Dissenters opposed the law primarily because of the expense. Politicians were working hard to balance the budget and many programs were being cut. Jörg Haider, chairman of the Freedom Party, strongly backed the child care policy so grumbling within the party was kept fairly quiet. Within the People's Party, however, dissent was more public, particularly within the Finance Ministry (*Frankfurter Allgemeine Zeitung*, May 18, 2000).

Most of the women within the People's Party, however, strongly favored the child care leave (Barbara Steininger, personal interview). The Austrian Women's Movement in particular worked hard to get the policy passed (Gertrude Brinek, personal interview). The Austrian Women's Movement is dominated by housewives who were not eligible for the parental leave but would benefit from the child care leave. It is worth noting that for this constituency, the lack of full job protection was not relevant. For housewives the new child care benefit has no significant drawbacks.

The women of the League of Workers and Employers thought the new leave was too long, but instead of objecting to that component of the leave, they concentrated on getting the maximum earnings limit raised so that women on leave could maintain a connection with their workplace (Gertrude Brinek, personal interview). They were successful in this regard and people on leave can now earn approximately three times what was allowed under the old parental leave law.

Both the Austrian Business League and its suborganization for women opposed the new policy because of the burden it imposed on employers

---

[5] The Social Democrats opposed the child care benefit both because of the expense and because the new law encouraged women to take a longer time off from work. The Social Democrats feared that women would be less able to find work after the benefit expired, particularly because the job protection clause was not extended for the full duration of the leave.

(Gertrude Brinek; Maria Rauch-Kallat, personal interviews). However, this League was not powerful enough to affect the final form of the policy.

The child care benefit had to be negotiated between the Freedom Party and the People's Party. While the Freedom Party pushed hard to ensure the law's passage, particular women's groups within the People's Party worked to shape the exact terms of the new benefit. Both the Austrian Women's Movement and the women's suborganization within the League of Workers and Employers had a significant role in forming the new policy.

Quotas

As in the German Christian Democratic Union (and differing from Christian Democratic parties in Italy and the Netherlands) the women's organization of the Austrian ÖVP succeeded in getting the main party to adopt a statement favoring a women's quota. Both the Austrian People's Party and the German CDU considered adopting women's quotas in the 1990s. In both countries, the adoption of a women's quota by a major regional organization (Vienna in the case of the Austrian People's Party, North Rhine-Westfalia in the case of the CDU) prepared the way for the possibility of a national quota. While neither party adopted the strongest quota measures considered, both parties created regulations at the party level to increase women's representation to a particular numerical percentage.

The Austrian People's Party in their current Basic Program (passed April 22, 1995) states:

> Equal representation from men and women in society also means equal represen-
> tation from men and women in politics. This equality should be pursued through a
> minimum quota of one third of all public offices [for women] and through a female-
> friendly political culture. (Basic Program, Austrian People's Party 1995: 16)[6]

The groundwork for the Austrian People's Party quota was laid at the Vienna regional organization of the party. The Vienna regional organization passed a women's quota in 1989. This quota went through because

---

[6] The party statutes, however, do not contain any language about promoting women (Party Statutes, Austrian People's Party). There is a fundamental difference between measures outlined in the party statutes, which are binding, and recommendations in the Basic Program, which are not. The Basic Program serves more as an electoral tool, while the party statutes regulate internal party life. At the party congress in 1995, the Austrian People's Party considered adopting a women's quota in the party statutes, but this measure was rejected.

the women pushing it were able to manipulate the agenda and set the vote for the quota at a time when they knew few participants in the party congress would be paying attention. The women pursuing the quota planned the vote for following a long and difficult series of elections. Most delegates to the party congress left the hall after the elections to get something to eat and the women involved were able to sneak the quota through (Maria Rauch-Kallat, personal interview). This Vienna quota made the idea of a national level quota more possible.

The women's suborganizations of the three Leagues prepared for a national level quota in the early 1990s (Gertrude Brinek, personal interview). The fact that the German CDU also began a serious quota debate at this time was not lost on the Austrian women, who were able to argue that having a women's quota was part of becoming a "modern" party (Gertrude Brinek, personal interview). Despite lobbying efforts and cooperation from the women's groups of the three Leagues and despite wanting to look modern and copy the CDU, the Austrian People's Party failed to adopt the quota as part of the party statutes. Instead, at the 1995 party congress, the party put language supporting a quota into its Basic Program. Unlike party statutes, the Basic Program is a nonbinding document.

As with the German CDU, the Austrian ÖVP was unwilling to adopt a strict quota in the party statutes. Christian Democratic parties are not very fertile ground for gender quotas. However, in both the German and the Austrian cases, it was the actions of the women's suborganizations within the parties that pushed gender quotas to the top of the agenda and forced the main parties to act. For Christian Democratic parties to have gender quotas at all is a noteworthy achievement. The contrast with the Christian Democratic parties in Italy and the Netherlands – neither of which implemented a women's quota at the party level – will become apparent shortly.

ITALY

The postwar Italian party system prior to 1994 had two large parties, the Christian Democrats (DC) and the Communist Party (PCI). Several significantly smaller parties also existed, including the Socialist Party and the neo-fascist party. Because the Communist Party was viewed by many voters as an unacceptable governing option, the Christian Democrats enjoyed a near monopoly over the government until the party's collapse in a wave of scandals in the early 1990s. The DC was rarely able to govern alone, however.

The DC is a corporatist catch-all party. One of the most notable features of the Italian Christian Democratic Party (DC) is that it was divided into institutionalized factions. These factions were recognized in the party statutes and had their own newspapers. In a corporatist economic system, the bargaining units have to represent genuine societal interests. Similarly, in a corporatist catch-all party, the subunits of the party must represent particular ideologies or policy directions. Whether the factions in the Italian DC were simply organizations for running clientelist relationship networks or whether factions also represented ideologies and policy positions is a question of significant debate among scholars of Italian political parties.[7] Leonardi and Wertman (1989) argue convincingly that mechanics of the factions in the DC were similar to the auxiliary organizations in the CDU. For example, increasing the membership of a particular faction increased that faction's representation within the party. Whether debate among factions was policy oriented varied over time. The factions of the DC represented particular ideologies and political directions frequently enough that the party can be considered a corporatist catch-all party (Leonardi and Wertman 1989). However, there was no women's faction within the DC and none of the factions took up the cause of women's issues.

The DC did create a women's auxiliary organization for the party, *the Women's Movement of the DC* (*Movimento Femminile*) in 1946 (Bertone 2002: 91). It is a separate body within the party. *Movimento Femminile* had its own Congresses, its own central committee and its own journal. It trained female activists and helped develop female leadership within the DC. It also helped develop the ideological positions of Catholic women (Bertone 2002: 100–2). One delegate of the Women's Movement was represented on the party's National Committee. In 1972, this was raised to 3–5 women on the National Committee (Katz and Mair 1992: 597).

Despite some similarities, the DC's Women's Movement was not as strong as the CDU's Women's Union or the Austrian Women's Movement. This internal representation alone did not make the DC a corporatist catch-all party. For example, the female representative on the DC's National Committee had voice, but not vote (Pircher 1990: 91). The DC also had a youth organization, but neither the women nor the youth took part in the bargaining among factions that distributed positions and power within the party. At the Women's Movement national congress in 1982,

---

[7] For more on factions within the DC, see Belloni and Beller (1978), Zuckermann (1979), Leonardi and Wertman (1989).

the DC women decided to lobby the party for more representation. This request caused significant conflict. Though the organization did get more representation at all levels of the party, the women sitting on the decision-making bodies would have no vote on political issues (Pircher 1990: 95). Furthermore, the party deemed it too difficult to integrate the women's organization into the factional distribution system that dominated the DC. Another telling sign of the weakness of the DC's Women's Movement is that during the 1970s, the peak of Italy's new women's movement, membership in the DC's women's organization experienced a serious decline (Pircher 1990: 102). During the same period, the CDU launched a successful membership drive and increased female membership. The CDU's Women's Union was seen as a reasonable alternative to the new women's movement. The DC's Women's Movement was not.

A look at policy outcomes in the three issue areas shows the limited influence of the DC's *Movimento Femminile*. As in other countries, abortion reform became an important topic in the 1970s. The DC maintained a hard-line position throughout the discussion. The DC voted with the neo-Fascists to defeat abortion reform in 1976. The DC abstained from voting on the 1978 law that legalized abortion in the first trimester, but immediately attempted to appeal that law through referendum. The appeal was a major failure. In Germany and Austria, the women's organizations of the Christian Democratic parties acted as moderating forces on abortion. These organizations emphasized measures other than punishment to limit abortion and were more sympathetic to women who found themselves seeking an abortion. Female Christian Democrats in Italy shared the same stance, but were unable to influence their party, which remained steadfastly opposed to abortion reform. Like Christian Democratic women elsewhere, Italian female Christian Democrats would have most preferred to be paid to stay home with their children. They were unable to convince their party to back this policy and Italian parental leave remains fairly short. The Italian DC also failed to implement or even recommend a gender quota despite very low levels of female representation. Later experimentation with gender quotas was at the national level, not the party level. The DC's *Movimento Femminile* was not an important influence within the party.

Abortion

The process of abortion reform sheds light on how little influence women have had on the Italian Christian Democratic Party. The DC maintained a very conservative stance on abortion throughout the debate. The party opposed abortion even in cases when the woman's life was in danger. Prior to the 1970s, the fascist-era law completely banning abortion remained in effect. In the early 1970s, as part of a broader movement of reform on gender issues, the feminist movement began demonstrating in favor of liberalizing abortion access. In 1975, the Italian Supreme Court declared the fascist-era law void, forcing some kind of parliamentary action (Calloni 2001: 185).

Abortion reform in Italy passed in a general era of reform on women's issues. In addition to the policies for working mothers discussed in the following, Italy legalized divorce, acknowledged equal rights and duties for men and women within marriage and provided for children born out of wedlock to be recognized (Calloni 2001: 185). It also became much easier to obtain contraception. These were major changes in a country where politics were often dominated by the Catholic Church.

The abortion debate in Italy was frequently framed as an issue of women's health (Calloni 2001: 186). Certainly the Supreme Court ruling contributed to this view – it clearly placed the mother's right to health over the fetus's right to life. The prevalence of illegal abortion in Italy also contributed to this perspective on the issue. Estimates of illegal abortions prior to 1978 (the year of legalization) range from 800,000 to three million per year, with as many as 20,000 women dying every year as a result of illegal abortion (Caldwell 1991: 50). An issue of this magnitude could not be ignored.

Abortion was also an extremely controversial issue in Italy. Feminist groups, political parties, and even Catholics found themselves internally divided over abortion (Calloni 2001: 188). Feminists groups split over whether legalization was sufficient or whether only full decriminalization would be adequate (Teske 2007: 29–30). Some Catholics wanted abortion to remain illegal while others supported a woman's right to choose (Calloni 2001: 188).

The Christian Democratic Party opposed liberalizing abortion access, even in cases in which the pregnant woman's life was in danger (Becalli 1994: 99). The DC voted with the neo-Fascists to defeat an abortion reform proposal in 1976 (Ergas 1982: 268). This vote was considered scandalous because all the other parties voted in favor of the reform. In the aftermath of the controversy (and under new leadership), the DC abstained from the next round of abortion proposals, and the Italian parliament passed abortion reform in 1978. This new law permitted abortion under certain cases, including "social circumstances" (Ergas 1982: 271).

The current law allows for abortion for the first ninety days of pregnancy for women over the age of eighteen. Women must request an abortion from a recognized person and then wait seven days before obtaining the procedure. Minors need permission from a parent or a doctor. Later abortions are allowed if the mother's health is in danger (Caldwell 1991: 93). As Caldwell describes it, this "cumbersome procedure ... results in a very liberal law" (Caldwell 1991: 93). In most cases, a woman can decide that she wants an abortion, but she must jump through a number of bureaucratic hoops to get one.

The law also contained a conscientious objection clause, which allows doctors and hospital staff to opt out of providing abortions (Caldwell 1991: 100). The Catholic Church embarked on a campaign to get doctors to sign up as objectors and 72 percent of them did so (Caldwell 1991: 101). Thus, even though the law on abortion is fairly liberal, access to abortion can still be problematic.

The Christian Democrats, working together with the pro-life movement, attempted to appeal the 1978 abortion law. In Italy, Article 75 of the Constitution permits popular referenda about particular laws. A law can only be repealed by referendum; no new legislation can be passed with this technique. The Christian Democrats' proposed referendum would have allowed abortion only for therapeutic reasons and would have given the power of decision to the doctor, not the woman (Calloni 2001: 191). The referendum failed. Only 32 percent of voters were in favor, while 60 percent were opposed (8 percent had blank or invalid ballots) (Calloni 2001: 192). This result was a serious defeat for the Christian Democrats. The DC was forced to apply a law it had utterly opposed.

Unlike the CDU, which modified its stance on abortion, partially as the female Christian Democrats became more accepting of it, the DC continued to strongly oppose legal abortion. Whereas the CDU allowed the social-liberal reform of the 1970s to stand, the DC attempted to repeal the 1978 abortion reform through a national referendum. Italians voted strongly in favor of the existing legislation. The insight to be gained here is that unlike the CDU, the DC lacked the links to society that would have prodded it to modernize its position on women's issues. The *Movimento Femminile* could have provided such a link except that the organization was powerless within the DC.

Parental Leave

Christian Democratic women had some influence over parental leave law, but only when they were able to forge a compromise in order to work with women on the left. They did not gain influence through their own political party. The technique of working with women on the left was successful in the reforms of 1950 and 1971 when the length of the leave being recommended was similar for Christian Democrats and women on the left. When Christian Democratic women began to advocate for their own vision of longer parental leaves, however, they lacked the backing of their former leftist allies and they were unsuccessful.

Italy currently provides for 20 weeks of maternity leave paid at 80 percent of a woman's salary (two months before the expected birth and three months after). Additionally, eligible Italians can take ten months of parental leave with six months paid at 30 percent of salary. If the father takes at least three months of leave, then an additional month can be taken for a total of eleven months (Fagan and Hebson 2006: 130). Ten months is relatively short for a country where the dominant ideology envisions mothers staying home with their children until they reach the age of three (Bertone 2002: 112–14). This policy has been in place since 2000.

In the early postwar period, Christian Democratic and Communist women worked together to introduce paid maternity leave (Caldwell 1991: 113). Italy was one of the first country's to introduce this policy in the postwar period. At the time it had one of the most progressive laws in Western Europe. In 1950 Italy implemented paid leave for six weeks prior to and eight weeks following the birth (Caldwell 1991: 113). Pay was at 80 percent of the woman's regular wage. Women from across the political spectrum worked together and succeeded in getting paid maternity leave.

The 1950 law was revised in 1971 to extend the policy in several ways (Caldwell 1991: 115). Eligibility was extended to workers in other sectors of the economy. The leave time was extended to two months before and three months after the birth. A parental leave was also added so that women could stay home an additional six months at 30 percent pay (Caldwell 1991: 115).[8]

How can we explain Italian parental leave? This legislation was a compromise between women's organizations. Women's organizations on the left wanted more daycare (crèches) while Catholic women's organizations advocated for extending maternity leave. The 1971 reform was part of a broader effort to reconcile the pressures of combining work and family. In 1968 Italy had introduced state-run Kindergartens (Bertone 2003: 237). In 1971 new laws expanded both maternity leave and public crèches (Bertone 2003: 241). The new policies were passed in the context

---

[8] The 1977 Parity Law gave fathers the right to take the leave if mothers were willing to abdicate their right (Bertone 2002: 134).

of severe labor unrest. These new policies resulted from pressure from the women's organizations of the Communist Party and the unions and from the Union of Italian Women, a socialist-oriented women's organization, as well as from the *Movimento Femminile* (Caldwell 1991: 115). In the early 1970s, women's organizations across the political spectrum were able to cooperate and make progress with new laws supporting their competing visions of appropriate roles for women (Bertone 2003: 242).

The women of the *Movimento Femminile* later began to advocate for longer leaves, similar to those eventually adopted in Germany and Austria (Bertone 2002: 114). The Catholic vision of the ideal combination of work and family saw children under the age of three at home with their mothers. However, these policies were not implemented in Italy. Women's organizations on the left were not in support of long parental leaves; instead they favored increasing child care. When the women of *Movimento Femminile*'s vision diverged from women of the left, they were unable to pass their preferred policy.

The Italian feminist movement was very powerful throughout the 1970s. But the new feminist movement arrived on the scene at a time when Catholic women's organizations were not very strong. An activist in the Catholic women's organization, Paola Gaiotti de Biase called this "a period of 'aphasia' due to the lack of a representative subject or place to develop a Catholic women's answer to feminism" (Gaiotte de Baise quoted in Bertone 2002: 130). The women of the DC did not have the same kind of organization available to them that the women of the CDU had. The CDU's Women's Union *was* used as a place to develop a Christian Democratic response to the feminist movement. The parental leave policies developed by the Women's Union in the 1970s were implemented into West German law in the 1980s. Italian Christian Democratic women, however, lacked a sufficiently powerful organization with which to counter Italian feminism.

After 1971, public discourse on women's issues changed from its focus on reconciling work and family to the topics of divorce and abortion (Bertone 2003: 237). On these issues women of the left and Catholic women were much more polarized. Women of the left eventually saw their policy preferences implemented on both issues.

Although many other western European countries expanded parental leave policies in the 1980s and 1990s, Italy did not until the European Union forced its hand. Italy expanded the leave to ten months in 2000 in response to a European Union directive. The additional months added in 2000 are not paid. One reason for this lack of change is the weakness of women within the Italian Christian Democratic Party. In this case, it is not surprising that a longer parental leave policy was not adopted in Italy.

Quotas

The *Movimento Femminile* was not successful in getting the Italian Christian Democratic Party to adopt gender quotas. The party considered working toward a gender quota at the National Congress in 1989, but no genuine progress was made on the issue before the DC collapsed in 1994. Italy later introduced a gender quota, but at the national, not the party level. After one election with the quota, the Italian Supreme court declared it unconstitutional.

Gender quotas certainly are possible in the Italian context. As in other countries, parties of the left did adopt quotas in Italy. The PCI started with a 25 percent women's quota for the party's Executive Board in 1986 (Guadagnini 1998: 215). In 1989 the PCI expanded this measure in order to aim for equal representation for men and women on all party bodies. For internal party elections, separate lists for men and women were used and one third of all seats were supposed to be given to women (Guadagnini 1998: 215). When the PCI transformed itself into the PDS, it adopted a 40 percent quota for each sex (Guadagnini 2005: 135). The PSI also introduced gender quotas for internal party bodies in the mid-1980s (Guadagnini 1993: 179). Gender quotas, therefore, were not unachievable in Italy, just within the DC itself.

In February 1989 the DC's National Congress approved an agenda stating that the party's National Council should change the party statutes in such a way as to permit gender quotas. No particular percentage was decided upon; the party is supposed to represent women at approximately their percentage of membership (nearly 40 percent) (Guadagnini 1993: 179). However, this pledge apparently did nothing to alter party behavior. In the Chamber of Deputies, 4.9 percent of DC parliamentarians were women in 1992 (Guadagnini 1993: 190). The DC made no further efforts at gender quotas before the party dissolved in the early 1990s.

The Italians did adopt a quota in the early 1990s, but it was not through the Christian Democratic Party. In conjunction with the new electoral law, quotas were adopted for municipal and provincial levels in March 1993 with the support of the Christian Democrats (Guadagnini 2005: 140). The new electoral law for the Chamber of Deputies was passed in August 1993. Seventy-five percent of the seats would now be elected through a major-itarian system (new for Italy, which had previously had a more pure proportional representation system). The remaining 25 percent of the seats would be elected proportionally and candidates should alternate, male and female. Christian Democrats were divided on the new law (Guadagnini 2005: 140–1). In any case, the Constitutional Court overturned the quota measures and ruled quotas unconstitutional in September 1995. Subsequently, parliament worked to amend the constitution in order to allow quotas, ultimately passing this law in February 2003 (Guadagnini 2005: 145). The amendment was supported by parties across the political spectrum. A number of proposals on how to implement quotas have recently been submitted, though none of them has passed.

Quotas are difficult policies to get parties or parliaments to adopt because a real quota will involve forcing men to give up political power. In Italy, women within the Christian Democratic Party were too weak to pass quotas despite the presence of a quota in the PCI, providing potential contagion from the left, and despite the moral pressure that arose from having such a low rate of female representation. Without a strong internal women's organization to back gender quotas, Christian Democratic parties are unlikely to do so.

THE NETHERLANDS

Since 1917 the Dutch electoral system has been one of proportional representation. The effective threshold for a party to gain a seat in parliament is very low at .67 percent (Koole and van de Velde 1992: 620). Unsurprisingly, the Netherlands has a multiparty system. Parties are divided by both religion and class and four ideological families have dominated Dutch politics: Calvinists, Catholics, Liberals, and Social Democrats (Koole and van de Velde 1992: 621). A variety of parties within these families has existed, sometimes with more than one party in a family existing simultaneously. The Netherlands is known for its system of "pillarization," which describes a society in which groups in society are separated not just by political parties, but by separate social spheres (Lijphart 1968). Calvinists, Catholics, Liberals, and Social Democrats historically lived in the same society, but apart from one another.

Major nonconfessional parties since World War II have included the Social Democratic or Labor Party (*Partij van de Arbeid*, PvdA), the People's Party for Freedom and Democracy, a liberal party (*Volkspartij voor Vrijheid en Democratie*, VVD), and Democrats '66, a progressive liberal party (*Democraten '66*, D'66). Several small far left parties merged in 1990 to create the Green Left (*Groen Links*, GL).

The Netherlands also has several confessional parties, most of which have roots in the pre–World War I era. The Catholic People's Party (*Katholieke Volkspartij*, KVP) and its pre–World War II predecessor played a pivotal role in government throughout the twentieth century. The KVP was part of the government from 1917 until 1994, and the Prime Minister was most frequently from this party.[9] The Anti-Revolutionary Party (*Anti-Revolutionaire Partij*, ARP) was a Calvinist party. Many of its members belonged to the Reformed Churches. The Christian Historical Union (*Christelijk-Historische Unie*, CHU) was another Protestant party. Most of its members belonged to the Dutch Reformed Churches. The CHU was formed from a group that split off from the ARP in 1908 (Koole and van de Velde 1992: 624). Despite this segregation, the three confessional parties frequently governed together. They began to work together as a confederation in the mid-1970s and formally merged in 1980 to form Christian Democratic Appeal (*Christen Demoratisch-Appel*, CDA) (Lucardie and ten Napel 1994: 53). The KVP and then the CDA governed continuously from 1917 until 1994. The CDA returned to the governing coalition in 2002.

Despite the political dominance of first the Catholic Party and later the Christian Democratic Party, the Netherlands had no parental leave policy prior to January 1991, and the time-off provided to parents to care for children is among the shortest in Europe (Bruning and Plantenga 1999: 204). Furthermore, the Netherlands is well-known for its very liberal abortion law and has been a popular destination for German women seeking abortions. Both of these policy outcomes are counter to what we might expect, given that religious parties have dominated the Netherlands for much of the twentieth century. The CDA also does not have a gender quota. The weak representation of women's organizations within the confessional parties and later within the CDA are an important part of the explanation for the lack of parental leave. While the abortion policy is surprising, this issue was handled largely outside of the domain of political parties. Although the CDA's women's organization demanded a gender quota in the mid-1980s, this organization was not powerful enough to force the CDA to implement one.

The history of confessional and Christian Democratic parties in the Netherlands is complicated. However, with the exception of the ARP, these parties are not corporatist catch-all parties. The CHU had a weak

---

[9] Prior to 1946, the Catholic People's Party was organized as the Roman Catholic State Party. After 1980, it fused with other confessional parties to form Christian Democratic Appeal.

internal organization (Irving 1979: 198). While a women's association existed within the party, it did not have much internal party influence. Of the two Protestant parties, the CHU was smaller, more conservative, and appealed more to elites, while also being more open to (classical) liberal ideas (Irving 1979: 196). Its organization was most like Duverger's cadre party.

The ARP, on the other hand, could be regarded as a corporatist catch-all party. Representatives from subsidiary organizations, including the women's association, sat on the party's national council (Irving 1979: 198). The "anti-revolutionary" part of the party's name refers to the party's rejection of the anticlerical position during the French Revolution (Irving 1979: 196). More committed to Calvinism than the CHU, the ARP has also emphasized a commitment to economic and social justice. Thus, the CHU was less religious, but more conservative politically while the ARP was more religious, but also more progressive politically. However, as will be seen in the following, the ARP's left-ward slant did not apply to women. The ARP's women's association was the least independent and least policy-oriented of the three confessional parties. Thus, in the one party that had a corporatist catch-all like structure, women were excluded.

The KVP was also not a corporatist catch-all party. The party did have social organizations for women and youth, but these organizations were not represented on the party's internal decision-making bodies (Irving 1979: 202). Internal social organizations had been represented in the decision-making hierarchy of the KVP's predecessor, the Roman Catholic State Party (RKSP), but that changed with the founding of the KVP after World War II (Irving 1979: 200). Like the other two confessional parties, the KVP had a women's association that was fairly independent from the main party. However, this organization was not represented within the party itself so women were again excluded from the policy-making process.

Beginning with discussions in the late 1960s, the three confessional parties formally merged into the CDA in 1980. The first shared electoral lists were not created until 1986. The CDA has four auxiliary organizations (Lepszy and Koecke 2000: 162). One of these organizations is the party's think tank, not a representative organization. The other three are organizations for women, youth, and local politicians. To better understand the CDA's women's organization, we need to understand the fusion of the three confessional parties. The depillarization process in the Netherlands was dramatic. As just one indicator for this process, in 1963

83 percent of Catholics voted for the KVP while by 1972 that had dropped to 38 percent (Lepszy and Koecke 2000: 139). The loss of voter support for the other confessional parties was less dire, but still severe. Already in the late 1960s, there were discussions within the KVP about the possibility of transforming the party into a Christian Democratic Party open to Protestants as well as Catholics (Lepszy and Koecke 2000: 141). The fusion of the three confessional parties then proceeded in stages until they finally fused into the CDA in 1980.

Fusing the women's organizations of the three parties was a complicated process. Each of the confessional parties had its own women's organization and these organizations had even cooperated on occasion. However, the three main parties had had different relationships with their respective women's organizations. In particular, the KVP and the CHU both had fairly independent women's organizations while the women's organization in the APR (the ARVC) was subservient to the main party (Van de Velde 1994: 105–6). As representatives of the three women's organizations met to discuss the merger, the ARP always sent a man to observe their discussions (Van de Velde 1994: 106). While the official position of the ARVC objected to the model of increased independence for the women's organization, this stance itself seems to have been influenced by the men of the ARP (Van de Velde 1994: 106). The main ARP worried that an independent women's organization would undermine party unity and they preferred a nonpolitical women's club (Van de Velde 1994: 106).

In 1978 the three women's organizations presented their vision of how a future CDA women's organization should operate. They asked for an independent CDA women's organization (Van de Velde 1994: 107). Furthermore, they wanted the women's organization anchored in the new party's statutes, which it had not been originally. Ultimately, the CDA's women's organization, the CDAV, was granted official status as an independent organization within the CDA (and was recognized in the party statutes). However, in contrast to other internal party groups, such as the one for youth, the women's organization was subject to certain restrictions. For example, unlike the CDU's Women's Union, the CDAV could not choose their own leadership; they could only make nonbinding suggestions to the main party. The CDAV was also not allowed to make political pronouncements outside of the main party. They CDA's Party Secretary and one other member of the party leadership (both very likely to be men) would be advisory members to the leadership of the CDAV (Van de Velde 1994: 107). Unsurprisingly, the CDAV is less powerful within the internal party hierarchy than the CDU's Women's Union and rarely criticizes the CDA leadership.[10]

Female members of the CDA are not automatically members of the CDAV and only about 10 percent of female membership joins the CDAV. However, for women in leadership positions in the party, a much higher percentage belongs to the CDAV (Van de Velde 1994: 115–16).

Abortion

Prior to the 1980s, the Dutch law governing abortion was the 1911 Morality Act, which permitted abortion only in cases in which the mother's life was in danger. Beginning in 1973, a group of physicians acting independently of the government made abortion available on demand. The state did not punish the doctors or the women seeking abortions, although the procedure was, strictly speaking, still illegal. After an extended parliamentary and societal debate, parliament passed a new law in 1981, which was implemented in 1984. The new law gave a woman the right to decide if she wanted an abortion, up until viability. There is a five day waiting period, but abortion is covered by the national health insurance. Women can seek abortion either in a hospital or in a private clinic (Ketting 1994).

How can we explain abortion policy in the Netherlands? Abortion reform was not initiated by parliament and the parties. Instead, when the abortion conflict arose in the Netherlands in the late 1960s and early 1970s, a group of doctors took matters into their own hands. The Foundation for Medically Responsible Interruption of Pregnancy (known by its Dutch acronym, Stimezo) began providing abortion on demand in the early 1970s. Parliamentary attempts to pass a law on abortion failed throughout the 1970s. Indeed abortion conflict nearly brought down the government and the ultimate policy was only passed with a miniscule majority after extraordinary parliamentary maneuvering. Because the availability of abortion changed dramatically through the actions of Stimezo, proposed reforms that would have restricted abortion came to be seen as rolling back an existing right. The CDA and the VVD (Liberal Party) passed laws in the early 1980s basically approving what Stimezo had already created (Outshoorn 1986a).

---

[10] The CDA's youth organization, the CDJA (Christen Democratisch Jongeren Appèl), by contrast, is autonomous of the CDA and elects its own chair (Lepszy and Koecke 2000: 166). Unlike the CDA's women's organization, the CDA's youth organization must be represented at all levels of the CDA. It is therefore not surprising that scholars have found the Netherlands to have a strong youth orientation in its social policies (Lynch 2006).

Although frequently in coalition together, the three confessional parties operated very much independently in determining their policy positions at this time. The KVP experienced intense in-fighting over the abortion issue. Abortion was a difficult issue for Catholic parties in the 1970s, even when these parties did not have a corporatist catch-all party organization. The KVP worked to develop its position on abortion from 1970 to 1972. At the party congress in 1970 the party adopted an indications model that would allow abortion for "medical-social" reasons if the mother's physical or psychological health were seriously threatened (Outshoorn 1986b: 187). The KVP organized a series of working groups on various morality laws, including one on abortion, but the abortion group could not reach a consensus on its position. The term "medical-social" seems to have been an attempt at a rhetorical glossing over of the party's position on the social indication.

The medical and psychological indications were widely accepted within the KVP. The KVP was divided on the social indication, however. The party also did not believe the woman should be allowed to decide for herself whether she needed an abortion or indeed, that she was even capable of making such a momentous decision without outside assistance. Instead, the KVP recommended a team of experts to advise doctors who were considering providing abortions (Outshoorn 1986b: 188). The decision would thus be twice removed from the woman herself.

The KVP women did not appear to be in favor of the social indication (Outshoorn 1986b: 188). They believed that a flexible handling of the law would allow adequate possibility for women in need of an abortion for a "social" reason to get one without having this be the explicit law. The KVP women rejected the very public approach of feminist groups such as Dolle Mina. They would have preferred to have this issue handled more quietly because they believed this approach would have better preserved a flexible interpretation of the law.

Not surprisingly, the KVP women's association did not play a major role in shaping KVP policy on abortion. The women's association was not represented within the party's decision-making process. The women did not hold an opinion significantly different from the main party. The organization was not very politically mobilized and not necessarily even internally united. The KVP struggled to reach some consensus on abortion, but the struggle was not based on conflict among internal interest groups.

The ARP seems to have had a somewhat easier time reaching a position as a party. The ARP organized discussion groups on abortion in the winter of 1969/70 (Outshoorn 1986b: 190). A strong majority of participants

favored some kind of reform that would allow abortion if certain indications were present and also that a team of doctors should decide whether
indications were present. There was some internal disagreement about the
acceptability of the social indication. The party adopted an "Action
Program" that allowed for abortion in case of a medical-social indication
(Outshoorn 1986b: 190). Internal dissent over allowing any kind of social
indication remained.

The CHU adopted the most progressive stance among the confessional
parties. Its scientific office issued a report stating that from an ethical
perspective the woman is the only one capable of making a decision
(Outshoorn 1986b: 191). Some CHU women agreed with this perspective.
The CHU also stated that the job of the government was to protect the
weaker of the two lives at stake, that of the unborn child. This stance was
criticized by CHU membership who saw the only adequate reason for
abortion as being when the mother's life was in danger (Outshoorn
1986b: 191). Still, to have some in the party advocating allowing the
mother to decide was unique among the confessional parties. As mentioned previously, the CHU is the confessional party most open to liberal
ideas.

None of these parties were corporatist catch-all parties representing
women. As expected, women within the parties did not play an important
role in formulating policy. In any case, the abortion issue seems to have cut
across subgroups and so the conflict was less regulated than it might have
been otherwise.

In 1971, the governing coalition, made up of the liberal VVD and the
confessional parties, proposed a bill on abortion reform. The proposal was
for an indications solution with abortion allowed for medical reasons. The
decision of whether the indications applied in a particular case would be
made by a team of experts (Outshoorn 1986a: 19). The bill was the result
of a summit conference among the governing parties.

The government proposal was severely criticized by women's groups,
particularly Dolle Mina. Furthermore, Stimezo had already begun providing abortion at private clinics, basically on demand. The government
proposal was unlikely to satisfy many. In any case, the government collapsed for unrelated reasons and new elections were held in 1972. The new
governing coalition consisted of the Labor Party, the KVP, and the ARP.

The new coalition was even more divided on abortion and was unable
to reach a coalition agreement on the issue. Instead it was decided to leave
the issue to parliament with the cabinet agreeing to pass whatever parliament approved (Outshoorn 1986a: 20). The plan under this highly

unusual procedure was to have a private bill submitted by members of the Labor Party go up against a bill proposed by the two confessional parties. The private bill was submitted but because the KVP was severely internally divided, progress on the confessional bill was slow (Outshoorn 1986a: 20). In the absence of societal pressure, this delay might have led to a de facto solution. Abortion was against the law but widely available at the clinics run by Stimezo. This sort of solution – in which law and practice differ quite significantly – was not uncommon in the Netherlands, but in the case of abortion, it did not hold up.

The choice of parliamentary procedure – to have the bill come from parliament rather than from the cabinet – opened the parliamentarians up to increased societal pressure and made traditional Dutch "Politics of Accommodation" more difficult to achieve (Lijphart 1968). Dutch pro-life groups were not satisfied with the emerging possibility that the law on the books would ban abortion but that the procedure would still be easily available (Outshoorn 1986a: 21). In response to pressure from these groups, KVP Justice Minister Van Agt tried to shut down private clinics performing second trimester abortions. Private members from the Liberal and Labor parties then submitted a bill that would have left the decision about abortion to a woman and her doctor – close to legalization – and this bill passed the Second Chamber. Because the Labor Party was in coalition with the KVP at this time, this move caused a huge rift within the coalition and threatened the stability of the government. The bill failed in the First Chamber when the Liberal Party, hoping for a future coalition with the confessional parties, withdrew its support. New elections were held in 1977.

The new governing coalition included all three confessional parties in an alliance now formally called the CDA, and the Liberals. Having suffered under the chaos of the approach to abortion in the previous legislative period, the government returned to what had been a more standard approach. The governing parties reached an agreement in a summit meeting. Lobbyists of all stripes were excluded from this process. In a very rare move on the abortion issue, whips imposed party discipline for the votes in parliament (Outshoorn 1986a). The government bill passed the Second Chamber with a majority of one in 1980 and the First Chamber with a majority of two in 1981 (Outshoorn 1986a)

The new law kept abortion a criminal act, but one that was not punishable if it happened before 20 weeks, therefore, basically a time limit model. The woman and her doctor were responsible for making the decision together and there was a five day waiting period. The new law legitimated the practice that had been in place since the mid-1970s. The parliamentary debate during this session was shifted to technical details and societal actors did not play a prominent role.

The parties were unable to make progress from 1973 to 1977 when the parliament (rather than the cabinet) was supposed to reach a decision. Extraordinary societal input and little way to regulate it meant that the parties were made incapable of acting coherently. During this period, 1973–7, the Dutch confessional parties in particular experienced the difficulties of a catch-all party with an empowered electorate.

It is important for this analysis to note that the parties were able to regain control over the debate in 1977. Because these parties are *not* corporatist catch-all parties, it is possible for them to both allow increased participation and then re-isolate themselves. When the strategy of a more open parliamentary debate led to chaos and the near collapse of the government, the parties returned to their usual modus operandi of the politics of accommodation. The parliamentary aspects of abortion reform were settled through cabinet level "summit style" politics (Outshoorn 2001: 219). Rank-and-file party members, interest groups, and civil servants were excluded from the debate. If the confessional parties had had a corporatist catch-all organization, they would not have had this kind of flexibility in structuring the debate.

After the act passed, parliament still needed to resolve some technical details in order to implement it. Although not expected to be controversial, the implementation was held up by the resistance of a group of hardliners within the CDA (Outshoorn 2001: 219). Ultimately, however, those in favor of the act prevailed and the necessary legislation for implementation (ensuring coverage by national health insurance and a licensing plan for the private clinics) was passed in 1984.

Parental Leave

The Netherlands did not have a parental leave policy until January 1991. Mothers had not been expected to be employed outside the home and therefore no parental leave was necessary (Knijn and Kremer 1997: 329). The parental leave policy that has emerged since the early 1990s is significantly different from the German child-raising leave. In the Netherlands, parents were initially only permitted to take part-time leave, in an effort to maintain the connection between the parent and his or her work place. To be eligible for this leave, parents had to have been working more than twenty hours per week for the same employer for at least one year. This restriction meant that only 25 percent of women and 70 percent of men could take the leave (Bruning and Plantenga 1999: 204).[11] The policy was relaxed in 1997 to allow more parents to take the leave, but parental leave in the Netherlands remained unpaid (Bruning and Plantenga 1999: 196). Reforms in 2001 extended eligibility for parental leave but only civil servants and workers for whom parental leave was covered in a collective wage agreement received paid parental leave (Knijn 2008: 162–3). The Dutch policy is clearly not intended to pay mothers to stay home with their children, although until recently Dutch women were employed at levels below the European average.

In some ways, the Netherlands would have been an ideal context for the emergence of long Christian Democratic-style parental leaves. The Dutch have deep-rooted values about young children remaining in the care of their mothers. The Dutch state has a tradition of subsidiarity especially in matters regarding children. The Catholic and later Christian Democratic Party was in the governing coalition continuously until 1994. Yet the country adopted a fairly modest parental leave policy fairly late. Policy makers have not made a sustained effort to extend the duration of parental leave or to make it paid.

There are several reasons for the lack of paid parental leave in the Netherlands. The CDA's women's organization – the most likely advocate for paid parental leave – is only weakly represented within the party. This organization did not have much influence over party leaders.

Some factors specific to the Dutch context also worked against the adoption of paid parental leave. Historically, very few women worked outside the home in the Netherlands. The Netherlands was a prime exemplar of the male breadwinner model (Knijn 1998; Plantenga 1996; Pfau-Effinger 2005). The Dutch welfare state – built on the assumption that mothers were home with their children – saw no need for parental leave.

As in other European countries, Dutch women began entering the paid labor force in more significant numbers in the 1970s and 1980s. This increase was dramatic in the 1990s and brought the Netherlands up to the European average for female labor force participation. One distinct feature of the female labor force in the Netherlands is the very strong tendency of women to work part time. The spectacular job creation in the Netherlands starting in the 1980s was part-time work, in jobs largely

---

[11] Of those eligible, 9 percent of Dutch men and 40 percent of Dutch women actually took parental leave. In Germany 96 percent of parents take the leave, nearly all of them women (Bruning and Plantenga 1999: 200).

filled by women. The increase in part-time work was supposed to promote flexibility, counteract unemployment, and increase women's economic independence (Plantenga 1996: 61). The tendency of women to work part time has both advantages and drawbacks. Part-time work does allow an easier combination of workplace and care responsibilities (Plantenga 1996: 68). On the other hand, even with recent improvements in the quality of part-time jobs, these are positions that tend to be less well paid and have much less of a career development path. It is troubling from a gender equity perspective that these types of jobs are filled predominantly by women. Furthermore, women tend to take up part-time work as a coping strategy in order to have time to do care work at home – though this arrangement may also be their preference (Plantenga 1996; Plantenga, Schippers, and Siegers 1999; Knijn 1998). The shift in the Dutch welfare state has been to a one and a half earner model, not a two earner model.

In 1990, political parties began to shift how the Dutch state approached the issue of working mothers. Prior to 1990, the state's policies were based on the assumption that mothers would not work outside the home. Since 1990, the Dutch have implemented a series of policies to facilitate combining work and family. The parental leave law of 1991 is just one of a series of policies passed in the Netherlands since the early 1990s. These laws include the 1990 Stimulation Measure on Child Care, the 1996 Working Time Act, the 1996 General Social Assistance Act,[12] the 2001 Work and Care Act, and the 2005 Child Care Provision Act. What is striking about these laws is that they do not follow the Christian Democratic vision of how women should combine employment and motherhood. That vision calls for young children to be in their mothers' care at home. It is true that the CDA was out of the governing coalition for the first time from 1994 to 2002 when several of these measures were passed. The Stimulation Measure on Child Care of 1990, however, rapidly increased available child care, especially for children under the age of three. Between 1990 and 1994, the government spent 300 million guilders, created 70,000 new child care facilities, and increased the number of children under the age of three in state-funded care from 2 percent to 8 percent (Bussemaker 1998: 74). This was the first piece of legislation explicitly designed to help working mothers (Gustafsson and Stafford 1995: 170). The 2005 Child Care Provision Act, passed with the support of the CDA, provides additional incentives for the creation of more child care spots.

---

[12] The General Social Assistance Act obligates single mothers to work once their youngest child reaches the age of five (Van Wel and Knijn 2001: 804).

In 2006 the Dutch government introduced the "life course saving scheme," which replaced most previously existing forms of leave, including parental leave. According to the "life course saving scheme," workers can set aside up to 12 percent of their gross annual salary and then draw on this money when they withdraw from the labor market for any reason they choose, including parental leave, elder care, sabbatical and early retirement (Knijn 2008: 164). People who use the "life course saving scheme" to fund their own parental leaves receive preferential tax treatment, but of course, this is not paid parental leave because workers are using their own earnings to pay for the leave. The repercussions of this policy are not clear yet, but if mothers continue to take parental leave at greater rates than fathers, they will pay for this choice by having to retire later (Knijn 2008: 164).

Taken as a whole, the Dutch work-family policies present a rather different vision of how to reconcile work and family responsibilities. These policies are favorable to part-time work following the birth of a child. Mothers seem to be expected to return to work rather quickly, albeit only part time. Part-time work is protected in the Netherlands much like full-time work. Differences in wages, benefits, and working conditions have largely been abolished and Dutch part-time workers are among the most content in Europe (van Oorschot 2004: 24).

This set of policies marks a significant shift in the Dutch approach to work and family. Previously, mothers had not been expected to work outside the home and had rarely done so. Indeed, women could be legally discriminated against based on pregnancy, childbirth, and marriage as late as 1973 (Gustafsson and Stafford 1995: 169). The change, which has been called a "pendulum shift" (Lewis 2001: 153) can be dated to 1990 and the release of a report by the Scientific Council for Government Policy (WRR) entitled *A Working Perspective*. The report argued that for women to become active in the labor force, they needed access to child care. The government (a coalition including the Christian Democrats and social democrats) used the WRR report to legitimate the new child care policy (Bussemaker 1998: 87). As of 1990, the Dutch government began implementing a series of policies that would support mothers' participation in the labor force rather than staying home with their children.

Another major reason for the policy change is the Dutch economy. In the early 1980s, the term "Dutch disease" was coined to describe the country's welfare state, seen as expensive and unsustainable. The OECD estimated "broad unemployment" to be 27 percent of the labor force (Visser and Hemerijck 1997: 9). Changes in policies toward working mothers were part of a larger agenda of increasing the size of the active labor force (Visser and Hemerijck 1997). The well-known "Dutch miracle" consisted of a series of active labor market policies designed to get more people into the work force. These policies were extraordinarily successful, particularly with regard to women. Dutch women entered the work force in large numbers for the first time, albeit primarily as part-time workers.

Why did the Dutch decide to send mothers to work instead of paying them to stay home? In a culture that has traditionally assigned an extremely high value to mothers' care, this decision was particularly surprising. It would have been possible, and perhaps even cheaper, to send mothers to work only after their youngest child reached the age of three. Indeed, single mothers are not expected to work until their children reach the age of five. In the cultural context of the Netherlands, it would not have been difficult to argue that a long care leave would help women maintain their relationship with the workplace, while still being able to remain at home with their young children. Furthermore, as has been argued repeatedly in the German case, lengthy parental leaves lessen the need for expensive child care for children under the age of three. Even in the context of economic distress, the CDA might have insisted on some sort of paid leave as a trade-off to increasing subsidies for child care. Similar trades have happened in Italy in the 1970s and in recent reforms in France.

A problem with getting paid parental leave in the Netherlands is the lack of a strong institutional actor advocating the policy. This stance would have been the natural domain of the CDA. Indeed, the CDA continues to support the spread of information on the dangers of day care to young children (Morgan 2006) and the population is quite receptive to this message. The lack of organizational representation for conservative women is one reason why the Netherlands did not implement lengthy care leaves. Christian Democratic women who most preferred this policy solution did not have a powerful voice within their own political party.

Quotas

The early 1980s saw a series of conflicts between the leadership of the CDA and the leadership of the CDAV. The main source of conflict was over whether the CDAV was simply an educational institution with the goal of training women (as the main CDA would have preferred) or whether it should engage in other activities such as advocating for particular policies (as the leaders of the CDAV would have preferred) (Van de Velde 1994:

109). The CDAV did ultimately try to work to increase women's representation within the party and even began advocating for a quota in the mid-1980s. However, because the CDAV was not well anchored in the party leadership, the main CDA was able to circumvent these efforts. In fact, when the main CDA began working on increasing female representation, they did it in such a way as to exclude the CDAV from the process.

For the elections of 1977, 1981, and 1982, the three confessional parties had maintained separate electoral lists. Having lists for three separate parties chosen by three separate selection processes naturally made it more difficult for the CDAV to have a significant effect on candidate selection because the CDAV would have to target each party individually. Nevertheless, for the 1982 election, the CDAV began sending informational packets to its leaders in the national constituency associations with suggestions on how to increase women's representation. The suggested goal of the national level CDAV was to try for a woman at every fourth spot on the electoral list (Van de Velde 1994: 114). This approach would have yielded 25 percent female candidates, on par with the quota the Social Democrats had at the time.

The fusion of the three confessional parties was sufficiently completed that by the 1986 election they nominated a single electoral list. This change made it easier for the CDAV to advocate for increasing women's representation. In May 1986, at its national meeting, the CDAV adopted an internal proposal demanding that on future party lists, one third of electable spots be reserved for women (Van de Velde 1994: 115). This clear request for a quota with a numerical target attached came earlier in the Netherlands than in the other countries under investigation here. However, the CDAV also acknowledged that this goal was probably unachievable. They used it at least partially as a rallying cry for women in general and CDAV members in particular to become more active in the party.

Independently from the actions of the CDAV, the main CDA was studying its relationship to the electorate. The party conducted three separate studies from 1981 to 1984. One study showed that while the CDA had an advantage with female voters, they had few female members of parliament and the party's image was older, grey, and male (Van de Velde 1994: 120–121). Subsequent studies recommended trying to modernize the party image, including the suggestion of selecting more female and more youthful candidates. These recommendations were not approved by the party as a whole, however.

Despite the CDAV's demand for a quota and despite the CDA's own interest in "modernizing" the party's image, little headway was made on the goal of increasing women's representation over the course of the 1986 election. The final CDA list had 15 percent women in the top 40 slots and 31 percent women overall on the list (Van de Velde 1994: 120). This was the most female candidates that the CDA had ever fielded, but over the course of the candidate selection process, female candidates had been steadily weeded out. Female sitting parliamentarians were evaluated less favorably than male sitting parliamentarians and newly proposed female candidates were less likely to have the strong backing of interest groups than were newly proposed male candidates (Van de Velde 1994: 119). Perhaps most importantly, in terms of internal representation within the CDA, factors such as achieving regional distribution and balancing candidates from the three predecessor parties were more important than achieving a particular balance of men and women (Van de Velde 1994: 119). In a sense, the three predecessor parties were acting like internal party factions, a situation that tends to be detrimental to women's chances of representation.

Rather than using the candidate selection process as a way to accommodate the demands of the CDAV, the main CDA was explicit about not empowering its women's organization. The CDAV had submitted a list of ten candidates who met the criteria proposed by the Executive Committee, but only two of these women made it on to the final party list (Van de Velde 1994: 120). The female candidates who made it onto the list were largely those selected by the main CDA and not by the CDAV. The CDA fared better than expected in the 1986 election so many of these female candidates were elected to parliament despite their lower positions on the party list (Van de Velde 1994: 120).

The CDA's own efforts to increase women's representation focused on nonquota methods. In 1988, the CDA used a government subsidy to hire someone to investigate the issue of female representation. Previously, this subsidy had been used to support the political parties' women's organizations and was therefore housed within the CDAV (Van de Velde 1994: 121). The new project was under the supervision of the main party. After this project discovered that 22.7 percent of CDA members were female, the party leadership decided to try to aim for 22.7 percent women in party offices (Van de Velde 1994: 122). However, the suggestion of giving "fully competent" women preferential treatment in obtaining office was rejected. Instead, the party focused on trying to recruit additional female members, on political education for women, and on urging lower levels of the party to voluntarily increase women's participation. The idea of any kind of quota for women was explicitly rejected (Van de Velde 1994: 122–123).

The CDAV had demanded a quota in 1986, but the organization did not have a sufficiently powerful position within the party to make its demands heard. Indeed, the CDA went to some effort to increase women's representation *without* the input (or increased representation of) the CDAV. This alternative path seems to have worked to increase women's representation. The CDA does well now at getting women into parliament, but the party accomplished this without a quota and without the participation of the CDAV.

CONCLUSION

This chapter demonstrates the importance of women's representation within the organization of political parties in cross-national perspective. It argues that in Austria, as in Germany, Christian Democratic women were well represented within their party. In the Austrian case, female Christian Democrats were able to exert a significant influence over their party's policy making on women's issue. In the Italian and Dutch Christian Democratic parties, this was not the case. The Italian DC was a corporatist catch-all party, but women were not included in its system of internal representation. The Dutch CDA has some features of a corporatist catch-all party, particularly in the way its predecessor parties have been represented within the CDA. The CDA's women's organization, however, does not have significant power within the party. In both Italy and the Netherlands, the voices of Christian Democratic women went unheard even in their own parties.

9

Conclusion

In September 1998, the Christian Democratic–Liberal coalition that had governed Germany for sixteen years was defeated in national elections. While the CDU itself was reluctant to acknowledge the problem, a primary reason behind this defeat was that the Christian Democrats lost the support of female voters, especially older women who had formed the party's most loyal support group (Molitor and Neu 1999). Certainly, many other factors contributed to the removal of the Christian Democrats from office: weariness with Helmut Kohl, a stalled economy with high unemployment, and the desire for something new. But if the CDU had managed to maintain its earlier levels of female support, Kohl and the Christian Democrats might have pulled out yet another victory.

In the 1998 Bundestag elections, the CDU/CSU's advantage with female voters effectively vanished. The Christian Democrats received only 0.1 percent more votes from women than from men. This was the smallest women's bonus ever, with the exception of 1980. The 1998 elections also marked the first time in the history of the Federal Republic that the majority of women ages 45 to 59 voted for parties of the left, rather than parties of the right (Molitor and Neu 1999: 257). However, the situation was even worse in 2002 when the CDU again polled worse with women than with men. When the party recovered some of this ground among women in 2005, it was able to reenter government.

Following the argument outlined in this book, limited female support for the CDU/CSU in 1998 and 2002 is not that surprising. In 1998, the Women's Union had been out of the dominant coalition for nine years. Although the Women's Union had been able to push through some moderate reforms, most of its proposals were defeated within the party. Kohl's

TABLE 9.1 *CDU/CSU Women's Bonus, 1969–1998*

Election Year	Women's Vote minus Men's Vote (in percentages)
1969	10.0
1972	3.0
1976	1.6
1980	−0.5
1983	1.5
1987	2.6
1990	2.9
1994	1.6
1998	0.1
2002	−1.4
2005	−0.2

For 1969–87 calculated from results in Ritter and Niehuss (1991: 224). 1990 results calculated from Claus Fischer(1997: 78). 1994 results calculated from Ritter and Niehuss (1995: 51). 1998 results calculated from Molitor and Neu (1999: 255). Election results from 2002 and 2005 calculated from information found at http://www.election.de/cgi-bin/news1.pl.

Minister of Women and Youth from 1994 to 1998, Claudia Nolte, was very conservative and made the CDU seem even further out of touch on women's issues. While the voices of the more progressive Women's Union were never silenced entirely, these voices had little influence over CDU actions. The election result reveals the danger of keeping a demographically powerful group out of the dominant coalition for too long. To some extent, the CDU showed that it recognized this danger when it elected Angela Merkel as its first female General Secretary in November 1998 and as the first female party chair in April 2000. And, of course, Merkel went on to win the 2005 election, albeit by the finest of margins.

This book has argued that in a corporatist catch-all party, as opposed to a classic catch-all party, party policy making is largely the product of internal organizations and alliances rather than just strategic positioning by leaders and the pursuit of electoral goals. All catch-all parties face a similar dilemma. They must appeal to a wide range of societal interest groups, many of which are likely to disagree with each other. The challenge for catch-all parties is to build a broad enough coalition to win elections. The traditional theory about catch-all parties says that two responses to this dilemma are possible. The first is that a catch-all party will offer a diluted ideology to voters while demobilizing membership, so that members cannot force a more extreme stance onto the party. The second possibility is that a catch-all party will attempt to offer a diluted ideology and demobilize membership, but will fail because entrenched membership forces the party into untenable extremist positions.

While the previous scenario may hold for some catch-all parties, it does not accurately depict the German CDU. Not all catch-all parties are alike. Party organizations differ from each other and these differences have real implications for party behavior. In particular, how conflict within a political party is handled influences the party's policy making. A corporatist catch-all party responds to societal change not by demo-bilizing membership in the manner of a classic catch-all party, but by mobilizing and incorporating new groups. This organizational strategy leads to a distinctive pattern of policy making. Policy in a corporatist catch-all party tends to emerge from the interplay of internal interest groups, as opposed to the party's founding ideology, strategic interaction with rival parties or the independent initiatives of party leaders. Certainly corporatist catch-all parties want to win elections, but the process by which they attempt to do so is significantly more complicated than responding directly to voter demands. Instead, societal demands are filtered through the party's internal organizational dynamic. Party response to voter demands depends on the prevailing pattern of internal representation and alliances.

This book has focused on how women are integrated into one particular corporatist catch-all party, the German CDU. The corporatist catch-all party structure also has implications for which groups are incorporated and for internal party democracy. The remainder of this conclusion considers in turn the implications for women of the corporatist catch-all party organization, the evidence from corporatist catch-all parties in other countries, and the implications of the corporatist catch-all party structure for internal party democracy.

IMPLICATIONS FOR WOMEN

The research in this book provides evidence that party organization matters. Christian Democratic women with party organizations at their disposal were significantly more likely to be able to get their party to advocate and implement their policy preferences. In Germany and Austria, Christian Democratic women were more influential within their political parties because the party's women's organizations could provide engaged activists and ideas. In Italy and the Netherlands, Christian Democratic women attempted but usually failed to get their parties to enact their policy preferences because they did not have party organizations to rely on.

If women are represented on a party's decision-making bodies, as in a corporatist catch-all party, then that party will tend to be more responsive to their demands. The difference can be significant, even in the case of a conservative, Christian party. Because the CDU is a *corporatist* catch-all party, not just a classic catch-all party or Christian party, women in Germany have made far greater gains than their counterparts in Italy and the Netherlands, where Christian Democratic parties offer no special representation to women's groups.

Another important insight from this research is that conservative women are not feminists. As obvious as that sounds, it is easy for scholars to make claims about what "women" want and then also to argue that any deviations from that ideal are driven by men. Conservative or Christian Democratic women have their own policy preferences, distinct from both feminist women on the left and Christian Democratic men.

Both the German CDU and the Austrian ÖVP are corporatist catch-all parties in which women are one of the represented groups. As is clear from the analysis, corporatist catch-all parties represent a variety of groups. It is the represented groups that are empowered during internal party bargaining over policy making. One possible arena for future research would be to investigate the reactions of these parties to demands from groups that are not recognized, such as immigrants and environmentalists. The hypothesis generated by this research would be that such groups would fare significantly less well than women in getting their voices heard within these parties.

IMPLICATIONS FOR PARTIES

The German Christian Democratic Union and the Austrian People's Party are both corporatist catch-all parties, but they are not the only corporatist catch-all parties. The comparisons thus far have all been to political parties on the right. The following analysis of two additional parties, both on the left, show that this type of party organization is more widespread. This examination of the French Socialist Party (PS) and the Hungarian Socialist Party (HSP) yields insights into the initial conditions that are likely to produce a corporatist catch-all party structure. The analysis of the French PS and the HSP deepen our understanding of two additional features of corporatist catch-all parties. First, these additional examples emphasize the importance of the party manager. Corporatist catch-all parties are more successful when they have the "right" kind of leadership. Konrad Adenauer, Helmut Kohl, and Angela Merkel have been adept at balancing the various groups within the CDU. François Mitterrand was able to "manage" the internal conflict in the French PS. Gyula Horn brought together conflicting groups within the HSP (Ágh 2002: 278). Under party management leadership, these corporatist catch-all parties were enormously successful at the polls.

This analysis also highlights a major pitfall of this form of organization: factionalism. Competition within these political parties is always to some extent about the career advancement of particular leaders and "their" suborganizations. When internal party competition shifts to become *exclusively* about the distribution of offices or other spoils, these parties become much less attractive to voters who then regard them as obsessed with fighting over trivial and self-serving matters.

The French Socialists

The French Socialist Party (prior to 1971 this party was called the *Section Française de l'Internationale Ouvrière* (SFIO), after 1971 it adopted the name *Parti Socialiste* (PS)) adopted a corporatist catch-all model as part of its strategy for becoming the major party of the Left in the French Fifth Republic.[1] By investigating why the party decided to make this organizational change, we can gain insight into the sorts of pressures that are likely to lead to the adoption of a corporatist catch-all party structure. The internal changes made by the French Socialist Party were part of a broader strategy. To understand the decisions made by party leaders, it is necessary to review some of the political context leading up to the 1970s.

The Socialists had been out of power since the founding of the Fifth Republic in 1958. The problem they faced was two-fold: their opponents on the right, the Gaullists, represented a near hegemonic force and the left was internally divided. The 1962 change to a directly elected president increased the payoff to a potential alliance on the Left. In May of 1968 widespread protests weakened the political right and led to the withdrawal of their leader, Charles de Gaulle.[2] The weakness of the right provided a political opening. None of the major political parties – including the SFIO

---

[1] Kitschelt uses different terminology but also points out the importance of this organization change (Kitschelt 1994: 234–6).

[2] On the other hand, the uprising of May 1968 increased the interest in "new politics" and threatened to divide the Left even further.

and the French Communist Party (PCF) on the left – backed the protesters. Therefore, a significant opportunity emerged for any party that could appeal to the 10 million people who had been on strike (Northcutt 1985: 28). However, the left still needed to improve its internal coherence before it would be strong enough to gain power.

The French left had been divided throughout the twentieth century with divisions not only between the Socialists and the Communists but among several smaller parties as well. The eventual emergence of a strong socialist party was certainly not a foregone conclusion. François Mitterrand, an independent leader on the left, had attempted to unite the left when he formed a coalition of parties, including the Communist Party, to back his candidacy for the presidency in 1965. Although Mitterrand polled 45 percent against de Gaulle in the 1965 presidential election, the coalition he had based his candidacy on broke apart. In the presidential election following de Gaulle's 1969 resignation, the SFIO candidate, Gaston Defferre, polled only 5 percent with votes on the left divided among several parties (Bell and Criddle 1988: 52). In the late 1960s, the French Socialists appeared to be developing into a marginal force that was, like the Italian Socialists, dwarfed by a more powerful Communist party.

The French Socialists faced a choice of strategies in their attempts to become a more significant political party. They could look to the right and form an alliance with groups in the center of the political spectrum or they could look to the left and cooperate with the French Communist Party (PCF). The lesson from the presidential elections of 1965 and 1969 seemed to be that uniting the parties of the left – and working with the Communists – was the most likely path to electoral success for the French Socialist Party (Machin and Wright 1977). The risk of this strategy, however, was that the smaller and less coherent Socialists would be over-run by a larger, better-organized Communist party.

From 1969 to 1971 the French Socialist Party embarked on an internal transformation that would allow it to cooperate with the Communists from a position of strength. Beginning with its July 1969 conference, the Socialist Party committed to a strategy of attempting to unify forces on the left, including negotiations with the French Communist Party, the PCF (Bell and Criddle 1988: 55). This was a clear rejection of the party's other choice, attempting to ally with parties in the political center.

Between 1969 and 1971 frustrated groups on the left came together in a new party, the *Parti socialiste* (PS). At the Épinay Congress in June 1971, the new party elected François Mitterrand First Secretary. The PS also adopted internal proportional representation for ideological factions (or currents) on the party's decision-making bodies (Bell and Criddle 1988: 64). Prior to the transformation, the old Socialist party's internal structure had been based on territorial units. The party's leadership had been able to use this organization to exclude opponents from having influence within the party (Bell and Criddle 1988: 64). After 1971 the units that were represented internally were primarily ideological currents (Sferza 2002: 170). A five percent threshold required for representation was chosen to be low enough to ensure some voice for internal party minorities (Bell and Criddle 1988: 65).

Under the PS's new structure, ideological currents compete with each other for votes at party congresses. The results of these internal elections determine membership on the party's National Council, which picks the top leadership. Ideological currents are generally led by powerful party leaders and are frequently (but not necessarily) rooted in a particular geographic territory (Knapp and Wright 2006: 191).

The new internal party structure was a key component in forging an internal coalition to support Mitterrand. Some of the currents backing Mitterrand were small enough that they would have been excluded under the previous form of organization (Bell and Criddle 1988: 64). These currents wanted to come together in an effort to win power, but were fearful of losing their identity within the larger Socialist Party. Internal representation was a solution for bringing these groups into the party while allowing them to maintain their original identities. Following these changes in internal organization, Mitterrand was elected leader of the PS.

The new internal structure gave the PS increased dynamism. The variety of ideologies represented within the party allowed the PS to appeal to diverse constituencies. The multiple ideological tendencies within the party also made the party appear open to internal debate, which was an exciting prospect. Membership increased from 75,000 in 1971 to 160,000 in 1977 (Northcutt 1985: 30).

With new leadership and a new internal structure, the PS commenced writing a new program and opened negotiations with the PCF. The Common Program of the Left was signed in 1972. The 'Union of the Left' (which included the PS, the PCF, and a third left-wing party, the MRG) went on to do well in the parliamentary elections of 1973 (Bell and Criddle 1988: 72–83). Backed by the Union of the Left, Mitterrand nearly won the presidency in 1974, gaining 49.2 percent of the vote, compared to Valéry Giscard d'Estaing's 50.8 percent (Bell and Criddle 1988: 82). For the Socialists, the strategy of an alliance with the Communists was paying off at the polls. While this alliance experienced some rough patches in the late 1970s,[3] it went on to victory when Mitterrand won the presidency in 1981, the first candidate of the left to be elected in the Fifth Republic.

While most corporatist catch-all parties adopt their internal structure at the party's founding (see Panebianco 1988), some do not. What does seem necessary for a party to adopt this form of organization is a similar strategic challenge – a party that wants to appeal to diverse societal constituencies while winning elections. The classic catch-all strategy is one response to this challenge, but not the only one. The French Socialist Party (PS) switched to a corporatist catch-all strategy in the period 1969–71. The move to a corporatist catch-all party structure was a major contributor to the PS's subsequent success (Sferza 2002). The adoption of a corporatist catch-all party structure in 1971 allowed the PS to widen and deepen its appeal simultaneously (Sferza 2002: 171). The representation of a range of ideological currents in the party meant many people in society felt attracted to the PS. Furthermore, being active within an ideological current had a real payoff as such activism would increase the internal power of that faction.

Although the PS has had its ups and downs since the early 1970s, it has established itself as one of the two major parties in France. The strategy adopted by the PS in the 1970s helped eliminate the Communists as a serious threat and changed the party landscape in France. France now has a largely bipolar system with a variety of smaller parties. Note that this change on the left dates *not* from 1958/61 and the founding of the Fifth Republic but from internal changes within the PS from 1969 to 1971.

The departure of Mitterrand did not change the importance of the PS for the French party system. It is true that the corporatist catch-all party structure became somewhat corrupted with time as factions became more personalized and less ideology-based (Sferza 2002). Some of the current travails of the French Socialist Party may be that the PS lacks a leader who is talented at managing the party's internal groups. The party has lost the last three presidential elections. Disaffected activists left the party in November 2008 to form the new Party of the Left in the wake of a severely contested leadership battle. Still, the PS improved its position in the parliamentary elections of June 2007. The UMP and the PS together received over 73 percent of the votes, providing evidence for renewed bipolarity of

---

[3] In 1976 the PS started outpolling the PCF. In the late 1970s, this alliance was increasingly marked by internal rivalry, especially as the PCF became willing to sacrifice the success of the Common Program in an effort to limit the power of the PS.

the French party system (Knapp and Sawicki 2008: 44). The current situation of the PS is comparable to that of the CDU in the early 1970s. Having now definitively lost national elections, the party must go through a process of renewal and it needs fresh leadership. If the CDU of the 1970s can provide any lessons for the French PS, it may be that the adoption of the corporatist catch-all party structure, which helped the PS move into the ranks of a top tier party, will also serve to guide the party through a period of reorientation.

The Hungarian Socialists

East Central Europe is a rather unlikely place to find corporatist catch-all parties. One of the legacies of the Communist period is a weak civil society and populations largely uninterested in being politically active (Howard 2003). In many East Central European countries, the democratic dreams of 1989/1990 have proved more difficult to achieve than expected because it has been hard to establish consolidated political parties with reasonably strong links to society in an era when parties can rely on the mass media to accomplish some of the tasks previously achieved through party organization (Mainwaring and Zoco 2007).

Broadly speaking, most of the new political parties coming out of the democratic transitions of Eastern and East Central Europe could initially be categorized as one of two types. Communist successor parties maintained the strong organizations and financial resources of their predecessor parties, but of course, these parties were tainted by their historic support for state socialism.[4] Genuinely new parties, on the other hand, lacked both organization and financial resources. Once the old regimes fell, new parties often found it difficult to establish themselves in newly democratic systems.

The Hungarian Socialist Party is an important exception to these trends (Ágh 1995: 497). While other Communist successor parties changed their names but little else, the Hungarian Socialist Party (HSP) went through a much more serious transformation. The HSP is one of the successor parties to the Hungarian Communist Party that was in power during the Soviet

---

[4] Grzymala-Busse (2002) notes that the Communist successor parties' ability to regenerate themselves depended on their pretransition history as well as their own actions. The Hungarian Socialist Party made the most decisive break with its past despite having the least need for such a break (because the Hungarian Communist Party was quite reform-oriented). Critically for the argument made here, the Hungarian Socialist Party also had relatively less need to centralize its internal organization after the transition (Grzymala-Busse 2002: 107).

period. However, the transition to democracy happened differently in Hungary than in other Eastern and Central European countries. The HSP emerged before the collapse of Communism and was a key player in bringing an end to the old system (Ágh 1995: 492). In this way it is unique among the Communist successor parties in East Central Europe.

The HSP made a much more complete break from the former Communist Party than most other Communist successor parties in Eastern Europe (Ágh 1995: 492).[5] All members of the former Communist Party were forced to reregister when the party changed its name to the Hungarian Socialist Party. This resulted in a massive membership exodus (Machos 2002: 20). The HSP accepted the assets of the former Communist Party, but then returned them to society rather than keeping them for the party's use (Ágh 1997: 429).

Despite being quite different from other post-Communist parties, the HSP was initially punished by voters for being part of the old regime. In the first democratic elections in 1990 the HSP received only 11 percent of the vote. However, the HSP went on to do much better in subsequent elections and has emerged as one of the two leading parties in Hungary.[6] The party led the governing coalition from 1994 to 1998, and again from 2002 until today. It was reelected to a new term most recently in 2006.

Like the French Socialists, the Hungarian Socialist Party (HSP) is also a corporatist catch-all party. Two aspects of the HSP's internal structure encouraged the party to adopt a corporatist catch-all party organization during the transition to democracy. First, as the only available party during the Communist period, the HSP had a very broad spectrum of supporters. This internal composition did not change even after the democratic transition; the HSP remained an internally heterogeneous party. The party has had candidates representing both business and labor interests. It has supporters from across Hungarian society, which leads to significant internal diversity and conflict (Ágh 1995: 502).

The second factor that led the HSP to adopt a corporatist catch-all party structure was the effort to make a clear break with the tradition of "democratic centralism." In trying to distinguish itself from its Communist predecessor, the HSP introduced a range of organizational reforms to decentralize power within the party. The local party organizations were given a great deal of autonomy and a range of societal groups were represented within the party (Ágh 1995: 493). Both local party

---

[5] Other parties have carried on the Communist tradition in Hungary (Hungarian Socialist Workers' Party, Hungarian Communist Workers' Party, Workers' Party of Hungary 2006).
[6] For election results see: http://www.abdn.ac.uk/cspp/hunelec.shtml.

organizations and a wide variety of functional groups are included in the main party's decision-making structures. In addition to territorial suborganizations, the HSP has internal groups called *sections*. Sections represent a range of societal groups including women, workers, teachers, farmers, local governments, doctors, businessmen, and the retired, among others (Ágh 1995: 507). The party also has internal groups for different political orientations called *platforms*. Additionally, societal organizations in cooperation with the party, such as a youth organization, are represented as well. Territorial subunits, sections, platforms, and affiliated societal organizations all receive representation on the party's decision-making bodies (Machos 2002: 59–62; 66).

The corporatist catch-all party structure may have helped the HSP manage its internal diversity after it was reelected in 1994.[7] The party's electoral results improved from 11 percent of the vote to 33 percent. Many of the deputies in 1994 won constituency seats rather than being elected through the party list and therefore were likely to be less loyal to the party and more committed to their local or social base (Ágh 1995: 503). Furthermore, once in government the HSP implemented economic austerity measures that provoked internal party conflict (Ágh 1997: 432). The corporatist catch-all party structure helped ameliorate internal party tension. For example, cabinet positions were distributed with an eye toward factional balance (Ziblatt 1998: 134).[8] The HSP has also increased the frequency of party congresses in an effort to reduce tensions between members and leaders and to channel membership input (Ágh 1997: 434).

Like the French PS (and for that matter like the German CDU and the Austrian ÖVP of the postwar era), the Hungarian HSP used the corporatist catch-all party structure to build and unite a large, internally diverse political party. This type of structure can help integrate a variety of groups into a single political party, thereby making that party into a major electoral player. All four of these parties were able to use the corporatist catch-all party strategy to transform themselves from secondary (small to medium-sized) parties to primary (large) parties within their respective party systems.

Part of the necessary context for the adoption of a corporatist catch-all party organization is a commitment to democracy. While these parties are not internally democratic in a way that would allow the full membership to

---

[7] Internal diversity can also lead to problems with internal party infighting. The HSP underwent a phase of intense factional conflict in the late 1990s, but then recovered (Machos 2002: 21).

[8] Some observers at the time suggested a "Hungarian solution" for the Polish left – which would have meant bringing the different tendencies on the left inside a single party rather than having multiple parties of the left in competition with each other (Ágh 1997: 436).

vote on party policy or elect party leadership, the value of democracy is an inherent part of party ideology. This insight draws our attention back to the paradox discussed in the opening pages of this book.

THE CORPORATIST CATCH-ALL PARTY AND DEMOCRATIC THEORY

In the introduction I noted that political parties can be seen as presenting an apparent paradox for democracy. Modern democratic nation states appear unable to function without parties and yet parties also force compromises with democracy itself. On the one hand, internally democratic political parties have the potential to empower activists who are likely to hold more extreme positions than voters (May 1973). If activists are empowered, and if their viewpoints differ significantly from voters, then they may force their parties to unelectable positions. The British Labour Party and the German Social Democratic Party have both fallen victim to this fate at times (Koelble 1991; Kitschelt 1994). On the other hand, if parties are not internally democratic – and Michels' Iron Law of Oligarchy predicts that they will not be – then wouldn't democracy itself be compromised because party leaders would escape popular control (Michels 1962)?

In order to specify the role of the corporatist catch-all party in understanding this dilemma, we must engage more thoroughly with democratic theory. The previous paradox is actually inherent to a particular vision of democracy, a vision I call here the competitive model. The competitive model of democracy takes economics as its inspiration for the functioning of the democratic system. It envisions an electoral marketplace in which rather than firms competing for customers, parties compete to win votes. Voters hold parties accountable for their past actions by either reelecting them or voting them out. In this model, democracy is about restraining government from deviating from citizens' interests. Accountability is critical. Voters control the government through their ability to vote the governing party out of power at election time. Competitive elections help express the popular will – to the extent that there is anything like a popular will in a mass public. Party competition in this model is the prime mechanism for both restraining and enabling the government.[9]

---

[9] Note that this is an idealized version of this model of democracy. Many authors subdivide competitive democracy into various subcategories. This analysis follows Teorell (1999) and Allern and Pedersen (2007) in considering these approaches together as the competitive model. It draws on the theories of Schattschneider (1942); Schumpeter (1942); Dahl (1956); Downs (1957); and Sartori (1987).

The competitive model favors representative government. The masses are not regarded as interested (from some perspectives they are also not seen as qualified) in governing directly. The limited participation involved in voting is sufficient for the people to control the government. Preferences are exogenous to the political system, that is, citizens know what political outcomes they desire, and their preferences are not significantly altered by political discourse or activity.

The primary tasks of political parties, according to the competitive model of democracy, are vote structuring, preference aggregation, and provision of accountability (Allern and Pedersen 2007: 72). Society itself is seen as divided and conflictual. The task of political parties is to aggregate interests. Most theorists find that parties that are internally cohesive are better able to manage the task of structuring the vote (Allern and Pedersen 2007; Katz 1997). If a party is not cohesive, it is difficult for voters to hold it responsible because it is unclear whether the party (or who within the party) is responsible for the actions and policies with which the voter is unhappy (Katz 1997: 38).[10]

Political parties in the competitive model of democracy do not need to be internally democratic. Indeed, internal democracy can create problems for the system's democratic functioning. Debates within a political party can blur that party's policy offering in the electoral marketplace and make voters unsure what they will get if they give that party their support. This makes democracy much less efficient. Furthermore, parties in this model are supposed to be responsible to *voters* not *members* so internal democracy would empower the wrong group (Allern and Pedersen 2007: 72).[11] Internally democratic political parties, therefore, are actually disadvantageous from the perspective of the competitive model because they are inefficient and because they make parties responsive to the wrong group. From this perspective, societal democracy trumps internal party democracy and the paradox is resolved.

At first glance, the corporatist catch-all party structure seems to exemplify the problems that internally democratic political parties pose for the

---

[10] Some versions of competitive democracy do not call for permanent cohesive parties. Ostrogorski (1902) and Madison can be seen as working within the tradition of the competitive model, yet these theorists argue against permanent parties. In addition to checking the government, these theorists are seeking ways to check a potentially overly powerful party or faction (Katz 1997).

[11] Possible exceptions include Katz's vision of Socialist popular sovereignty and Duverger's binary democracy. In these versions, internal democracy leads to the program and then the program is not to be deviated from (Katz 1997).

competitive model. After all, corporatist catch-all parties institutionalize internal party conflict. With multiple, often conflicting, interests given representation and voice within the party, a corporatist catch-all party's programmatic offering is likely to be blurrier than that of a cohesive, internally disciplined party. Furthermore, in a corporatist catch-all party, leaders respond to members as well as to voters. From the perspective of most theorists of competitive democracy, a corporatist catch-all party would be at best useless and at worst harmful.

The competitive model itself, however, has some notable problems. Because it is extremely difficult for new parties to form, the electoral marketplace is much closer to an oligopolistic market than a market with perfect competition (Ware 1979: 40–52). The terms of competition under oligopoly are quite different than in a competitive market. Just as oligopolists have no incentive to engage in price competition with each other, parties may not have sufficient incentive to redefine the arena of political conflict (Ware 1979: 45). This dynamic implies that parties may not respond to changing demands from voters. If parties have a shared disinterest in addressing new questions, these issues may be kept out of the political arena (Carmines and Stimson 1989). For the model to work, when a new issue emerges or when there is a shift in the distribution of voter preferences, parties should move to capture those voters and increase their vote share. However, if appealing to new voters (or using a new issue to appeal to voters) risks sacrificing existing constituencies, parties might not change their positions. Aside from the possibility of collusion among parties, one can imagine a situation in which all established parties simply share a disinterest in raising a particular issue (Katz and Mair 1995; 1996). From this perspective, the competitive model is significantly flawed even from its own internal logic (Ware 1979 as discussed in Teorell 1999: 366–7).

What is more, even well-intentioned party elites might not have the means to discover new issues or latent voting groups. Party leaders do not have perfect information about the electorate. Of course, if a party loses an election, it may try a new strategy, but it would be preferable to have information about changes in the electorate prior to a lost election. Parties can also make use of opinion polling, but that approach requires that party elites know what to ask, which may not be the case. The competitive model may break down because party leaders have insufficient information.

Democratic political parties are Ware's solution to this problem. Because it is so difficult to form a new political party, voters do not have an effective exit option. Using Hirschman's framework, Ware proposes internally democratic parties to give voters "voice" within the party and allow new political concerns to percolate up to party leadership (Hirschman 1970; Ware 1979: 78). Internal party democracy would create a mechanism to force party leaders to respond to new issues and changing societal demands.

As Teorell points out, however, Ware's analysis suffers from certain flaws (Teorell 1999: 367). Ware assumes that the views of party activists will match those of the electorate – that is, that a new demand from the electorate will somehow make it into the party membership. But he offers no evidence to support this viewpoint and May (1973) argues that party members will tend to hold more extreme views than voters.[12] If party members differ significantly from voters then membership may not be able to offer a voice within the party to new voter concerns. The party could continue to ignore them.

A corporatist catch-all party is one possibility for overcoming these difficulties within the competitive model. The groups within a corporatist catch-all party are internally differentiated. Therefore, they represent multiple points of view and a wide spectrum of positions within the party. A corporatist catch-all party grants recognition to multiple sides of a debate in most cases.

Furthermore, because a variety of groups are represented within the party and because no group can be eliminated, corporatist catch-all parties tend toward moderate rather than extremist policy making. The membership of a corporatist catch-all party may be more politically engaged than voters, but in the aggregate they are not necessarily more extreme than voters because multiple political positions are represented within the party. The problem of potential differences between membership views and voter views is therefore less acute.

Additionally, the corporatist catch-all party provides party elites with a connection to society, thereby giving them information about public concerns. The corporatist catch-all party structure helps keep the party in touch with changing demands from society.

These features of a corporatist catch-all party begin to address all three of the concerns about the competitive model raised previously. The internal party groups provide the party elites with closer contact with societal-level concerns. This information is likely to be more detailed than would be possible with opinion polls. Furthermore, within the party the possibility exists for continued discussion about a particular topic. While intentional

---

[12] Ware also does not address the efficiency problem. This problem may be more theoretical than empirical, however (Wattenberg 2000: 71–76; Allern and Pedersen 2007: 73).

collusion would still be possible, it is less likely given the ability of the party's internal party groups to raise new issues.

Because representation is guaranteed, leaders have to listen to a variety of viewpoints whether they want to or not. A corporatist catch-all party provides a message transmitter from societal demands to the leadership of the party. Corporatist catch-all parties can help provide political parties under the competitive model of democracy with an increased connection to society, thereby helping to overcome Ware's critique that competition under this model tends toward oligopoly. The corporatist catch-all party structure provides a possibility for internally democratic political parties even under the competitive model of democracy.

EXPANDING DEMOCRATIC HORIZONS

In addition to helping resolve the dilemma that emerges under the competitive model of democracy, the corporatist catch-all party structure can help realize some of the values held by the deliberative model of democracy. This section first explains the deliberative model. It then explores how the corporatist catch-all party might be able to help realize some of the values held by this model.

The deliberative model of democracy is based on the idea that rational discussion should precede political decision making. Deliberation can be seen as reasoned debate in which the participants remain open to reasonable arguments from people with whom they do not initially agree. Indeed, theorists of deliberative democracy argue that, far from being exogenous, people may not know their true preferences until they have engaged in deliberation. It is through discussion with others that we can judge which ideas are best. Gutmann and Thompson define deliberative democracy as "a form of government in which free and equal citizens (and their representatives), justify decisions in a process in which they give one another reasons that are mutually acceptable and generally accessible, with the aim of reaching conclusions that are binding in the present on all citizens but open to challenge in the future" (Gutmann and Thompson 2004: 7).

The deliberative model of democracy assumes that real conflict exists in society. In keeping with the competitive model, deliberative democrats also favor voting as part of reaching agreement, but voting alone is not seen as sufficient. Deliberation should precede (and thereby legitimate) elections. Deliberation should occur "under conditions promoting reasoned reflection open to both affected and competent parties" (Allern and Pedersen 2007: 80). Reasoned debate means that participants go into the discussion with open minds. They must be willing to consider the question at hand from others' perspectives, though they do not ultimately have to reach consensus.

The deliberative model assumes that preferences will be formed in part through the process of deliberation. But unlike the participatory model, the deliberative model of democracy does not require widespread participation.[13] It is left up to citizens to decide whether and how to participate. Limited participation is fine as long as it fits the requirements of the deliberative model – that is, open and reasoned debate. Thus, deliberative democracy is more easily combined with representative government than participatory democracy is (Gutmann and Thompson 1996: 128–64; Teorell 1999: 372).

There are several points to deliberation. It should make political decision making more legitimate because decisions are made through a process of reasoned discussion rather than simply reflecting the relative power of different groups. It should encourage citizens to take a broader perspective because they will hear the views of others explained. While deliberation cannot force agreement, it should help participants recognize the value in their opponents' positions. Finally, deliberation should increase the quality of decision making. Talking through the issue at hand with rational arguments may allow participants to find more common ground than they had previously had. When citizens deliberate, they can "expand their knowledge, including both their self-understanding and their collective understanding of what will best serve their fellow citizens" (Gutmann and Thompson 2004: 10–12).

Deliberative democracy naturally requires a forum in which deliberation can take place. Some theorists of deliberative democracy have focused more on theorizing about the process of deliberation itself while spending relatively little attention on the institutional underpinnings of deliberation. However, inventing a real-life arena in which to deliberate is not a trivial undertaking. Attempting to structure deliberation for decision making in a nation state inhabited by millions of people for decisions on thousands of topics is daunting to say the least. Luckily we already have institutions designed to respond to the political demands of citizens in democracies: political parties.[14]

---

[13] A third model of democracy, the participatory model, is not treated extensively here. While it can be argued that the corporatist catch-all party structure encourages participation, this type of party organization does not facilitate the widespread participation required by the participatory model. As discussed in the following, the corporatist catch-all party organization does encourage a wide spectrum of participants from across society, a value shared by the participatory and deliberative models.

[14] One institution for deliberation which has received a lot of attention is Fishkin's deliberative poll (Fishkin 1991; 1995). Fishkin's proposal is to have a randomly sampled

Given the extraordinary amount of literature on deliberative democracy, it is surprising how little of it discusses a role for political parties. The lack of attention to political parties is especially surprising because two important early essays by theorists of deliberative democracy called for a significant role for political parties (Cohen 1989; Manin 1987).

When considering the interaction of deliberative democracy and political parties, much of the theoretical work that exists focuses on the role for political parties in a larger deliberative democracy. Thus Manin (1987) argues that parties can help limit the agenda, because it is not possible to deliberate on everything. Johnson continues in this vein arguing that "It is, therefore, perhaps more appropriate to claim that deliberation structures disagreement rather than to insist that it induces agreement" (Johnson 2006: 49). By narrowing the range of discussion and getting actors to agree on a shared understanding of the problem at hand (though not necessarily on the ideal solution), political parties can also help structure preferences in such a way that voting rules will actually produce stable majorities (Johnson 2006). Additionally, both Cohen (1989) and Christiano (1996) argue that parties can help move the terms of the debate to issues of more general concern rather than particular interests because parties must try to appeal to broad segments of society. What these theorists have in common, then, is that parties may be beneficial actors within a larger deliberative society.[15]

Another possibility is to consider parties themselves as deliberative arenas.[16] Deliberation within a political party would presumably bestow many of the advantages of this form of decision making on the party's decision-making process. Activists might differ from party leaders in their opinions, but party leaders would not be required to follow activist

collection of individuals come together to deliberate on a particular issue or issues. The results of the deliberation represent both the views of the population at large and the process of deliberation. Teorell proposes using Fishkin's deliberative poll for intra-party decision making (Teorell 1999). Deliberative polls within a political party might decide on issues such as the party's policy stances, party finance rules, or even candidate selection. While Teorell's proposal might also realize some of the aims of deliberative democracy, the point here is that the corporatist catch-all party structure may already be accomplishing this goal.

[15] See Budge (2000), however, for the alternative perspective that parties are actually incompatible with deliberative democracy because partisans are necessarily (by definition) already committed to a particular standpoint and therefore are not beginning deliberation with the requisite openness to other positions.

[16] As discussed previously, Teorell argues in favor of deliberation within political parties, advocating "deliberative procedures for the exchange of arguments between party leaders and members" (Teorell 1999: 373). Allowing for deliberation within political parties would provide a mechanism for these parties to access public opinion between elections.

preferences in policy making. Party leaders would be required, however, to justify to membership their divergence from member preferences in a reasonable manner. The same would hold for membership – they would be required to give reasons when advocating their preferences.

The structure of the corporatist catch-all party seems particularly suitable for realizing the goals of deliberative democracy. The corporatist catch-all party structure encourages more extensive interaction between leaders and members within recognized internal party groups. If leaders of a particular group are to increase their power vis-à-vis leaders of other groups, they need a large and active membership of their own group. One way to accomplish this task is through increased engagement and discussion with their members. Both leaders and members of internal groups therefore have the motivation to engage in deliberation.

Furthermore, persuasion – reasoned debate – is the only instrument available to leaders and members in their attempts to convince each other of desirable policy stances for their group. Members are not under any requirement to obey 'their' leaders. Leaders must therefore appeal to their members on the basis of rational discussion. Similarly, leaders are not required to follow the dictates of the members of their group, but it may be to their advantage to engage the membership in deliberation. This structure accomplishes similar goals to the internal deliberative poll with the advantage that it is already in place in some parties. This kind of internal party debate is at least in line with the aims of deliberative democracy. Deliberation within a corporatist catch-all party is fairly widespread. Reasoned debate is the primary mode of exchange. Leadership is not bound to follow the demands of membership but it is required to justify deviation away from those demands.

As just discussed, another advantage of the corporatist catch-all party model is that it represents a wide range of viewpoints within the party. This practice is in keeping with the values held by the deliberative model of democracy. The quality of deliberative decision-making will be significantly reduced if some viewpoints are not heard. A corporatist catch-all party ensures that many voices participate in the party's internal debate.

One area in which a corporatist catch-all party does not fulfill the requirements of deliberative democracy is the question of "open minds." Participants in the internal party discussion may commit to their views fairly early in the process and may not be open to being persuaded through the process of deliberation. On the other hand, this is likely to be true of most matters that people care about in most forums for discussion.

Conclusion

In the classic catch-all party literature, party members exist primarily as a constraint on the ability of enlightened leaders to pursue party modernization and the optimal electoral strategy. The case of the German CDU demonstrates, by contrast, that a political party – even a catch-all party – need not sacrifice internal democracy and ignore or restrain its members in order to be "modern" and successful at the polls. As the case studies discussed in this book demonstrate, increasing membership participation has often benefited the German CDU. New members have brought new ideas and helped the party stay in tune with a changing society.

Furthermore, at least some of the more demanding requirements of deliberative democracy can be fulfilled through democratic political parties. The structure of the corporatist catch-all party creates a dynamic in which leadership encourages rather than discourages membership participation. It is certainly not the case that corporatist catch-all parties are the cure for all democratic deficits. Even if that were true, it is no simple matter to change the internal organization of a political party. However, given the generally pessimistic outlook regarding the ability of political parties to continue to sustain democracy, any sign of hope is worth noting.

Appendix

List of Cited Interviews

Bendig, Kristel, business manager of the CDU Women's Union, interview, Bonn, August 26, 1998.

Böhmer, Maria, Member of the Bundestag, deputy chair of the CDU/CSU Bundestag caucus, chair of the Women's Union of Rhineland-Palatinate, chair of the Women's Union since 2001, interview, Bonn, November 20, 1998.

Breuer, Bernhard, Christlich Demokratische Arbeitnehmerschaft Deutschlands, interview, Bonn, September 25, 1998.

Brinek, Gertrude, Member of the Nationalrat 1994–2008, interview, Vienna, June 17, 2003.

Diemers, Renate, Member of the Bundestag 1990–2002, active in the Women's Union since 1963, interview, Bonn, October 28, 1998.

Geissler, Heiner, Member of the Bundestag 1980–2002, CDU General Secretary 1977–1989, Minister for Youth, Family and Health 1982–1985, interview, Bonn, November 7, 1998.

Hassenbach, Claudia, business manager of the CDU Women's Union, interview, Berlin, June 18, 2008.

Hellwig, Renate, Member of the Bundestag 1980–98, Parliamentary Secretary for the Ministry for Youth, Family and Health, interview, Bonn, November 6, 1998.

Henry-Hutmacher, Christine, Konrad Adenauer Foundation, expert in family and women's policy, interview, St. Augustin, September 29, 1998.

Hesse, Beate, Ministry for Family Affairs, Senior Citizens, Women and Youth, unit for women and career, interview, Bonn, August 19, 1998.

Holzapfel, Elke. Member of the Bundestag 1997–8, deputy chair of the Women's Union, interview, Berlin, June 7, 2008.

Karwatzki, Irmgard, Member of the Bundestag 1976–2005, chair of the Women's Union in North-Rhine-Westfalia 1991–9, interview, Bonn, June 25, 1998.

Kempen, Yvonne, press office of the Bundestag, board of directors of the Women's Union, interview, Bonn, August 5, 1998.

Klug, Annelies, business manager of the Women's Union 1973–85, interview, Bonn, November 19, 1998.

Kollenberg, Udo, assistant to Helga Wex and Heiner Geissler at the Ministry for Family Affairs, various positions, interview, Bonn, August 14, 1998.

Lüders, Birgit, CDU Women's Union, unit on family policy, interview, Bonn, October 1, 1998.

Pack, Doris, Member of the Bundestag 1974–83, 1985–9, Member of the European Parliament 1989–2008, deputy chair of CDU Women's Union, phone interview, July 1, 2008.

Pollmann, Hanne, business manager of the German Women's Council, interview, Bonn, November 24, 1998.

Rauch-Kallat, Maria, Chair of Austrian Women's Movement since 2002, General Secretary of the Austrian People's Party 1999–2003, Minister for Women (cabinet position changed names several times) 1992–4, 2003–7, interview, Vienna, June 18, 2003.

Ristau-Winkler, Malte, Federal Ministry for Family Affairs, Seniors, Women and Youth, Director General, interview, Berlin, June 27, 2008.

Roesgen, Helga, assistant to Hannelore Rönsch (Member of the Bundestag 1983–2002, Minister for Family Affairs and Senior Citizens 1991–4), interview, Bonn, July 9, 1998.

Schulz, Jochen, Christlich Demokratische Arbeitnehmerschaft Deutschlands, interview, Bonn, September 25, 1998.

Sothmann, Bärbel, Member of the Bundestag 1990–2002, Chair of the CDU's Group of Women of the CDU/CSU parliamentary caucus 1994–2000, interview, Bonn, June 19, 1998.

Steininger, Barbara, scholar, University of Vienna, interview, Vienna, June 12, 2003.

Süssmuth, Rita, Member of the Bundestag 1987–2002, Minister for Youth, Family, Women and Health 1985–1988, chair of the CDU Women's Union 1986–2001, interview, Bonn, December 8, 1998.

Walter, Stephan, Ministry for Women and Youth 1991–4, assistant to Christian Wulff on women's issues, interview, Hannover, November 17, 1998.

Welskop-Deffaa, Eva Maria, Federal Ministry of Family Affairs, Senior Citizens, Women and Youth, Head of Department of Equality Policy, interview, Berlin, June 24, 2008.

Zieschang, Tamara, chair of CDU's student organization (Ring Christlich-Demokratischer Studenten, interview, Bonn, August 24, 1998.

List of References

Addis, Elizabeth. 2000. "Gender in the Reform of the Italian Welfare State" in Maria Jose Gonzalez, Teresa Jurado, and Manuela Naldini (eds.), *Gender Inequalities in Southern Europe: Women, Work and Welfare in the 1990s*, London: Frank Cass, pp. 122–49.

Agence France Press, various dates.

Ágh, Atilla. 1995. "Partial Consolidation of the East-Central European Parties: The Case of the Hungarian Socialist Party," *Party Politics*, Vol. 1, No. 4, pp. 491–514.

Ágh, Atilla. 1997. "Defeat and Success as Promoters of Party Change: The Hungarian Socialist Party after Two Abrupt Changes," *Party Politics*, Vol. 3, No. 3, pp. 427–44.

Ágh, Atilla. 2002. "The Dual Challenge and the Reform of the Hungarian Socialist Party," *Communist and Post-Communist Studies*, Vol. 35, Issue 3, pp. 269–88.

Allern, Elin H. and Karina Pedersen. 2007. "The Impact of Party Organisational Changes on Democracy," *West European Politics*, Vol. 30, Issue 1, pp. 68–92.

Altbach, Edith. 1984. "The New German Women's Movement," in Edith Altbach, J. Clause, D. Schultz, and N. Stephan (eds.), *German Feminism: Readings in Politics and Literature*, 3–26. Albany: State University of New York Press.

Anderson, Margaret Lavinia. 1981. *Windthorst: A Political Biography*. New York: Oxford University Press.

Ansell, Christopher K. and M. Steven Fish. 1999. "The Art of Being Indispensible: Noncharismatic Personalism in Contemporary Political Parties," *Comparative Political Studies*, Vol. 32, No. 3, pp. 283–312.

Associated Press Germany, various dates.

Banaszak, Lee Ann. 1998. "East-West Differences in German Abortion Opinion," *Public Opinion Quarterly*, Vol. 62, No. 4, pp. 545–82.

Banaszak, Lee Ann, Karen Beckwith, and Dieter Rucht. 2003. *Women's Movements Facing the Reconfigured State*. Cambridge: Cambridge University Press.

Bardi, Luciano and Leonardo Morlino. 1992. "Italy," in Richard S. Katz and Peter Mair (eds.), *Party Organizations: A Data Handbook on Party Organizations in Western Democracies, 1960–1990*. London: Sage Publications, pp. 458–618.

Basic Program, Austrian People's Party. 1995. Basic Program. Passed at the ÖVP's National Congress on April 22, 1995.

Basic Program, Austrian People's Party. 1999. Party Statutes, version from April 23, 1999.

Beccalli, Bianca. 1994. "The Modern Women's Movement in Italy," *New Left Review*, Issue 204, pp. 86–112.

Becker, Winifried. 1987. *CDU und CSU 1945–1950: Vorläufer, Gründung und regionale Entwicklung bis zum Entstehen der CDU-Bundespartei*. Mainz: Hase und Koehler.

Bell, David S. and Byron Criddle. 1988. *The French Socialist Party: The Emergence of a Party of Government*. Second edition. Oxford: Clarendon Press.

Belloni, Frank P. and Dennis C. Beller (eds.). 1978. *Faction Politics: Political Parties and Factionalism in Comparative Perspective*. Santa Barbara: ABC-CLIO.

Bertone, Chiara. 2002. *Whose Needs? Women's Organizations' Claims on Child Care in Italy and Denmark*. Aalborg: FREIA, Aalborg University.

Bertone, Chiara. 2003. "Claims for Child Care as Struggles Over Needs: Comparing Italian and Danish Women's Organizations," *Social Politics*, Vol. 10, No. 2, pp. 229–55.

Bettio, Francesca and Janneke Plantenga. 2004. "Comparing Care Regimes in Europe," *Feminist Economics*, Vol. 10, No. 1, pp. 85–113.

Betz, Hans-Georg. 1994. *Radical Right-Wing Populism in Western Europe*. New York: St. Martin's Press.

Betz, Hans-Georg and Stefan Immerfall. 1998. *The New Politics of the Right: Neo-Populist Parties and Movements in Established Democracies*. New York: St. Martin's Press.

Bimbi, Franca. 2000. "The Family Paradigm in the Italian Welfare State (1947–1996)" in Maria Jose Gonzalez, Teresa Jurado, and Manuela Naldini (eds.), *Gender Inequalities in Southern Europe: Women, Work and Welfare in the 1990s*, London: Frank Cass, pp. 72–88.

Blyth, Mark and Richard S. Katz. 2005. "From Catch-all Politics to Cartelisation: The Political Economy of the Cartel Party," *West European Politics*, Vol. 28, Issue 1, pp. 33–60.

Bösch, Frank. 2001. *Die Adenauer-CDU: Gründung, Aufstieg und Krise einer Erfolgspartei, 1945–1969*. Stuttgart: Deutsche Verlags-Anstalt.

Bösch, Frank. 2002. *Macht und Machtverlust: Die Geschichte der CDU*. Stuttgart: Deutsche Verlags-Anstalt.

Boysen, Jacqueline. 2005. *Angela Merkel: Eine Karriere*. Berlin: Ullstein.

Bremme, Gabriele. 1956. *Die politische Rolle der Frau in Deutschland: Eine Untersuchung über den Einfluß der Frauen bei Wahlen und ihre Teilnahme in Partei und Parlament*. Gottingen: Vandenhoeck & Ruprecht.

Bruning, Gwennaële and Janneke Plantenga. 1999. "Parental Leave and Equal Opportunities: Experiences in Eight European Countries," *Journal of European Social Policy*, Vol. 9, No. 3, pp. 195–209.

Buchhaas, Dorothee. 1981. *Die Volkspartei: Programmatische Entwicklung der CDU, 1950–1973*. Düsseldorf: Droste Verlag.

Budge, Ian. 2000. "Deliberative Democracy versus Direct Democracy – Plus Political Parties!" in Michael Saward (ed.), *Democratic Innovation: Deliberation, Representation and Association*. London and New York: Routledge, pp. 195–209.

Budge, Ian and Hans Keman. 1990. *Parties and Democracy: Coalition Formation and Government Functioning in Twenty States*. Oxford: Oxford University Press.

Bundesministerium für Familie, Senioren, Frauen und Jugend. 1998. *Frauen in der Bundesrepublik Deutschland*. Bonn: Bundesministerium für Familie, Senioren, Frauen und Jugend.

Bundesministerium für Familie, Senioren, Frauen und Jugend. 2006. *Erziehungsgeld, Elternzeit.* Berlin: Bundesministerium für Familie, Senioren, Frauen und Jugend.

Der Bundeswahlleiter – *Veröffentlichungen zur Wahl zum 17. Deutschen Bundestag am 27.* September 2009 [cited January 7, 2010]. Available from http://www.bundeswahlleiter.de/de/bundestagswahlen/BTW_BUND_09/ veroeffentlichungen/.

Burgess, Katrina and Steven Levitsky. 2003. "Explaining Populist Party Adaptation in Latin America: Environmental and Organizational Determinants of Party Change in Argentina, Mexico, Peru and Venezuela," *Comparative Political Studies*, Vol. 36, No. 8, pp. 881–911.

Bussemaker, Jet. 1998. "Rationales of Care in Contemporary Welfare States: The Case of Childcare in the Netherlands," *Social Politics*, Vol. 5, No. 1, pp. 70–96.

Bussemaker, Jet and Kees van Kersbergen. 1999. "Contemporary Social-Capitalist Welfare States and Gender Inequality," in Diane Sainsbury (ed.), *Gender and Welfare State Regimes.* Oxford: Oxford University Press, pp. 15–46.

Butler, David, and Donald E. Stokes. 1974. *Political Change in Britain: The Evolution of Electoral Choice*, Second Edition. London: Macmillan.

Caldwell, Leslie. 1991. *Italian Family Matters: Women, Politics and Legal Reform.* London: Macmillan.

Calloni, Marina. 2001. "Debates and Controversies on Abortion in Italy," in Dorothy McBride Stetson (ed.), *Abortion Politics, Women's Movements, and the Democratic State.* Oxford: Oxford University Press, pp. 181–203.

Campbell, Angus, Philip Converse, Warren E. Miller, and Donald E. Stokes. 1960. *The American Voter.* New York: Wiley.

Carmines, Edward G. and James A. Stimson. 1989. *Issue Evolution: Race and the Transformation of American Politics.* Princeton: Princeton University Press.

Caul, Miki L. 1999. "Women's Representation in Parliament: The Role of Political Parties," *Party Politics*, Vol. 5, No. 1, pp. 79–98.

CDU. 1975. "Woman and Society," from CDU National Party Congress Protocol.

CDU. 1985. "A New Partnership," from CDU National Party Congress Protocol.

CDU-Bundesgeschäftsstelle. 1965. *Frau und Arbeitswelt – morgen. Kongress berufstätiger Frauen der CDU vom 2.–4. Dezember 1964 in Bochum.* Bonn: Presse- und Informationsdienste der Christlich Demokratischen Union Deutschlands, Verlagsgesellschaft, mgH.

CDU-Bundesgeschäftsstelle. 1973. "Grundsatzprobleme der Familienpolitik: Anhörung von Sachverständigen der Kommission der CDU/CSU-Bundestagsfraktion, der CDU und CSU 'Familie' Vorsitzender: Dr. Hermann Götz, MdB, und 'Frauen' Vorsitzende: Dr. Helga Wex, MdB. Am 24. September 1973." Bonn.

CDU-Bundesgeschäftsstelle. 1974. "Die Familie – Unsere Zukunft," *Argumente, Dokumente, Materialien.* Familienpolitischer Kongress der CDU am 4./5. Oktober 1974 in Münster.

CDU-Bundesgeschäftsstelle. 1991. "Dokumentation: Positionen zum verbesserten Schutz des ungeborenen Kindes in Deutschland."

CDU-Bundesgeschäftsstelle. 1991. Minutes from the meetings of the Commission "Schutz des ungeborenen Kindes," Konrad-Adenauer-Haus, various dates.

CDU National Party Congress. 1975, 1985, 1986, 1988, 1989, 1994 (February), 1994 (November), 1995 (October), 1996 (October). Protocol of the National Party Congress. Bonn: Presse- und Informationsdienste der Christlich Demokratischen Union Deutschlands, Verlagsgesellschaft, mgH.

CDU Statutes.[cited April 12, 2010]. Available from http://www.cdu.de/doc/pdfc/080121-CDU-statut.pdf

Chandler, William M. 1988. "Party System Transformations in the FRG," in Steven B. Wolinetz (ed.), *Parties and Party Systems in Liberal Democracies*. London and New York: Routledge.

Chandler, William M. 1989. "The Christian Democrats," in Peter H. Merkl (ed.), *The Federal Republic of Germany at Forty*. New York and London: New York University Press, pp. 287–313.

Chandler, William M. 1993. "The Christian Democrats and the Challenge of Unity," in Stephen Padgett (ed.), *Parties and Party Systems in the New Germany*. Dartmouth Publishing Company Ltd.: England.

Christiano, Thomas. 1996. *The Rule of the Many*. Boulder, CO: Westview Press.

Clemens, Clay. 1989. *Reluctant Realists: The CDU/CSU and West German Ostpolitik*. Durham: Duke University Press.

Clemens, Clay. 1993. "Disquiet on the Eastern Front: The Christian Democratic Union in Germany's New Länder," *German Politics*, Vol. 2, No. 2, pp. 200–23.

Clemens, Clay. 1994. "The Chancellor as Manager: Helmut Kohl, the CDU and Governance in Germany," *West European Politics*, Vol. 17, Issue 4, pp. 28–51.

Clemens, Clay. 1998. "Party Management as a Leadership Resource: Kohl and the CDU/CSU" *German Politics*, Vol. 7, No. 1, pp. 90–117.

Cohen, Joshua. 1989. "Deliberation and Democratic Legitimacy," in Alan Hamlin and Philip Pettit (eds.), *The Good Polity*. Oxford: Basil Blackwell, pp. 17–34.

Collier, Ruth Berins and David Collier. 1979. "Inducements versus Constraints: Disaggregating 'Corporatism,'" *American Political Science Review*, Vol. 73, Issue 4, pp. 967–86.

Cox, Gary W. 1997. *Making Votes Count: Strategic Coordination in the World's Electoral Systems*. Cambridge: Cambridge University Press.

Crow, Barbara. 2000. *Radical Feminism: A Documentary Reader*. New York: New York University Press.

Czarnowski, Gabriele. 1994. "Abortion as Political Conflict in Unified Germany," *Parliamentary Affairs*, Vol. 47, No. 2, pp 252–68.

Däubler-Gmelin, Herta and Renate Faerber-Husemann. 1987. *§218–Der tägliche Kampf um die Reform. Mit einem dokumentarischen Anhang von Dorothea Brück über Angriffe auf die Reform des §218 seit der "Wende."* Bonn: Verlag Neue Gesellschaft.

Dahl, Robert. 1956. *A Preface to Democratic Theory*. Chicago: University of Chicago Press.

Dahlerup, Drude. 2006. *Women, Quotas and Politics*. London and New York: Routledge.

Daly, Mary. 1973. *Beyond God the Father: Toward a Philosophy of Women's Liberation*. Boston: Beacon Press.

Daly, Mary. 1978. *Gyn/Ecology: The Metaethics of Radical Feminism*. Boston: Beacon Press.

Daly, Mary. 1984. *Pure Lust: Elemental Feminist Philosophy*. Boston: Beacon Press.

Davidson-Schmich, Louise K. 2006. "Implementation of Political Party Gender Quotas: Evidence from the German Länder, 1990–2000," *Party Politics*, Vol. 12, No. 2, pp. 211–32.

ddp, Nachrichtenagentur, various dates.

Detterbeck, Klaus. 2005. "Cartel Parties in Western Europe?" *Party Politics*, Vol. 11, No. 2, pp. 173–91.

Dittrich, Karl. 1983. "Testing the Catch-all Thesis: Some Difficulties and Problems," in Hans Daalder and Peter Mair (eds.), *Western European Party Systems, Continuity and Change*. London: Sage, pp. 257–66.

Domes, Jürgen. 1964. *Mehrheitsfraktion und Bundesregierung: Aspekte des Verhältnisses der Fraktion der CDU/CSU im zweiten und dritten Deutschen Bundestag zum Kabinett Adenauer*. Cologne: Westdeutscher Verlag.

Doormann, Lottemi. 1980. *Wartet nicht auf bess're Zeiten: Frauenpolitik aus Bonn und Alternativen der Frauenbewegung*. Cologne: Pahl-Rugenstein Verlag.

Doormann, Lottemi. 1983. "Die neue Frauenbewegung: Zur Entwicklung seit 1968," in F. Hervé (ed.), *Geschichte der deutschen Frauenbewegung*. Cologne: Pahl-Rugenstein, pp. 237–72.

Downs, Anthony. 1957. *An Economic Theory of Democracy*. New York: Harper and Row.

Duverger, Maurice. 1954. *Political Parties: Their Organization and Activities in the Modern State*. London: Methuen.

Duverger, Maurice. 1955. *The Political Role of Women*. Paris: UNESCO.

Echols, Alice. 1990. *Daring to Be Bad: Radical Feminism in America, 1967–75*. Minneapolis: University of Minnesota Press.

Edelman, Murray. 1964. *The Symbolic Uses of Politics*. Urbana and Chicago: University of Illinois Press.

Edinger, Lewis J. and Brigitte L. Nacos. 1998. *From Bonn to Berlin: German Politics in Transition*. New York: Columbia University Press.

Egen, Peter. 1971. *Die Entstehung des Evangelischen Arbeitskreises der CDU/CSU*. Phd Dissertation. Bochum University.

Eisenstein, Zillah. 1986. *The Radical Future of Liberal Feminism*. Boston: Northeastern University Press.

Elder, Charles D. and Roger W. Cobb. 1983. *The Political Use of Symbols*. New York and London: Longman.

Engelbrech, Gerhard, Hannelore Gruber and Maria Jungkunst. 1997. "Erwerbsorientierung und Erwerbstätigkeit ost- und westdeutscher Frauen unter veränderten gesellschaftlichen Rahmenbedingungen," *Miteilungen aus der Arbeitsmarkt- und Berufsforschung*. Stuttgart: Verlag W. Kohlhammer.

Ergas, Yasmine. 1982. "1968–1979. Feminism and the Italian Party System: Women's Politics in a Decade of Turmoil," *Comparative Politics*, Vol 14, Issue 3, pp. 253–79.

Esping-Andersen, Gøsta. 1990. *The Three Worlds of Welfare Capitalism*. Princeton: Princeton University Press.

Esping-Andersen, Gøsta. 1999. *Social Foundations of Postindustrial Economies*. Oxford: Oxford University Press.

Fagan, Colette and Gail Hebson (eds.). 2006. '*Making Work Pay' Debates from a Gender Perspective: A Comparative Review of Some Recent Policy Reforms in Thirty European Countries*. Brussels: European Commission, Directorate-General for Employment, Social Affairs and Equal Opportunities.

Falke, Wolfgang. 1982. *Die Mitglieder der CDU: Eine empirische Studie zum Verhältnis von Mitglieder- und Organisationsstruktur der CDU 1971–1977*. Berlin: Duncker & Humblot.

Feist, Ursula and Hans-Jürgen Hoffmann. 1999. "Dokumentation und Kurzanalyzen: Die Bundestagswahlanalyse 1998: Wahl des Wechsels," *Zeitschrift für Parlamentsfragen*, Heft 2, pp. 215–51.

Ferree, Myra Marx. 1987. "Equality and Autonomy: Feminist Politics in the United States and West Germany," in Mary Fainsod Katzenstein and Carol McClurg Mueller (eds.), *The Women's Movements of the United States and Western Europe: Consciousness, Political Opportunity, and Public Policy*. Philadelphia: Temple University Press, pp. 171–95.

Ferree, Myra Marx. 1993. "The Rise and Fall of 'Mommy Politics': Feminism and Unification in (East) Germany," *Feminist Studies*, Vol. 19, No. 1, pp. 89–115.

Ferree, Myra Marx. 1994. "'The Time of Chaos Was the Best': Feminist Mobilization and Demobilization in East Germany," *Gender and Society*, Vol. 8, No. 4, pp. 597–623.

Ferree, Myra Marx. 1995. "Patriarchies and Feminisms: The Two Women's Movements of Unified Germany," *Social Politics*, Vol. 2, No. 1, pp. 10–24.

Ferree, Myra Marx. 1997. "German Unification and Feminist Identity," in Joan W. Scott, Cora Kaplan, and Debra Keates (eds.), *Transitions, Environments, Translations: Feminisms in International Politics*. New York: Routledge, pp. 46–55.

Ferree, Myra Marx. 2006. "Angela Merkel: What Does it Mean to Run as a Woman?" *German Politics and Society*, Vol. 24, No. 1, pp. 93–107.

Ferree, Myra Marx. Forthcoming. *Sisterhood Since the Sixties: German Feminism, American Liberalism, and Global Gender Politics*. Stanford: Stanford University Press.

Ferree, Myra Marx, William Anthony Gamson, Jürgen Gerhards, and Dieter Rucht. 2002. *Shaping Abortion Discourse: Democracy and the Public Sphere in Germany and the United States*. Cambridge: Cambridge University Press.

Feuchtwanger, E. J. 1993. *From Weimar to Hitler: Germany, 1918–33*. New York: St. Martin's Press.

Firestone, Shulamith. 1970. *The Dialectic of Sex*. New York: Bantam Books.

Fischer, Claus. 1997. *Wahlergebnisse in der Bundesrepublik Deutschland und in den Ländern, 1946–1997, insgesamt und nach Alter und Geschlecht*. Sankt Augustin: Konrad Adenauer Foundation.

Fishkin, James. 1991. *Democracy and Deliberation: New Directions for Democratic Reform*. New Haven, CT and London: Yale University Press.

Fishkin, James. 1995. *The Voice of the People: Public Opinion and Democracy*. New Haven, CT and London: Yale University Press.

FOCUS magazine, various dates.

Frankfurter Allgemeine Zeitung, various dates.

Frankfurter Rundschau, various dates.

Frauen Union der CDU. 1991. *Leitsaetze der Frauen-Union zur Neuregelung des §218 StGB 1991.* beschlossen vom Bundesvorstand der Frauen-Union am 12. Juli 1991.

Frauen-Union der CSU (ed.). 1997. *50 Jahre Frauen-Union in Bayern.* Augsburg: Hofmann-Druck GmbH.

French, Marilyn. 1985. *Beyond Power: On Women, Men and Morals.* New York: Summit Books.

Friedan, Betty. 1974. *The Feminine Mystique.* New York: Dell.

Fröhlich, Ute. 1983. "The Old and New Women's Movements in the Federal Republic of Germany," in Ingeborg Drewitz (ed.), *The German Women's Movement: The Social Role of Women in the 19th Century and the Emancipation Movement in Germany.* Bonn: Hohwacht.

Galtry, Judith and Paul Callister. 2005. "Assessing the Optimal Length of Parental Leave for Child and Parental Well-being – How Can Research Inform Policy?" *Journal of Family Issues*, Vol. 26, No. 2, pp. 219–46.

Gante, Michael. 1991. *§218 in der Diskussion: Meinungs- und Willensbildung, 1945–1976.* Dusseldorf: Droste Verlag GmbH.

General Anzeiger, various dates.

Gerhard, Ute. 1982. "A Hidden and Complex Heritage: Reflections on the History of Germany's Women's Movements," *Women's Studies International Forum*, Vol. 5, No. 6, pp. 561–7.

Green Party statutes.

Grzymala-Busse, Anna. 2002. *Redeeming the Communist Past: The Regeneration of Communist Parties in East Central Europe.* Cambridge: Cambridge University Press.

Guadagnini, Marila. 1993. "A 'Partitocrazia' Without Women: the Case of the Italian Party System," in Joni Lovenduski and Pippa Norris (eds.), *Gender and Party Politics*, pp. 168–204.

Guadagnini, Marila. 1998. "The Debate on Women's Quotas in Italian Electoral Legislation," *Swiss Political Science Review*, Vol. 4, No. 3, pp. 97–102.

Guadagnini, Marila. 2005. "Gendering the Debate on Political Representation in Italy: a Difficult Challenge," in Joni Lovenduski (ed.), *State Feminism and Political Representation*, Cambridge: Cambridge University Press, pp. 130–52.

Gurland, Arcadius Rudolph Lang. 1980. *Die CDU/CSU: Ursprünge und Entwicklung bis 1953.* Dieter Emig (ed.). Frankfurt am Main: Europäische Verlagsanstalt.

Gustafsson, Siv S. and Frank P. Stafford. 1995. "Links between Early Childhood Programs and Maternal Employment in Three Countries," *The Future of Children*, Vol. 5, No. 3, pp. 161–74.

Gutmann, Amy and Dennis Thompson. 1996. *Democracy and Disagreement.* Cambridge, MA: Harvard University Press.

Gutmann, Amy and Dennis Thompson. 2004. *Why Deliberative Democracy?* Princeton: Princeton University Press.

Hank, Karsten, Michaela Kreyenfeld, and C. Katharina Spiess. 2004. "Kinderbetreuung und Fertilität in Deutschland," *Zeitschrift für Soziologie*, Vol. 33, No. 3, pp. 228–44.

Harmel, Robert and Kenneth Janda 1994, "An Integrated Theory of Party goals and Party Change," *Journal of Theoretical Politics*, Vol. 6, No. 3, pp. 259–87.

Harmel, Robert, Uk Heo, Alexander Tan & Kenneth Janda. 1995. "Performance, Leadership, Factions and Party Change: an Empirical Analysis," *West European Politics*, Vol.18, Issue 1, pp. 1–13.

Haungs, Peter. 1992. "Die CDU: Prototyp einer Volkspartei," in Alf Mintzel and Heinrich Oberreuter (eds.), *Parteien in der Bundesrepublic Deutschland*. Bonn: Bundeszentrale für politische Bildung, pp. 172–216.

Haus der Geschichte der Bundesrepublik Deutschland (ed.). 1997. Ungleiche Schwestern? Frauen in Ost- und Westdeutschland: Anspruch und Alltag Gemeinsamkeiten und Unterscheide. Catalog to the exhibit of the same name.

Haussman, Melissa and Birgit Sauer (eds.). 2007. *Gendering the State in the Age of Globalization: Women's Movements and State Feminism in Postindustrial Democracies*. Lanham, MD: Rowman & Littlefield Publishers, Inc.

Heidenheimer, Arnold J. 1960. *Adenauer and the CDU: The Rise of the Leader and the Integration of the Party*. The Hague: Martinus Nijhoff.

Helms, Ludger. 2000. "Is there Life after Kohl? The CDU Crisis and the Future of Party Democracy in Germany," *Government and Opposition*, Vol. 35, Issue 4, pp. 419–38.

Helwerth, Ulrike and Gislinde Schwarz. 1995. *Von Muttis und Emanzen: Feministinnen in Ost- und Westdeutschland*. Frankfurt am Main: Fischer.

Hinich, Melvin J. and Michael C. Munger. 1997. *Analytical Politics*. Cambridge: Cambridge University Press.

Hirschman, Albert O. 1970. *Exit, Voice and Loyalty*. Cambridge, MA: Harvard University Press.

Hochgeschurz, Marianne. 1995. "Zwischen Autonomie und Integration – Die neue (west)deutsche Frauenbewegung," in Florence Hervé (ed.), *Geschichte der deutschen Frauenbewegung*. Cologne: PapyRossa Verlag.

Hoecker, Beate. 1995. *Politische Partizipation von Frauen: Kontinuität und Wandel des Geschlechterverhältnisses in der Politik – ein einführendes Studienbuch*. Opladen: Leske + Budrich.

Holz, Petra. 2004. *Zwischen Tradition und Emancipation: CDU-Politikerinnen in der Zeit von 1946 bis 1960*. Königstein: U. Helmer.

Howard, Marc Morjé. 2003. *The Weakness of Civil Society in Post-Communist Europe*. Cambridge: Cambridge University Press.

Inglehart, Ronald. 1977. *The Silent Revolution: Changing Values and Political Styles among Western Publics*. Princeton: Princeton University Press.

Inglehart, Ronald and Pippa Norris. 2003. *Rising Tide: Gender Equality and Cultural Change Around the World*. Cambridge: Cambridge University Press.

Irving, R. E. M. 1979. *The Christian Democratic Parties of Western Europe*. London: George Allen & Unwin.

Jarausch, Konrad. 1994. *The Rush to German Unity*. New York: Oxford University Press.

Jesse, Eckhard. 1985. *Wahlrecht zwischen Kontinuität und Reform: Eine Analyse der Wahlrechtssystemdiskussion und der Wahlrechtsänderungen in der Bundesrepublik Deutschland 1949–1983*. Düsseldorf: Droste.

Johnson, James. 2006. "Political Parties and Deliberative Democracy?" in Richard S. Katz and William J. Crotty (eds.), *Handbook of Party Politics*. London: Sage.

Juristen-Vereinigung Lebensrecht e. V. (ed.). 1985. *Schriftenreihe der Juristen-Vereinigung Lebensrecht e. V. zu Köln*, Nr. 1. Cologne.

Kaden, Albrecht. 1964. *Einheit Oder Freiheit? Die Wiedergründung der SPD 1945/46*. Berlin/Bonn: Verlag J.H.W. Dietz Nachfolger GmbH.

Kalyvas, Stathis N. 1996. *The Rise of Christian Democracy in Europe*. Ithaca: Cornell University Press.

Kamenitsa, Lynn. 2001. "Abortion Debates in Germany," in Dorothy McBride Stetson (ed.), *Abortion Politics, Women's Movements, and the Democratic State*. Oxford: Oxford University Press, pp. 111–34.

Kamenitsa, Lynn and Brigitte Geissel. 2005. "WPAs and Political Representation in Germany," in: Joni Lovenduski (ed.), *State Feminism and Political Representation*. Cambridge: Cambridge University Press, pp. 106–29.

Kaplan, Gisela. 1992. *Contemporary Western European Feminism*. New York: New York University Press.

Katholische Nachrichten Agentur, various dates.

Katz, Richard. 1997. *Democracy and Elections*. Oxford: Oxford University Press.

Katz, Richard and Peter Mair (eds.). 1992. *Party Organizations: A Data Handbook on Party Organizations in Western Democracies, 1960–1990*. London: Sage Publications.

Katz, Richard, and Peter Mair. 1995. "Changing Models of Party Organization and Party Democracy: The Emergence of the Cartel Party," *Party Politics*, Vol. 1, No. 1, pp. 5–28.

Katz, Richard and Peter Mair. 1996. "Cadre, Catch-all or Cartel? A Rejoinder," *Party Politics*, Vol. 2, No. 4, pp. 525–34.

Katzenstein, Mary. 1987. "Comparing the Feminist Movements of the United States and Western Europe: An Overview," in Mary Fainsod Katzenstein and Carol McClurg Mueller (eds.), *The Women's Movements of the United States and Western Europe: Consciousness, Political Opportunity, and Public Policy*. Philadelphia: Temple University Press, pp. 3–20.

Katzenstein, Mary and Carol McClurg Mueller (eds.). 1987. *The Women's Movements of the United States and Western Europe: Consciousness, Political Opportunity, and Public Policy*. Philadelphia: Temple University Press.

Katzenstein, Peter. 1987. *Policy and Politics in West Germany: The Growth of a Semisovereign State*. Philadelphia: Temple University Press.

Keller-Kühne, Angela and Sabine Klein (eds.). 1998. *50 Jahre Frauen-Union der CDU: Katalog zur Ausstellung*. Bad Honnef: Archiv für Christlich-Demokratische Politik der Konrad-Adenauer-Stiftung, e.V.

Kensinger, Loretta. 1997. "(In)Quest of Liberal Feminism," *Hypatia*, Vol. 12, No. 4, pp. 178–97.

Ketting, Evert. 1994. "Netherlands," in Bell Rolston and Anna Eggert (eds.), *Abortion in the New Europe: A Comparative Handbook*. Westport, CT: Greenwood Press, pp. 173–86.

Kirchheimer, Otto. 1966. "The Transformation of the Western European Party Systems," in Joseph LaPalombara and Myron Weiner (eds.), *Political*

Parties and Political Development. Princeton: Princeton University Press, pp. 177–200.

Kitschelt, Herbert. 1989. "The Internal Politics of Parties: The Law of Curvilinear Disparity Revisited," *Political Studies*, Vol. 37, Issue 3, pp. 400–21.

Kitschelt, Herbert. 1994. *The Transformation of European Social Democracy*. Cambridge: Cambridge University Press.

Kitschelt, Herbert. 1995. *The Radical Right in Western Europe: A Comparative Analysis*. In collaboration with Anthony J. McGann. Ann Arbor: University of Michigan Press.

Kitschelt, Herbert. 2000. "Citizens, Politicians, and Party Cartelization: Political Representation and State Failure in Post-Industrial Democracies," *European Journal of Political Research*, Vol. 37, Issue 2, pp. 149–79.

Kittilson, Miki Caul. 2006. *Challenging Parties, Changing Parliaments: Women and Elected Office in Contemporary Western Europe*. Columbus: The Ohio State University Press.

Klein, Ethel. 1987. "The Diffusion of Consciousness in the United States and Western Europe," in Mary Fainsod Katzenstein and Carol McClurg Mueller (eds.), *The Women's Movements of the United States and Western Europe: Consciousness, Political Opportunity, and Public Policy*. Philadelphia: Temple University Press, pp. 23–43.

Kleinmann, Hans-Otto. 1993. *Geschichte der CDU, 1945–1982*. Stuttgart: Deutsche Verlags-Anstalt.

Klein-Schonnefeld, Sabine. 1994. "Germany," in Bill Rolston and Anna Eggert (eds.), *Abortion in the New Europe: A Comparative Handbook*. Westport, CT: Greenwood, pp. 113–38.

Knapp, Andrew and Vincent Wright. 2006. *The Government and Politics of France*. Fifth Edition. London: Routledge.

Knapp, Andrew and Frédéric Sawicki. 2008. "Political Parties and the Party System," in Alistair Cole, Patrick Le Galès, and Jonah D. Levy (eds.), *Developments in French Politics 4*. London: Palgrave Macmillan, pp. 42–59.

Knijn, Trudie. 1998. "Social Care in the Netherlands," in Jane Lewis (ed.), *Gender, Social Care and Welfare State Restructuring in Europe*. Aldershot: Ashgate.

Knijn, Trudie. 2008. "Private Responsibility and Some Support. Family Policies in the Netherlands," in Ilona Ostner and Christoph Schmitt (eds.), *Family Policies in the Context of Family Change: The Nordic Countries in Perspective*, Wiesbaden: VS Verlag für Sozialwissenschaften, pp. 155–73.

Knijn, Trudie and Monique Kremer. 1997. "Gender and the Caring Dimension of Welfare States: Toward Inclusive Citizenship," *Social Politics*, Vol. 4, No. 3, pp. 328–61.

Koelble, Thomas A. 1991. *The Left Unraveled: The Impact of the New Left on the British Labour Party and the West German Social Democratic Party, 1968–1988*. Durham: Duke University Press.

Kolinsky, Eva. 1991. "Political Participation and Parliamentary Careers: Women's Quotas in West Germany," *West European Politics*, Vol. 14, Issue 1, pp. 56–72.

Kolinsky, Eva. 1993. "Party Change and Women's Representation in Unified Germany," in Joni Lovenduski and Pippa (eds.), *Gender and Party Politics*. London: Sage.

Kolinsky, Eva. 1998. "Women, Work and Family in the New Länder: Conflicts and Experiences," *German Politics*, Vol. 7, No. 3, pp. 101–25.

Konrad-Adenauer-Stiftung (ed.). 1991. "Tagungsprotokoll," from *Schutz des ungeborenen Kindes: Fachtagung der Konrad-Adenauer-Stiftung am 25. und 26. April 1991 in St. Augustin*. St. Augustin: Konrad-Adenauer-Stiftung.

Konrad-Adenauer-Stiftung (ed.). 1992. "Tagungsprotokoll," from *Schutz des ungeborenen Kindes: Fachtagung der Konrad-Adenauer-Stiftung am 28. und 29. November 1991 in St. Augustin*. St. Augustin: Konrad-Adenauer-Stiftung.

Koole, Ruud. 1996. "Cadre, Catch-all or Cartel? A Comment on the Notion of the Cartel Party," *Party Politics*, Vol. 2, No. 4, pp. 507–23.

Koole, Ruud and Hella van de Velde. 1992. "The Netherlands," in Richard S. Katz and Peter Mair (eds.), *Party Organizations: A Data Handbook on Party Organizations in Western Democracies, 1960–1990*. London: Sage Publications, pp. 619–731.

Köpl, Regina. 2001. "State Feminism and Policy Debates on Abortion in Austria," in Dorothy McBride Stetson (ed.), *Abortion Politics, Women's Movements, and the Democratic State: A Comparative Study of State Feminism*. Oxford: Oxford University Press, pp. 17–38.

Kramer, Gertrud and Johannes Kramer. 1976. "Der Einfluss der Sozialausschüsse der Christlich-Demokratischen Arbeitnehmerschaft auf die CDU: Ein Beitrag zur Parteientheorie," *Aus Politik und Zeitgeschichte* B **46**–7, pp. 17–46.

Kreyenfeld, Michaela, and Karsten Hank. 2000. "Does the Availability of Child Care Influence the Employment of Mothers? Findings from Western Germany," *Population Research and Policy Review*, Vol. **19**, No. 4, pp. 317–37.

Krook, Mona Lena. 2009. *Quotas for Women in Politics: Gender and Candidate Selection Reform Worldwide*. New York: Oxford University Press.

Krug, Stefanie, and Ulrich Rauter. 1998. "Einleitung," in Gesellschaft für Informationstechnologie und Pädagogik am IMBSE (eds.), *Beschäftigungsrisiko Erziehungsurlaub: Die Bedeutung des "Erziehungsurlaubs" für die Entwicklung der Frauenerwerbstätigkeit*. Opladen/Wiesbaden: Westdeutscher Verlag, pp. 9–20.

Lang, Sabine. 1997. "The NGOization of Feminism: Institutionalization and Institution Building within the German Women's Movements," in Joan W. Scott, Cora Kaplan, and Debra Keates (eds.), *Transitions, Environments, Translations: Feminisms in International Politics*. New York: Routledge, pp. 101–20.

Langguth, Gerd. 2001. *Das Innenleben der Macht: Krise und Zukunft der CDU*. Berlin: Ullstein Verlag.

Langguth, Gerhard. 2005. *Angela Merkel*. Munich: Deutscher Taschenbuch Verlag.

Laver, Michael and Norman Schofield. 1990. *Multiparty Government: The Politics of Coalition in Europe*. Oxford: Oxford University Press.

Lehmbruch, Gerhard. 1979. "Liberal Corporatism and Party Government," in Philippe C. Schmitter and Gerhard Lehmbruch (eds.), *Trends Toward Corporatist Intermediation*. London: Sage Publications, pp. 147–84.

Lehner, Oskar. 1994. "Austria," in Bill Rolston and Anna Eggert (eds.), *Abortion in the New Europe: A Comparative Handbook*. Westport, CT: Greenwood, pp. 1–17.

Leitner, Sigrid, Ilona Ostner, and Christoph Schmitt. 2008. "Family Policies in Germany," in Ilona Ostner and Christoph Schmitt (eds.), *Family Policies in the Context of Family Change: The Nordic Countries in Perspective*, Wiesbaden: VS Verlag für Sozialwissenschaften, pp. 175–202.

Leonardi, Robert and Douglas A. Wertman. 1989. *Italian Christian Democracy: The Politics of Dominance*. New York: St. Martin's Press.

Lepszy, Norbert and Christian Koecke. 2000. "Der niederländische Christlich-demokratische Appell (CDA)," in Hans-Joachim Veen (ed.), *Christlich-demokratische und konservative Parteien in Westeuropa, 5*. Paderborn: Ferdinand Schöningh, pp. 119–260.

Leslie, John. 2002. *Parties and Other Social Functions*, PhD Dissertation, Department of Political Science, University of California, Berkeley.

Leslie, John, and Sarah Elise Wiliarty. 2009. "Gate Crashers and Engraved Invitations: Integrating Women Activists in the SPD and CDU from the 1960s to the 1980s," in Elizabeth McLeay, Kate MacMillan and John Leslie (eds.), *Women and Politics in New Zealand*. Wellington, New Zealand: Victoria University Press.

Levitsky, Steven. 2001. "Organization and Labor-Based Party Adaptation: the Transformation of Argentine Peronism in Comparative Perspective," *World Politics*, Vol. 54, No. 1, pp. 27–56.

Lewis, Jane. 2001. "The Decline of the Male Breadwinner Model: Implications for Work and Care," *Social Politics*, Vol. 8, No. 2, pp. 152–69.

Lewis, Jane, Trudie Knijn, Claude Martin and Ilona Ostner. 2008. "Patterns of Development in Work/Family Reconciliation Policies for Parents in France, Germany, the Netherlands, and the UK in the 2000s," *Social Politics*, Vol. 15, No. 3, pp. 261–86.

Ley, Richard. 1978. *Föderalismusdiskussion innerhalb der CDU/CSU: Von der Parteigründung bis zur Verabschiedung des Grundgesetzes*. Mainz: Hase und Koehler.

Lijphart, Arend. 1968. *The Politics of Accommodation*. Berkeley: University of California Press.

Lipset, Seymour Martin. 1960. *Political Man: The Social Bases of Politics*. Garden City, NY: Doubleday.

Lipset, Seymour Martin and Stein Rokkan. 1967. "Cleavage Structures, Party Systems, and Voter Alignments. An Introduction," in Lipset and Rokkan, (eds.), *Party Systems and Voter Alignments. Cross-National Perspectives*. New York: Free Press, pp. 1–64.

Lösche, Peter and Walter, Franz. 1992. *Die SPD: Klassenpartei, Volkspartei, Quotenpartei*. Darmstadt: Wissenschaftliche Buchgesellschaft.

Lovenduski, Joni. 1986. *Women and European Politics: Contemporary Feminism and Public Policy*. Amherst: University of Massachusetts Press.

Lovenduski, Joni and Joyce Outshoorn (eds.). 1986. *The New Politics of Abortion*. London: Sage Publications.

Lovenduski, Joni. 2005a. "Introduction: State Feminism and the Political Representation of Women," in Joni Lovenduski (ed.), *State Feminism and Political Representation*. Cambridge: Cambridge University Press, pp. 1–19.

Lovenduski, Joni (ed.). 2005b. *State Feminism and Political Representation*. Cambridge: Cambridge University Press.

Lovenduski, Joni and Pippa Norris (eds.). 1993. *Gender and Party Politics*. London: Sage Publications.

Lovenduski, Joni and Vicki Randall. 1993. *Contemporary Feminist Politics: Women and Power in Britain*. Oxford: Oxford University Press.

Lucardie, Paul and Hans-Martien ten Napel. 1994. "Between Confessionalism and Liberal Conservatism: the Christian Democratic Parties of Belgium and the Netherlands," in David Hanley (ed.), *Christian Democracy in Europe: A Comparative Perspective*. London and New York: Pinter Publishers, pp. 51–70.

Lutz, Hedwig. 2004. *Wiedereinsteig und Beschäftigung von Frauen mit Kleinkindern: Ein Vergleich der bisherigen Karenzregelung mit der Übergangsregelung zum Kinderbetreuungsgeld*. Vienna: Österreichisches Institut für Wirtschaftsforschung.

Lynch, Julia. 2006. *Age in the Welfare State: The Origins of Social Spending on Pensioners, Workers, and Children*. Cambridge: Cambridge University Press.

Machin, Howard and Vincent Wright. 1977. "The French Left Under the Fifth Republic: The Search for Identity in Unity," *Comparative Politics*, Vol. 10, No. 1, pp. 3–67.

Machos, Csilla. 2002. *Organisationsstrukturen linken Parlamentsparteien in Ostmitteleuropa*. Erkrath: Toennes Satz + Druck GmbH.

Madison, James. n.d. *The Federalist*. New York: Random House, number 10.

Maguire, G. E. 1998. *Conservative Women: A History of Women and the Conservative Party, 1874–1997*. London: Palgrave Macmillan.

Mainwaring, Scott and Edurne Zoco. 2007. "Political Sequences and the Stabilization of Interparty Competition – Electoral Volatility in Old and New Democracies," *Party Politics*, Vol. 13, No. 2, pp. 155–78.

Mair, Peter. 1990. "Continuity, Change and the Vulnerability of Party," in Peter Mair and Gordon Smith (eds.), *Understanding Party System Change in Western Europe*. London: Frank Cass, pp. 169–87.

Maleck-Lewy, Eva. 1994. *Und wenn ich nun Schwanger bin? Frauen zwischen Selbstbestimmung und Bevormundung*. Berlin: Aufbau Taschenbach.

Maleck-Lewy, Eva. 1997. "The East German Women's Movement After Unification," in Joan W. Scott, Cora Kaplan, and Debra Keates (eds.), *Transitions, Environments, Translations: Feminisms in International Politics*. New York: Routledge, pp. 121–7.

Manin, Bernard. 1987. "On Legitimacy and Political Deliberation," *Political Theory*, Vol. 15, pp. 338–68.

Markovits, Andrei S. 1986. *The Politics of West German Trade Unions: Strategies of Class and Interest Representation in Growth and Crisis*. Cambridge: Cambridge University Press.

Markovits, Andrei S., and Philip S. Gorski. 1993. *The German Left: Red, Green and Beyond*. New York: Oxford University Press.

Matland, Richard E. and Donley T. Studlar. 1996. "The Contagion of Women Candidates in Single-Member Districts and Proportional Representation Systems: Canada and Norway," *Journal of Politics*, Vol. 58, No. 3, pp. 707–33.

May, John. 1973. "Opinion Structure of Political Parties: The Special Law of Curviliear Disparity," *Political Studies*, Vol. 21, pp. 135–51.

Mazur, Amy G. 1995. *Gender Bias and the State: Symbolic Reform at Work in Fifth Republic France*. Pittsburgh: University of Pittsburgh Press.

Mazur, Amy G. (ed.). 2001. *State Feminism, Women's Movements, and Job Training: Making Democracies Work in a Global Economy*. New York and London: Routledge.

McKay, Joanna. 2004. "Women in German Politics: Still Jobs for the Boys?" *German Politics*, Vol. 13, No. 1, pp. 56–80.

Melich, Tanya. 1998. *The Republican War against Women: An Insider's Report from behind the Lines*. Updated edition. New York: Bantam Books.

Mesner, Maria. 1994. *Frauensache? Zur Auseinandersetzung um den Schwangerschaftsabbruch in Österreich nach 1945*. Vienna: J&V.

Meyer, Sibylle and Eva Schulze. 1998. "After the Fall of the Wall: The Impact of the Transition on East German Women," *Political Psychology*, Vol. 19, No. 1, pp. 95–116.

Michels, Robert. 1962. *Political Parties: A Sociological Study of the Oligarchical Tendencies of Modern Democracies*. New York: The Free Press.

Miethe, Ingrid. 1999. "From 'Mother of the Revolution' to 'Fathers of Unification': Concepts of Politics among Women Activists Following German Unification," *Social Politics*, Vol. 6, No. 1, pp. 1–22.

Mill, John Stuart. 1970. "The Subjection of Women," in Alice X. Rossi, ed., *Essays on Sex Equality*. Chicago: University of Chicago Press.

Millet, Kate. 1970. *Sexual Politics*. Garden City, NY: Doubleday.

Moeller, Robert G. 1993. *Protecting Motherhood: Women and the Family in the Politics of Postwar West Germany*. Berkeley: University of California Press.

Molitor, Ute. 1992. *Wählen Frauen anders?: zur Soziologie eines frauenspezifischen politischen Verhaltens in der Bundesrepublik Deutschland*. Baden-Baden: Nomos Verlagsgesellschaft.

Molitor, Ute and Viola Neu. 1999. "Das Wahlverhalten der Frauen bei der Bundestagswahl 1998: Kaum anders als das der Männer," *Zeitschrift für Parlamentsfragen*, Vol. 2, pp. 252–67.

Morgan, Kimberly. 2006. *Working Mothers and the Welfare State: Religion and the Politics of Work-Family Policies in Western Europe and the United States*. Stanford: Stanford University Press.

Morgan, Kimberly J., and Kathrin Zippel. 2003. "Paid to Care: The Origins and Effects of Care Leave Politics in Western Europe," *Social Politics*, Vol. 10, No. 1, pp. 49–85.

Müller, Wolfgang C. 1997. "Die Österreichische Volkspartei," in Herbert Dachs, Peter Gerlich, Herbert Gottweis, Franz Horner, Helmut Kramer, Volkmar Lauber, Wolfgang C. Müller, Emmerich Tálos (eds.), *Handbuch des politischen Systems Österreichs: Die Zweite Republik*. Vienna: Manzsche Verlags- und Universitätsbuchhandlung, pp. 265–85.

Müller, Wolfgang C. and Barbara Steininger. 1994. "Christian Democracy in Austria: the Austrian People's Party," in David Hanley (ed.), *Christian Democracy in Europe*. London: Francis Pinter, pp. 87–100.

Müller, Wolfgang C. and Kaare Strøm. 1999. *Policy, Office, or Votes? How Political Parties in Western Europe Make Hard Decisions*. Cambridge: Cambridge University Press.

Mushaben, Joyce Marie. 1995. "Second-class Citizenship and its Discontents: Women in the New Germany," in Peter H. Merkl (ed.), *The Federal Republic of Germany at Forty-Five*. New York: New York University Press, pp. 80–98.

Mushaben, Joyce Marie. 1997. "Concession or Compromise? The Politics of Abortion in United Germany," *German Politics*, Vol. 6, No. 3, pp. 70–88.

Mushaben, Joyce Marie. 2006. "Deconstructing Gender in German Politics: The 'Extreme Make-Over' of Chancellor Angela Merkel," paper prepared for Thirteenth German Studies Association Conference, Pittsburgh, September 28-October 1, 2006.

Nave-Herz, Rosemarie. 1997. *Die Geschichte der Frauenbewegung in Deutschland*. Bonn: Bundeszentrale für politische Bildung.

Neidhardt, Friedhelm. 1996. "Öffentliche Diskussion und politische Entscheidung. Der deutsche Abtreibungskonflikt 1970–1994," in Friedhelm Neidhardt (ed.), *Protest – öffentliche Meinung – Politik*. Berlin: Wissenschaftszentrum Berlin für Sozialforschung, pp. 59–80.

Neue Züricher Zeitung, various dates.

Neumann, Sigmund. 1956. "Towards a Comparative Study of Political Parties," in Sigmund Neumann (ed.), *Modern Political Parties*. Chicago: Chicago University Press, pp. 395–421.

Norris, Pippa. 2005. *Radical Right: Voters and Parties in the Electoral Market*. Cambridge: Cambridge University Press.

Northcutt, Wayne. 1985. *The French Socialist and Communist Party under the Fifth Republic, 1958–1981*. New York: Irvington Publishers, Inc.

Ostrogorski, Moisei. 1902. *Democracy and the Organization of Political Parties*. New York: Macmillan.

Outshoorn, Joyce. 1986a. "The Rules of the Game: Abortion Politics in the Netherlands," in Joni Lovenduski and Joyce Outshoorn (eds.), *The New Politics of Abortion*. London: Sage Publications, pp. 5–26.

Outshoorn, Joyce. 1986b. *De politieke strijd rondom de abortuswetgeving in Nederland 1964–1984*. Den Haag: VUGA.

Outshoorn, Joyce. 2001. "Policy-Making on Abortion: Arenas, Actors, and Arguments in the Netherlands," in Dorothy McBride Stetson (eds.), *Abortion Politics, Women's Movements, and the Democratic State*. Oxford: Oxford University Press, pp. 205–27.

Outshoorn, Joyce (ed.). 2004. *The Politics of Prostitution: Women's Movements, Democratic States, and the Globalization of Sex Commerce*. Cambridge: Cambridge University Press.

Padgett, Stephen. 1994. "Introduction: Chancellors and the Chancellorship," in Stephen Padgett (ed.), *Adenauer to Kohl: The Development of the German Chancellorship*. Washington, DC: Georgetown University Press.

Panebianco, Angelo. 1988. *Political Parties: Organization and Power*. Cambridge: Cambridge University Press.

Pappi, Franz Urban. 1973. "Parteiensystem und Sozialstruktur in der Bundesrepublik," *Politische Vierteljahresschriften*, Vol. 14, no. 2, pp. 191–213.

Parliamentary Democracy – Inter-Parliamentary Union (IPU) [cited January 7, 2010]. Available from http://www.ipu.org/english/home.htm

Pelinka, Anton and Sieglinde Rosenberger. 2003. *Österreichische Politik: Grundlagen – Strukturen – Trends*. Vienna: WUV.

Pelinka, Anton. 1998. *Austria: Out of the Shadow of the Past*. Boulder, CO: Westview Press.

Pfau-Effinger, Birgit. 2005. "Culture and Welfare State Policies: Reflections on a Complex Interrelation," *Journal of Social Policy*, Vol. 34, Part 1, pp. 3–20.

Pircher, Erika. 1990. "Fallbeispiel 2: Frauenbewegung der Democrazia Cristiana," in Anton Pelinka, Erika Pircher, and Sieglinde Rosenberger (eds.), *Organisationsformen von Fraueninteressen in Parteien westlicher Demokratien – unter besonderer Berücksichtigung christlich-demokratischer und konservativer Parteien*. Innsbruck: Unpublished manuscript.

Plantenga, Janneke. 1996. "For Women Only? The Rise of Part-Time Work in the Netherlands," *Social Politics*, Vol. 3, No. 1, pp. 57–71.

Plantenga, Janneke, Joop Schippers and Jacques Siegers. 1999. "Towards an Equal Division of Paid and Unpaid Work: The Case of the Netherlands," *Journal of European Social Policy*, Vol. 9, No. 2, pp. 99–110.

Pridham, Geoffrey. 1977. *Christian Democracy in Western Germany: The CDU/CSU in Government and Opposition, 1945–1976*. London: Croom Helm.

Prinzing, Marlis. 2006. *Lothar Späth: Wandlungen eines Rastlosen*. Zurich: Orell Füssli Verlag AG.

Przeworski, Adam and John Sprague. 1986. *Paper Stones: A History of Electoral Socialism*. Chicago: University of Chicago Press.

Rattinger, Hans. 1994. "Attitudes Towards the Abortion Law in Germany, 1990–1992: Determinants and Political Implications," *German Politics*, Vol. 3, No. 2, pp. 249–64.

Ritter, Gerhard A. and Merith Niehuss. 1991. *Wahlen in Deutschland, 1946–1991: Ein Handbuch*. Munich: Verlag C. H. Beck.

Ritter, Gerhard A. and Merith Niehuss. 1995. *Wahlen in Deutschland, 1990–1994*. Munich: Verlag C. H. Beck.

Rohnstock, Katrin. 1994. *Stiefschwestern: Was Ost-Frauen und West-Frauen voneinander denken*. Frankfurt am Main: Fischer.

Rosenberger, Sieglinde. 1990. "Fallbeispiel 1: Die Österreichesche Frauenbewegung (ÖFB)," in Anton Pelinka, Erika Pircher, and Sieglinde Rosenberger (eds.), *Organisationsformen von Fraueninteressen in Parteien westlicher Demokratien – unter besonderer Berücksichtigung christlich-demokratischer und konservativer Parteien*. Innsbruck: Unpublished manuscript.

Rucht, Dieter. 2003. "Interactions between Social Movements and States in Comparative Perspective," in Lee Ann Banaszak, Karen Beckwith, and Dieter Rucht (eds.), *Women's Movements Facing a Reconfigured State*. Cambridge: Cambridge University Press, pp. 242–74.

Rymph, Catherine E. 2006. *Republican Women: Feminism and Conservatism from Suffrage through the Rise of the New Right*. Chapel Hill: University of North Carolina Press.

Saalfed, Thomas. 2005. "Political Parties," in Simon Green and William E. Paterson (eds.), *Governance in Contemporary Germany: The Semisovereign State Revisited*. Cambridge, Cambridge University Press, pp. 46–77.

Sartori, Giovanni. 1987. *The Theory of Democracy Revisited. Part I and II*. Chatham, NJ: Chatham House Publishers.

SPD Statutes. [cited April 12, 2010]. Available from http://www.spd.de/de/pdf/rechtliches/071026_spd-statut.pdf

Scarrow, Susan. 1996. *Parties and Their Members: Organizing for Victory in Britain and Germany*. Oxford: Oxford University Press.

Scarrow, Susan. 2006. "Party Subsidies and the Freezing of Party Competition: Do Cartel Mechanisms Work?" *West European Politics*, Vol. 29, Issue 4, pp. 619–39.

Schattschneider, E. E. 1942. *Party Government*. New York: Holt, Rinehart, and Winston.

Schenk, Herrad. 1981. *Die feministische Herausforderung*. Munich: Verlag C. H. Beck.

Schindler, Peter. 1999. *Datenhandbuch zur Geschichte des Deutschen Bundestages 1949 bis 1999*. Baden-Baden: Nomos Verlagsgesellschaft.

Schlesinger, Joseph A. 1991. *Political Parties and the Winning of Office*. Ann Arbor: University of Michigan Press.

Schley, Nicole. 2005. *Angela Merkel: Deutschlands Zukunft ist weiblich*. Munich: Knaur Taschenbuch Verlag.

Schmidt, Ute. 1987. *Zentrum oder CDU: Politischer Katholizismus zwischen Tradition und Anpassung*. Opladen: Westdeutscher Verlag.

Schmidt, Ute. 1997. *Von der Blockpartei zur Volkspartei? Die Ost-CDU im Umbruch, 1989–1994*. Opladen: Westdeutscher Verlag.

Schmitter, Philippe C. 1979. "Still the Century of Corporatism?" in Philippe C. Schmitter and Gerhard Lehmbruch (eds.), *Trends Toward Corporatist Intermediation*. London: Sage Publications, pp. 7–52.

Schönbohm, Wolfgang. 1985. *Die CDU wird moderne Volkspartei: Selbstverständnis, Mitglieder, Organisation und Apparat 1950–1980*. Stuttgart: Klett-Cotta.

Schroeder, Wolfgang. 1998. "Das katholische Milieu auf dem Rückzug: Der Arbeitnehmerflügel der CDU nach der Ära Kohl," in Tobias Dürr and Rüdiger Soldt (eds.), *Die CDU nach Kohl*. Frankfurt am Main: Fischer Taschenbuch Verlag GmbH, pp. 175–91.

Schumpeter, Joseph. 1942. *Capitalism, Socialism and Democracy*. London: Allen and Unwin.

Schwarzer, Alice. 1981. *10 Jahre Frauenbewegung: So fing es an!* Cologne: EMMA-Verlag.

Sehrbrock, Ingrid. 1990. Letter to CDU Business Office (CDU-Bundesgeschäftsstelle). 11 July 1990. Women's Union Archive, Konrad-Adenauer-Haus. Bonn.

Sferza, Serenella. 2002. "Party Organization and Party Performance: The Case of the French Socialist Party," in Richard Gunther, José Ramón-Montero, and

Juan J. Linz (eds.), *Political Parties: Old Concepts and New Challenges*. New York: Oxford University Press.

Shepsle, Kenneth. 1991. *Models of Multiparty Electoral Competition*. New York. Harwood Academic Publishers.

Smith, Gordon. 1982. "The German *Volkspartei* and the Career of the Catch-all Concept," in Herbert Döring and Gordon Smith (eds.), *Party Government and Political Culture in West Germany*. New York: St. Martin's, pp. 59–76.

Smith, Gordon. 1990. "Core Persistence: System Change and the 'People's Party,'" in Peter Mair and Gordon Smith (eds.), *Understanding Party System Change in Western Europe*. London: Frank Cass, pp. 157–68.

Speil, Wolfgang. 1991. *Betriebliche Wirkungen des Erziehungsurlaubs*. Hannover: Materialien des Instituts für Entwicklungsplanung und Strukturforschung 151.

Der Spiegel, various dates.

Statistisches Bundesamt. 1987. *Frauen in Familie, Beruf und Gesellschaft: Ausgabe 1987*. Mainz: Verlag W. Kohlhammer GmbH.

Statistisches Bundesamt. 2005. "Wahl zum 16. Deutschen Bundestag am 18. September 2005." Wiesbaden.

Stern, various dates.

Stetson, Dorothy McBride (ed.). 2001a. *Abortion Politics, Women's Movements, and the Democratic State*. Oxford: Oxford University Press.

Stetson, Dorothy McBride. 2001b. "Introduction: Abortion, Women's Movements, and Democratic Politics," in Dorothy McBride Stetson (ed.), *Abortion Politics, Women's Movements, and the Democratic State*. Oxford: Oxford University Press, pp. 1–16.

Stetson, Dorothy McBride and Amy G. Mazur (eds.). 1995. *Comparative State Feminism*. Thousand Oaks, CA: Sage Publications.

Stock, Wolfgang. 2005. *Angela Merkel: Eine politische Biographie*. Munich: Olzog Verlag.

Strøm, Kaare. 1990. "A Behavioral Theory of Competitive Political Parties," *American Journal of Political Science*, Vol. 34, No. 2, pp. 565–98.

Stuttgarter Nachrichtung, various dates.

Stuttgarter Zeitung, various dates.

Süddeutsche Zeitung, various dates.

Süssmuth, Hans. 1990. *Kleine Geschichte der CDU-Frauen-Union: Erfolge und Rückschläge 1948–1990*. Baden-Baden: Nomos Verlagsgesellschaft.

tageszeitung, various dates.

Teorell, Jan. 1999. "A Deliberative Defence of Intra-Party Democracy," *Party Politics*, Vol. 5, Issue 3, pp. 363–82.

Teske, Erin. 2007. *More Coffins than Cradles: Low Fertility in Bologna, Italy*. Middletown, CT: Unpublished Manuscript.

Thompson, Mark R. and Ludmilla Lennartz. 2006. "The Making of Chancellor Merkel," *German Politics*, Vol 15, No. 1, pp. 99–110.

Tong, Rosemarie Putnam. 1998. *Feminist Thought: A More Comprehensive Introduction*. Second Edition. Boulder, CO: Westview Press.

Trzcinski, Eileen. 1998. "Gender and German Unification," *Affilia-Journal of Women and Social Work*, Vol. 13, No. 1, pp. 69–101.

Tucker, Robert. 1970. "The Theory of Charismatic Leadership," in Dankwart A. Rustow (ed.), *Philosophers and Kings: Studies in Leadership*. New York: Braziller.

Uertz, Rudolf. 1981. *Christentum und Sozialismus in der frühen CDU: Grundlagen und Wirkungen der christlich-sozialen Ideen in der Union, 1945–1949*. Stuttgart: Deutsche Verlags-Anstalt.

Van Oorschot, Wim. 2004. "Balancing Work and Welfare: Activation and Flexicurity Policies in the Netherlands, 1980–2000," *International Journal of Social Welfare*, Vol. 13, pp. 15–27.

Van de Velde, Hella. 1994. *Vrouwen van de partij: De integratie van vrouwen in politieke partijen in Nederland, 1991–1990*. Leiden: DSWO-Press.

Van Wel, Frits and Trudie Knijn. 2001. "The Labor Market Orientation of Single Mothers on Welfare in the Netherlands," *Journal of Marriage and Family*, Vol. 63, No. 3, pp. 804–15.

Visser, Jelle and A. Hemerijck. 1997. *A Dutch Miracle: Job Growth, Welfare Reform, and Corporatism in the Netherlands*. Amsterdam: Amsterdam University Press.

Von Beyme, Klaus. 1996. "Party Leadership and Change in Party Systems: Towards a Postmodern Party State?" *Government and Opposition*, Vol. 31, No. 2, pp. 135–59.

Von Schwartzenberg, Margritta. 2002. *Wirtschaft und Statistik*. Wiesbaden: Statistisches Bundesamt, pp. 823–7.

Von Wahl, Angelika. 2006a. "Gender Equality in Germany: Comparing Policy Change across Domains," *West European Politics*, Vol. 29, Issue 3, pp. 461–88.

Von Wahl, Angelika. 2006b. "Women and Political Representation in Germany: The Not-So-Unlikely Rise of Angela Merkel," paper prepared for Thirteenth German Studies Association Conference, Pittsburgh, September 28-October 1, 2006.

Von Wahl, Angelika. 2008. "From Family Policy to Reconciliation Policy: How the Grand Coalition Reforms the German Welfare State," *German Politics and Society*, Vol. 26, No. 3, pp. 25–9.

Wagner, Gert, Kartsen Hank and Katja Tillmann. 1995. *Ausserhäusige Kinderbetreuung in Ostdeutschland – 1990 und 1994 im Vergleich zu Westdeutschland*. Diskussionspapier aus der Fakultät für Sozialwissenschaft der Ruhr-Universität Bochum, No. 95–18. Available http://www.ruhr-uni-bochum.de/sowi.

Ware, Alan. 1979. *The Logic of Party Democracy*. New York: St. Martin's Press.

Wattenberg, Martin P. 2000. "The Decline of Mobilization," in Russell J. Dalton and Martin P. Wattenberg (eds.), *Parties without Partisans: Political Change in Advanced Industrialized Democracies*. Oxford: Oxford University Press, pp. 64–76.

Die Welt, various dates.

Wieck, Hans Georg. 1953. *Die Entstehung der CDU und die Wiederbegründung des Zentrums im Jahre 1945*. Düsseldorf: Droste Verlag.

Wieck, Hans Georg. 1958. *Christliche und Freie Demokraten in Hessen, Rheinland-Pfalz, Baden und Württemberg, 1945/46*. Düsseldorf: Droste Verlag.

Wiliarty, Sarah Elise. 2008a. "Angela Merkel's Path to Power: The Role of Internal Party Dynamics and Leadership," *German Politics*, Vol. 17, No. 1, pp. 81–96.

Wiliarty, Sarah Elise. 2008b. "Chancellor Angela Merkel – A Sign of Hope or the Exception that Proves the Rule?" *Politics and Gender*, Vol. 4, No. 3, pp. 485–96.

Wilson, Frank L. 1994. "The Sources of Party Change: The Social Democratic Parties of Britain, France, Germany, and Spain," in Kay Lawson (ed.), *How Political Parties Work: Perspectives from Within*. Westport, CN: Praeger Press, pp. 263–83.

Wingen, Max. 1997. *Familienpolitik: Grundlagen und aktuelle Probleme*. Bonn: Bundeszentrale für politische Bildung.

Wolinetz, Steven B. 1979. "The Transformation of Western European Party Systems Revisited," *West European Politics*, Vol. 2, Issue 1, pp. 4–28.

Wolinetz, Steven B. 1991. "Party System Change: The Catch-all Thesis Revisited," *West European Politics*, Vol. 14, Issue 1, pp. 113–28.

Wollstonecraft, Mary. 1975. *A Vindication of the Rights of Woman: An Authoritative Text, Backgrounds, Criticism*. Carol H. Poston (ed.), New York: W. W. Norton.

Yoder, Jennifer A. 1999. *From East Germans to Germans? The New Postcommunist Elites*. Durham: Duke University Press.

Young, Brigitte. 1998. "The Strong German State and the Weak Feminist Movements," *German Politics*, Vol. 7, No. 2, pp. 128–150.

Young, Brigitte. 1999. *Triumph of the Fatherland: German Unification and the Marginalization of Women*. Ann Arbor: University of Michigan Press.

Young, Lisa. 1998. "Party, State and Political Competition in Canada: The Cartel Model Reconsidered," *Canadian Journal of Political Science*, Vol. 31, No. 2, pp. 339–58.

Young, Lisa. 2000. *Feminists and Party Politics*. Ann Arbor: University of Michigan Press.

Ziblatt, Daniel F. 1998. "The Adaptation of Ex-Communist Parties to Post-Communist East Central Europe: a Comparative Study of the East German and Hungarian Ex-Communist Parties," *Communist and Post-Communist Studies*, Vol. 31, No. 2, pp. 119–37.

Zuckerman, Alan S. 1979. *The Politics of Faction: Christian Democratic Rule in Italy*. New Haven and London: Yale University Press.

Index